React Interview Guide

Learn all you need to know to ace any React interview and land your dream job

Sudheer Jonna

Andrew Baisden

<packt>

BIRMINGHAM—MUMBAI

React Interview Guide

Group Product Manager: Rohit Rajkumar

Publishing Product Manager: Nitin Nainani

Book Project Manager: Aishwarya Mohan

Senior Content Development Editor: Debolina Acharyya

Technical Editor: Simran Udasi

Copy Editor: Safis Editing

Proofreader: Safis Editing

Indexer: Rekha Nair

Production Designer: Vijay Kamble

DevRel Marketing Coordinators: Nivedita Pandey, Namita Velgekar, and Anamika Singh

First published: November 2023

Production reference: 1181023

Published by Packt Publishing Ltd.

Grosvenor House

11 St Paul's Square

Birmingham

B3 1RB, UK

ISBN 978-1-80324-151-7

www.packtpub.com

To my wife, Poojitha, and my son, Viraj; without their support, this book would not have been completed as early as it has.

– Sudheer Jonna

To the programming tech community, for all the support and motivation; you are the innovators shaping the future. This book is a tribute to your outstanding dedication to making a living from working in tech. I hope this book serves to inspire the next generation of programmers to join this remarkable journey.

– Andrew Baisden

Contributors

About the authors

Sudheer Jonna is a lead software developer, writer, and solution architect within JavaScript and Java programming languages. Sudheer has worked on many large-scale applications, prioritizing robust architecture and high performance. He has extensive knowledge of single-page applications (ReactJS/VueJS/Angular), backend API development, SQL, and cloud and containerization technologies, enabling him to assist many developers in advancing their careers. He is also the author of four other books, and a blogger, speaker, and trainer.

Andrew Baisden is a software developer and technical writer skilled in using the JavaScript and Python programming languages. Andrew has worked for a variety of companies in various industries throughout his career. His skills and knowledge as a technical writer have helped and inspired many developers to start their careers in tech and advance their existing skills. He has an audience on social media of over 30K and actively contributes to the community.

About the reviewers

Anthony "Kharioki" Wagura is a software engineer with years of experience building across web, mobile, and blockchain teams, primarily in early-stage start-ups. With expertise in Javascript, React, React Native, GraphQL, NodeJS, and TypeScript, Anthony has built numerous web and mobile projects, including ticket management apps, ride-sharing platforms, e-commerce solutions, and fitness applications. Anthony is an active contributor to open source projects and has done a few talks on developing mobile applications with React Native. Most recently, Kharioki has been venturing into start-ups and has recently launched a start-up in the travel and tourism industry. His hobbies are woodworking and swimming.

Emmanuel Demey works with the JavaScript ecosystem on a daily basis. He spends his time sharing his knowledge with anyone and everyone, with his first goal at work being to help the people he works with. He has spoken at French conferences (such as Devfest Nantes, Devfest Toulouse, Sunny Tech, and Devoxx France) about topics related to the web platform, such as JavaScript frameworks (Angular, React.js, and Vue.js), accessibility, and Nest.js. He has been a trainer for 10 years at Worldline and Zenika (two French consulting companies). He is also the co-leader of the Google Developer of Lille group and the co-organizer of the Devfest Lille conference.

Venkat Rohith Saripalli is an experienced frontend developer with a strong grasp of various technologies such as React, Redux, Redux Saga, JavaScript, CSS, Sass, styled-components, responsive design, and web components. Rohith is also skilled in using Jest and Testing Library for testing applications. He also has a sound knowledge of TypeScript, Redux Toolkit, and Node.js, which he has utilized in his development projects.

Kirill Ezhemenskii is an experienced software engineer, a frontend and mobile developer, a solution architect, and the CTO at a healthcare company. He's a functional programming advocate and an expert in the React stack, GraphQL, and TypeScript. He's also a React Native mentor.

Table of Contents

Part 2: Mastering the Core React Technical Interview

2

Understanding ReactJS Fundamentals and Its Features   35

3

Hooks: Bring State and Other Features into Function Components   75

4

Handling Routing and Internationalization   103

5

Advanced Concepts of ReactJS   119

Part 3: Going Beyond React and Advanced Topics

6

7

8

Testing and Debugging the React Application   179

9

Rapid Development with Next.js, Gatsby, and Remix Frameworks   199

Part 4: Hands-On with Programming Tasks

10

Cracking Any Real-World Programming Task   217

11

Building an App Based on React, Redux, Styled Components, and the Firebase Backend   231

12

Building an App Based on the Next.js Toolkit, Authentication, SWR, GraphQL, and Deployment   265

Preface

Hello there! *The Complete ReactJS Interview Guide* is a book that will assist developers in getting ready for a React interview in order to land a job. You will discover several tactics and ideas to ace your upcoming React interview in this book.

This book will cover all the different steps when getting ready for a React interview, starting from the preparation phase and going all the way to building some real-world projects, where you will gain insight to help you complete the take-home programming assignments in the final chapters.

The React ecosystem is quite vast, so many topics will be discussed throughout so that you get a fairly broad understanding of many of the most talked-about features and concepts related to React. Some of the topics we will touch on include state, components, Hooks, and testing.

Who this book is for

Aspiring web developers, programmers, and React developers can gain practical knowledge on how to perform well in React interviews.

The three main personas who are the target audience of this book are as follows:

- **Aspiring web developers**: Developers who are new to programming and want to learn React from the ground up and wish to crack React interviews

- **Programmers**: Any programmer who wishes to expand their knowledge and skillset by learning about React and how to do well in interviews

- **React developers**: They will gain insight into upgrading their existing React skills, leading to further career progression as a React developer

What this book covers

Chapter 1, Brace Yourself for Interview Preparation, provides an introduction to how to best prepare for upcoming React-based interviews. It will cover preparing a résumé and cover letter, as well as tips on creating a GitHub profile or website. The chapter will also discuss how to find work on job boards and LinkedIn and how meetups and referrals can assist with job searches. Additional interview tips are recommended.

Chapter 2, Understanding ReactJS Fundamentals and Its Major Features, provides an overview of some of the core fundamentals of ReactJS, covering many of the main topics, which include the JSX language, state, and props, as well as class and functional components. The chapter will also explain event handling, the virtual DOM, data flow, the context API, and how to do server-side rendering.

Chapter 3, Hooks: Bring State and Other Features into Functional Components, provides an overview of the various hooks that are available to use in ReactJS alongside their use cases. At the end of the chapter, you will learn how to create your own custom hooks.

Chapter 4, Handling Routing and Internationalization, provides an overview of how to handle routing and internationalization. The chapter primarily covers the React Router library and how to do page routing within a React application. Numerous topics are covered, including routes, links, parameters, translation, and how to pass arguments and placeholders.

Chapter 5, Advanced Concepts of ReactJS, provides an overview of advanced concepts in ReactJS. This chapter goes into detail on how to use error boundaries, portals, debugging with the Profiler API, strict mode, and concurrent rendering. The chapter also covers code splitting in addition to using React when in a mobile environment.

Chapter 6, Redux: The Best State Management Solution, provides an overview of how we can use Redux inside of our React applications. The chapter discusses the Flux pattern and Redux, going over their core principles and how to use them to manage the state within an application. With the help of this chapter, you will also learn about Redux middleware, Saga, Thunk, DevTools, and testing.

Chapter 7, Different Approaches to Apply CSS in ReactJS, provides an overview of how we can incorporate CSS into our React applications. There are different implementations, such as using processors, CSS Modules, CSS-in-JS, and styled-components, all of which will be discussed.

Chapter 8, Testing and Debugging the React Application, provides an overview of the concepts of testing and debugging within a React application. The chapter will go into detail on using React testing helpers, as well as the steps to perform a setup and teardown. Setups and teardowns are done while writing tests because we frequently need to do configurations before the tests run, and also at the end after the tests have finished running.

As well as data fetching and mocking, you will also gain knowledge on how to create events and timers and how we can use the React DevTools to do our debugging and analysis.

Chapter 9, Rapid Development with Next.js, Gatsby, and Remix Frameworks, provides an overview of how it's possible to use React to build full stack applications. The chapter aims to give an insight into using frameworks such as Next.js, Remix, and Gatshy to develop their React applications. You will also learn how to do static site generation, server-side rendering, and add page metadata.

Chapter 10, Cracking Any Real-World Programming Task, provides an overview of how to prepare for upcoming programming take-home assignments or code challenges when going through an interview process. You will learn how to set up a development environment and about the right tools and templates for a project. It is also important for you to learn about the benefits of choosing the right architecture, the reasons for good code testing, and how to share the project on GitHub, which will be covered here.

Chapter 11, Building an App Based on React, Redux, Styled Components, and the Firebase Backend, provides an overview of how to build a React application that connects to a Firebase database. The chapter will go into detail about how to best plan the architecture for the application, how to create the business logic and presentation layer, and how to set up the testing layer. When everything has been completed, you will learn how to deploy the application to GitHub so that it can be viewed publicly online.

Chapter 12, Building an App Based on NextJS Toolkit, Authentication, SWR, GraphQL, and Deployment, provides an overview of how to build a React application that has an authentication layer. The chapter will go into detail about how to best plan the architecture for the application and, in this case, use SWR and GraphQL, followed by the creation of the business logic and presentation layer, and setting up the testing layer. When everything has been completed, you will learn how to deploy the application to GitHub so that it can be viewed publicly online.

To get the most out of this book

Readers should have knowledge of JavaScript or any similar programming languages, frameworks, or libraries. Prior knowledge of React is welcome but not required. Having a basic understanding of programming concepts and methodologies is recommended.

Software/hardware covered in the book	Operating system requirements
React 18	Windows, macOS, or Linux
TypeScript 3.7	
ECMAScript 11	

Readers should have a programming setup with an **integrated development environment (IDE)**, a **command-line interface (CLI)** application, and any tools, frameworks, libraries, or packages installed, such as NodeJS, npm, and Next.js.

If you are using the digital version of this book, we advise you to type the code yourself or access the code from the book's GitHub repository (a link is available in the next section). Doing so will help you avoid any potential errors related to the copying and pasting of code.

Download the example code files

You can download the example code files for this book from GitHub at `https://github.com/PacktPublishing/React-Interview-Guide`. If there's an update to the code, it will be updated in the GitHub repository.

We also have other code bundles from our rich catalog of books and videos available at https://github.com/PacktPublishing/. Check them out!

Conventions used

There are a number of text conventions used throughout this book.

Code in text: Indicates code words in text, database table names, folder names, filenames, file extensions, pathnames, dummy URLs, user input, and Twitter handles. Here is an example: "The child components can consume the context using the useContext hook."

A block of code is set as follows:

```
import { useContext } from 'react';
import { UserContext } from './context';
function MyChildComponent() {
  const currentUser = useContext(UserContext);
  return <span>{currentUser}</span>;
```

Any command-line input or output is written as follows:

```
git status
git add .
git commit -m "vercel graphql endpoint for uri"
git push
```

Bold: Indicates a new term, an important word, or words that you see on screen. For instance, words in menus or dialog boxes appear in **bold**. Here is an example: "In the same way, when the API throws an error due to service unavailability, the respective root cause can be tracked through the **DebugValue** label."

> **Tips or important notes**
> Appear like this.

Get in touch

Feedback from our readers is always welcome.

General feedback: If you have questions about any aspect of this book, email us at `customercare@packtpub.com` and mention the book title in the subject of your message.

Errata: Although we have taken every care to ensure the accuracy of our content, mistakes do happen. If you have found a mistake in this book, we would be grateful if you would report this to us. Please visit `www.packtpub.com/support/errata` and fill in the form.

Piracy: If you come across any illegal copies of our works in any form on the internet, we would be grateful if you would provide us with the location address or website name. Please contact us at `copyright@packt.com` with a link to the material.

If you are interested in becoming an author: If there is a topic that you have expertise in and you are interested in either writing or contributing to a book, please visit `authors.packtpub.com`.

Share Your Thoughts

Once you've read, we'd love to hear your thoughts! Scan the QR code below to go straight to the Amazon review page for this book and share your feedback.

`https://packt.link/r/1803241519`

Your review is important to us and the tech community and will help us make sure we're delivering excellent quality content.

Download a free PDF copy of this book

Thanks for purchasing this book!

Do you like to read on the go but are unable to carry your print books everywhere?

Is your eBook purchase not compatible with the device of your choice?

Don't worry, now with every Packt book you get a DRM-free PDF version of that book at no cost.

Read anywhere, any place, on any device. Search, copy, and paste code from your favorite technical books directly into your application.

The perks don't stop there, you can get exclusive access to discounts, newsletters, and great free content in your inbox daily

Follow these simple steps to get the benefits:

1. Scan the QR code or visit the link below

https://packt.link/free-ebook/9781803241517

2. Submit your proof of purchase
3. That's it! We'll send your free PDF and other benefits to your email directly

Part 1:
Getting Ready for Interviews

In this part, you will learn how to prepare yourself for React.js interviews. The chapter will cover how job seekers should prepare their résumés and cover letters, as well as covering the importance of having a GitHub account and portfolio website. Then, we will gain some knowledge about meetups and referrals and how they can help with finding work. We will finish by learning some additional interview tips.

This part has the following chapter:

- *Chapter 1, Bracing Yourself for Interview Preparation*

1

Bracing Yourself for Interview Preparation

Finding a career that fits your abilities, interests, and objectives can be difficult in today's ever-changing employment environment. It's essential to devote time and energy to perfecting the art of interview preparation if you want to stand out from the crowd and obtain your ideal job. This chapter acts as your full road map, equipping you to confidently navigate the way to your next professional opportunity by providing useful guidance and essential insights into each stage of the interview process. In the next chapters, we are going to explore common interview questions for React developers as we get ourselves job-ready for working in this industry as JavaScript developers skilled in using the React framework.

As we go on an actual job hunt, we look at a number of resources to find chances, including LinkedIn, meetings, and referrals. We go through methods for utilizing your professional network, enhancing your internet profile, and accessing the untapped job market so that you have the knowledge and resources necessary to find a wide range of opportunities and develop enduring relationships. In this chapter, we will start by talking about your resume and cover letter, which are the foundation of your job application. These crucial records give prospective employers a summary of your qualifications and a look into your professional demeanor. To capture the hiring manager's interest, we go into detail on creating appealing content, customizing your resume and cover letter to the job's needs, and improving their overall presentation.

Because we will be applying for React roles, it's important that we tailor our resume appropriately so that it gives us the best chance of getting our resume in front of a hiring manager's eyes. This can be achieved by including relevant buzzwords such as *React*, *Redux*, and *Next.js*, which are all related to the React ecosystem, strengthening our profile further as it becomes apparent that we are a candidate worth checking out due to the fact that we use the tools and technologies they most likely have on their job descriptions.

The next strategy to follow would be to have a process that can enhance our job search and make us more hirable. This can include doing things such as the following:

- Having a GitHub profile
- Creating a personal website portfolio

This is especially important in the creative and technological sectors, where employers frequently want concrete evidence of your skill. We offer advice on the following areas:

- Choosing projects
- Perfecting your profile
- Building an interesting portfolio

With this information, we can showcase our technical expertise and also capture the essence of our individuality, which is great for highlighting our best work that makes us a stand-out candidate.

Finally, we provide priceless interview advice to help you succeed when it counts. We cover everything, leaving no stone unturned in our pursuit to ensure that you are well prepared for interviews, from preparing for behavioral and technical questions to mastering the art of communication and negotiation.

Starting this trip can be exciting and difficult, but if you have the correct attitude and follow the advice in this chapter, you can embrace the process and come out on top. So, be ready, and let's start your road to mastering interview preparation.

In this chapter, we will cover the following topics:

- Preparing your resume and cover letter
- Building your GitHub profile or website portfolio
- Finding jobs to apply for
- Understanding the role of meetups and referrals
- Exploring interview tips

Preparing your resume and cover letter

We will be going through the process of creating a good resume and cover letter in this section, which is essential if you want to give yourself the best possible chance of doing well during the interview stage of your job search as a React developer. This is an area that can essentially have a big impact on whether or not you find yourself in a position where you have a constant stream of job opportunities coming your way. Having a good resume combined with an equally good cover letter is the first step to covering all of your bases—so to speak—by preparing you for any challenging outcome you might encounter.

Differentiating between a resume and a cover letter

We are now going to talk about the difference between a resume and a cover letter, so let's get started. Essentially, a resume is a form of Word or PDF document that basically showcases a person's work history. This is where you will be presenting all of your career experience up to the most recent date. Resumes can cover areas of interest such as your education, work experience, achievements, and skills. The main purpose of having a resume in the first place is to present your knowledge and qualifications to companies for whom you are trying to get hired, in the hopes that your profile will be strong enough to get you an interview. The first step is always to convince a hiring manager that you are a candidate worth shortlisting.

Cover letters, on the other hand, are documents that are no longer than one page. Their sole purpose is to accompany your resume, and both are oftentimes submitted at the same time for a role. A cover letter is not as formal as a resume, meaning that you can be a lot more expressive with your wording here. This is your chance to introduce yourself to the company and explain why above all else you are the stand-out candidate they should seriously consider hiring. We should use cover letters to highlight our best skills and experiences, with the goal of ultimately convincing the hiring manager and company that our resume and personality make us a potential good culture fit and that we deserve to be invited for an interview, at least so that we can prove ourselves. You can find a great example of a cover letter in *Figure 1.1*:

Dear [Employer's Name],

I am writing to express my strong interest in the React Developer position at [Company Name], as advertised. With a deep passion for frontend development and an extensive background in React, I am excited about the opportunity to contribute to your team's innovative projects and collaborate with fellow professionals who share my enthusiasm for cutting-edge technology.

Allow me to introduce myself: I am an accomplished frontend developer with [X] years of experience specializing in React. Through my hands-on experience in building dynamic and responsive web applications, I have honed my proficiency in creating elegant, user-friendly interfaces that seamlessly integrate with backend systems. My expertise also extends to modern JavaScript frameworks, HTML, CSS, and version control systems like Git.

Upon reviewing the job description for the React Developer role, I am confident that my skills and experience align well with the requirements. My proficiency in developing reusable components, optimizing application performance, and employing state management libraries perfectly complements the technical expectations outlined in the job posting. Additionally, my familiarity with testing methodologies and tools ensures the delivery of high-quality, bug-free code that meets your company's standards.

I have conducted thorough research into Company Name] and am genuinely impressed by your commitment to pushing the boundaries of web development. Your emphasis on innovation, user experience, and continuous improvement resonates with my own professional values. The projects showcased on your website, particularly [specific project or initiative], exemplify the kind of impactful work I am eager to participate in. Moreover, the positive feedback and recognition Company Name] have received within the industry further solidify my desire to contribute to your team's success.

I am enthusiastic about the opportunity to interview for the React Developer position at [Company Name]. I am confident that my skills and passion for web development will allow me to make a meaningful impact on your projects and contribute to your company's ongoing success. I am eager to discuss my experiences and learn more about how I can contribute to Company Name's mission during an interview.

Thank you for considering my application. I am excited about the prospect of joining [Company Name] and contributing to your team's achievements. Please feel free to contact me at [Your Phone Number] or [Your Email Address] to schedule an interview at your earliest convenience. I look forward to further discussing my qualifications and learning more about the exciting projects at Company Name.

Sincerely, [Your Name]

Figure 1.1: Cover letter

The significance of having an excellent resume and cover letter

Let's now discuss the importance of having a good resume and cover letter and why they are essential for job searchers. It is far too easy to believe that you can make do with just a generic resume, believing that it is not a high priority and that your time would be better spent on other areas of the job search process such as doing job applications. We are going to break this down even further so that we can highlight the areas where having a stand-out resume and cover letter can work in your favor.

To do that, we will navigate the importance of making a good first impression, learn how to pass the screening process, understand which customizations to look into, learn how to sell your brand, and learn how to train yourself to go into an interview with confidence.

How to make a good first impression

When people meet us for the first time, they don't really know anything about us. This essentially gives us a blank canvas where we are able to really sell ourselves to a new person and convince them that we are high value and worth getting to know. Resumes and cover letters are pretty much the introduction documents akin to saying "hi" to someone new or shaking hands when you have met someone new whom you would like to know. With well-written documents, we are able to set ourselves apart from the other candidates and hopefully put ourselves at the top of the shortlist.

In my experience, you need to be as friendly as possible and go into that interview with charisma and as much belief and positivity as you can create. Sometimes, it can be hard if, for whatever reason, you are feeling low or bad on the day, but you have to find a way to overcome it. I have gone to interviews when I was not feeling the greatest, and it negatively impacted the interview. Similarly, I have had interviews go well because I was in the right frame of mind on the day and knew what I was going to say. A strategy that works well for me is listening to music or meditating beforehand. Feeling relaxed or fired up for a challenge is really going to give you the strength you need to put your best persona forward on the day.

Passing the screening process

This is our time to show our potential new employer how good a professional we are. Resumes and cover letters are used to screen new candidates to see which ones are worth interviewing. If the content we are putting forward is poorly written, outdated, fake, or has too many grammatical, spelling, and other inaccuracies, then we are highly unlikely to get to the interview stage. In these instances, it can be common to experience rejections or even ghosting when you never hear back from them. Of course, there are many reasons why this could be happening; we just ran through a few scenarios.

I can remember an instance when I had a resume that had some spelling errors on it that I did not even notice and nobody mentioned. You would think that the spellchecker in Word would show them all, but that was not the case. I had some words that were all in capital letters, and the spellchecker did not see the typos. That's why it's essential that you double- and triple-check what you are writing. Even getting someone else to proofread it is a good option. They might spot something you missed.

Customizing your resume and cover letter

It's now time for us to learn about customizations and how having a tailor-made resume and cover letter can increase your job prospects even more. If you create a tailor-made resume and cover letter for each role you apply for, then you can demonstrate that you have taken the time to read through their job description and that you are capable of showcasing how your current technology stack is a perfect match for the job. A custom profile is always going to stand out from a generic one. Sure—it might take a bit longer to create something custom for each application, but if that leads to even a few interviews, then it was clearly worth the effort.

I have had much success with doing this over the years, with my tailor-made resumes leading to more interviews compared to the generic ones that I just used everywhere. So, let's say that I am applying for a React role. To better my chances of success, I would try to highlight all the React experience that I have. So, I would add links to projects that I have created in React either on GitHub or a live website. I am also a technical writer, so adding links to articles on React that I have published would help me stand out even more.

I could also take this a step further, and for each relevant role I could mention something about React, such as—for example—"integrated a Redux store and optimized the performance of the application, leading to faster load times for users." Adding in keywords such as *Next.js*, *Vercel*, *Netlify*, *AWS*, and other technologies will improve our profile further because it shows that we are well versed in modern technical stacks.

Selling your brand

We are brands. This is an important concept that should be realized as we walk through life. Every time we meet somebody new, we have a chance to forge a new connection that can open up doors to even more life experiences. We use resumes and cover letters for marketing purposes because we are essentially selling ourselves and our ethos to new people. This gives us the chance to highlight our experiences, life achievements, and technical abilities, which are very hard to gauge from a normal job application.

This realization has led to me applying this mindset to everything in my life. Whether that is the content I create on social media or the emails that I send to clients, it's all about having this brand and business professional ethos. People are more likely to believe in you if you can prove that you are a credible person.

Going in with confidence

When we put in the time and effort to create a well-made resume and cover letter, it can do wonders for our confidence. The more confidence you can show at the start, the higher the likelihood that you are going to perform well in the interviews. It really does make a difference when we go into something high on confidence, as opposed to feeling negative and downbeat. We attract what we put out into the world. The more positivity we can output, the more positivity that will come back our way.

I can't think of many successful interviews I had when I went there downbeat and lacking confidence. People can really pick up on this energy, which is why it's so important to be in the right frame of mind prior to going for that interview. There have been times when I was feeling low after facing multiple rejections and ghosting experiences, which happens to all of us. In those situations, it's probably best to take a break from interviews, which is what I forced myself to do. The confidence will return over time. If you are getting burnt out, as I did, take a break.

In the next section, we will learn about the different types of resumes that we can create. Every job is different, so it's important to learn about the variety of resumes that we have available to us and which ones are the most appropriate for each job.

Exploring types of resumes

It is critical to select a resume format that best emphasizes your talents and experiences and is relevant to the position you are looking for.

There are several varieties of resumes, such as chronological, functional, combination, targeted, and creative. Each one serves a different purpose. We are going to learn about the differences between them so that we can factor this in when it is time to create our own.

Chronological resume

The most popular resume format is a chronological resume. We can see an example of this type of resume in *Figure 1.2*:

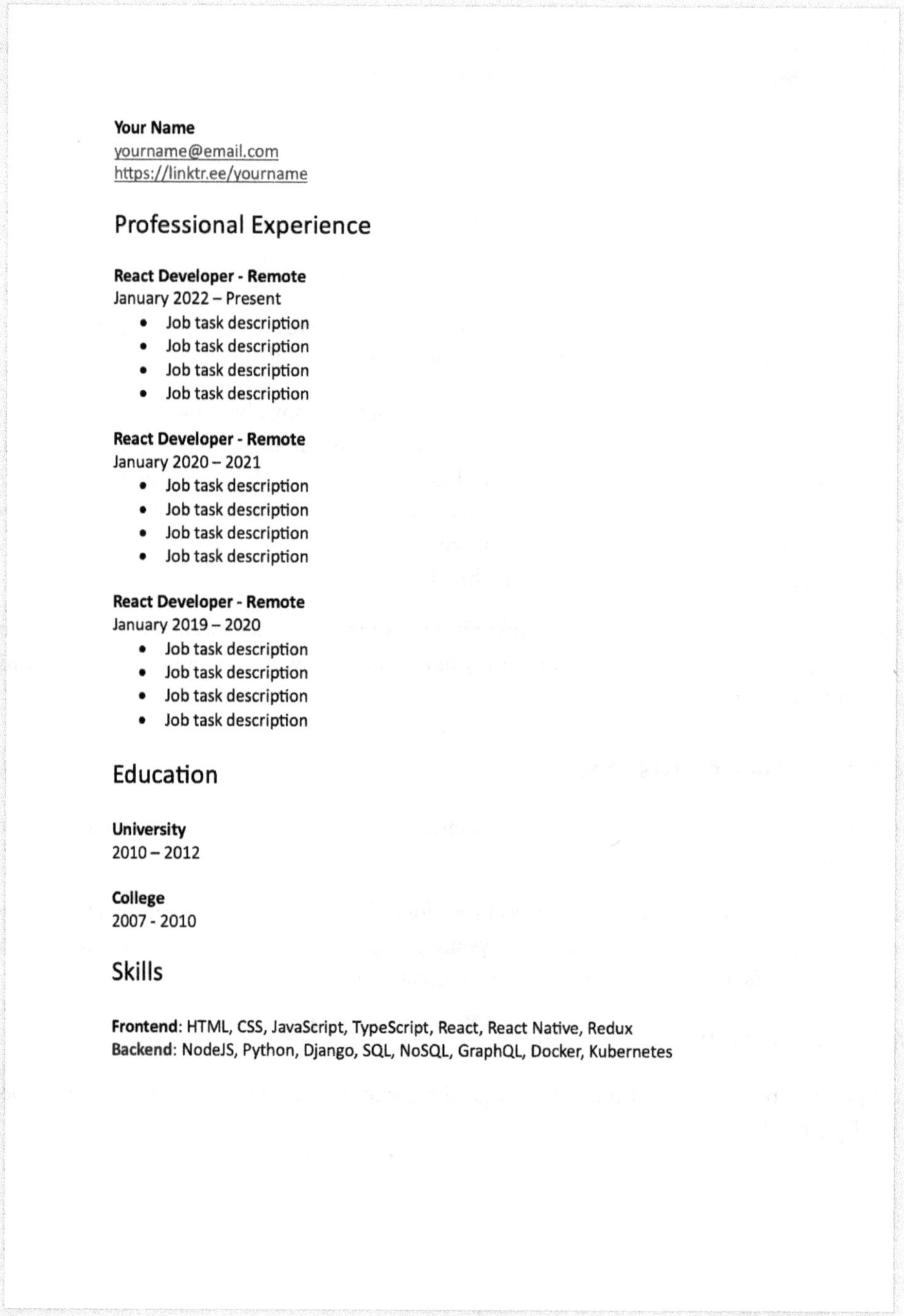

Your Name
yourname@email.com
https://linktr.ee/yourname

Professional Experience

React Developer - Remote
January 2022 – Present
- Job task description
- Job task description
- Job task description
- Job task description

React Developer - Remote
January 2020 – 2021
- Job task description
- Job task description
- Job task description
- Job task description

React Developer - Remote
January 2019 – 2020
- Job task description
- Job task description
- Job task description
- Job task description

Education

University
2010 – 2012

College
2007 - 2010

Skills

Frontend: HTML, CSS, JavaScript, TypeScript, React, React Native, Redux
Backend: NodeJS, Python, Django, SQL, NoSQL, GraphQL, Docker, Kubernetes

Figure 1.2: Chronological resume

You start with your most recent position and go backward; it presents your employment history in reverse chronological order. This method displays your professional development and demonstrates how your talents have advanced over time. This style is well liked by job seekers and is my personal preference because it provides a concise and easy-to-understand account of employment history, enabling hiring managers to rapidly evaluate credentials and potential.

A normal chronological resume will begin with the candidate's contact information in the header, then go on to a professional overview or objective statement, followed by a thorough listing of their job history. Each position will be documented with the title, employer, dates of employment, major duties and achievements, and any relevant skills or certifications acquired while holding that position.

Candidates with a solid work history and a distinct professional trajectory benefit most from chronological resumes since they can display their development and advancement over time. This style, however, might not be appropriate for persons who have little or no job experience, have had a long period of unemployment, or are trying to change careers or roles.

Functional resume

Instead of emphasizing your employment experience, a functional resume concentrates on your talents and competencies. We can see an example of this type of resume in *Figure 1.3*:

Your Name
yourname@email.com
https://linktr.ee/yourname

Skills and Abilities

Customer Service

- Expertise Description

Content Creation

- Expertise Description

Product Management

- Expertise Description

Professional Experience

Recruitment Consultant - London
January 2022 – Present
- Job task description
- Job task description

Sales Advisor - London
January 2020 – 2021
- Job task description
- Job task description

Marketing Assistant - London
January 2019 – 2020
- Job task description
- Job task description

Education

University
2010 – 2012

College
2007 - 2010

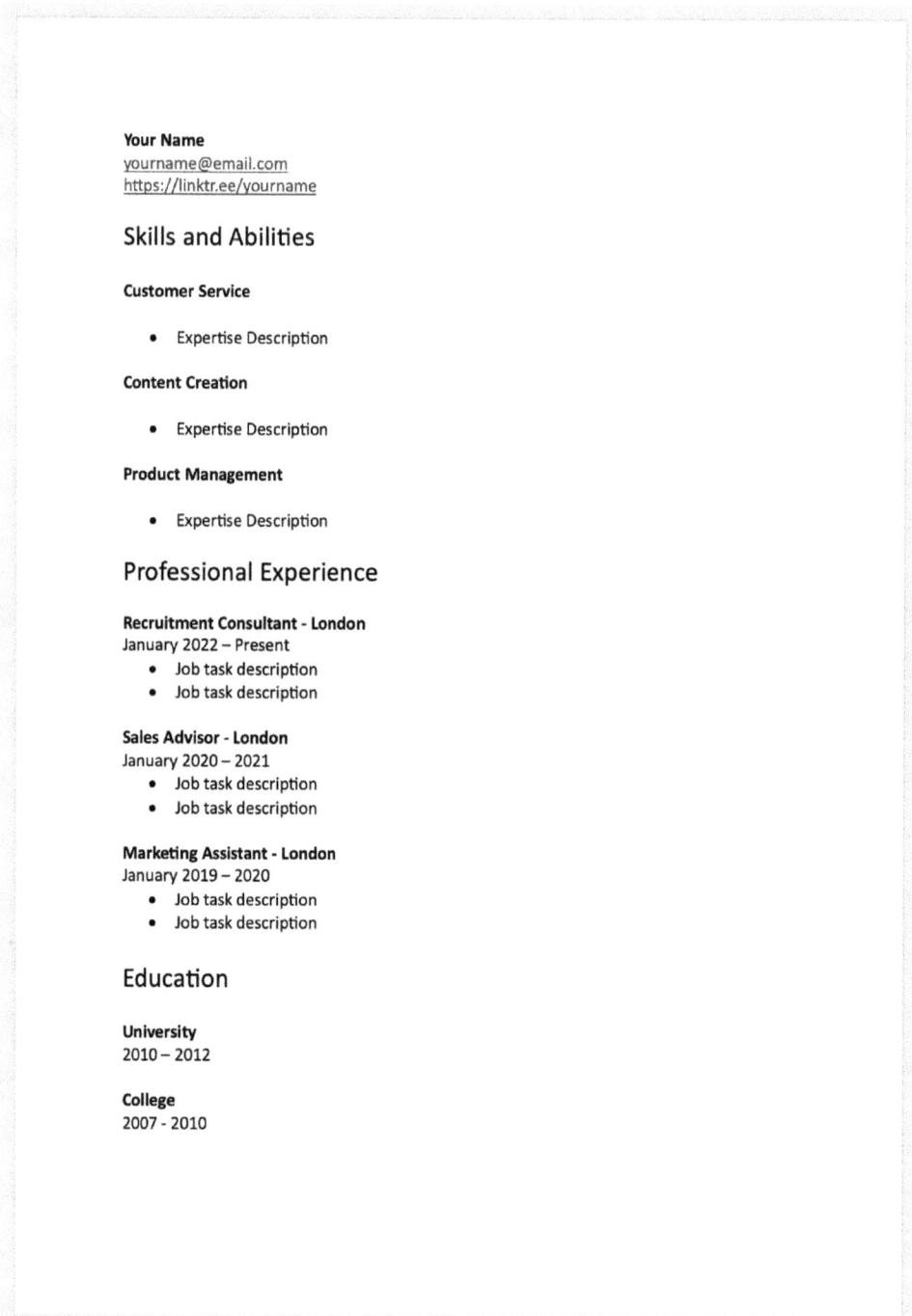

Figure 1.3: Functional resume

It showcases your successes and talents, and people have gaps in their employment history frequently choose to use this type.

A functional resume still includes the applicant's employment history, but it is presented in a streamlined style without dates or job titles. Instead, the emphasis is on the accomplishments and talents that are most pertinent to the position they are applying for. Often, these abilities are categorized into groups, such as communication, leadership, problem-solving, and technical capabilities.

A quick synopsis or objective statement that emphasizes the applicant's top qualifications might be included at the start of a functional resume. The resume's last section could also include information about education and other relevant credentials. Although functional resumes can be an effective way to highlight a candidate's abilities and accomplishments, some hiring managers might be wary of this style since it may be seen as an effort to hide a lack of experience or employment gaps. As a result, it's crucial to make sure the functional resume is customized to the precise job needs and is presented in an open and truthful way.

Combination resume

This resume format incorporates aspects of both functional and chronological resumes. The resume includes a section on your job history as well as highlighting your accomplishments and talents. For job seekers with a varied work history, this style is especially helpful because it highlights both their previous experience and talents.

We can see an example of this type of resume in *Figure 1.4*:

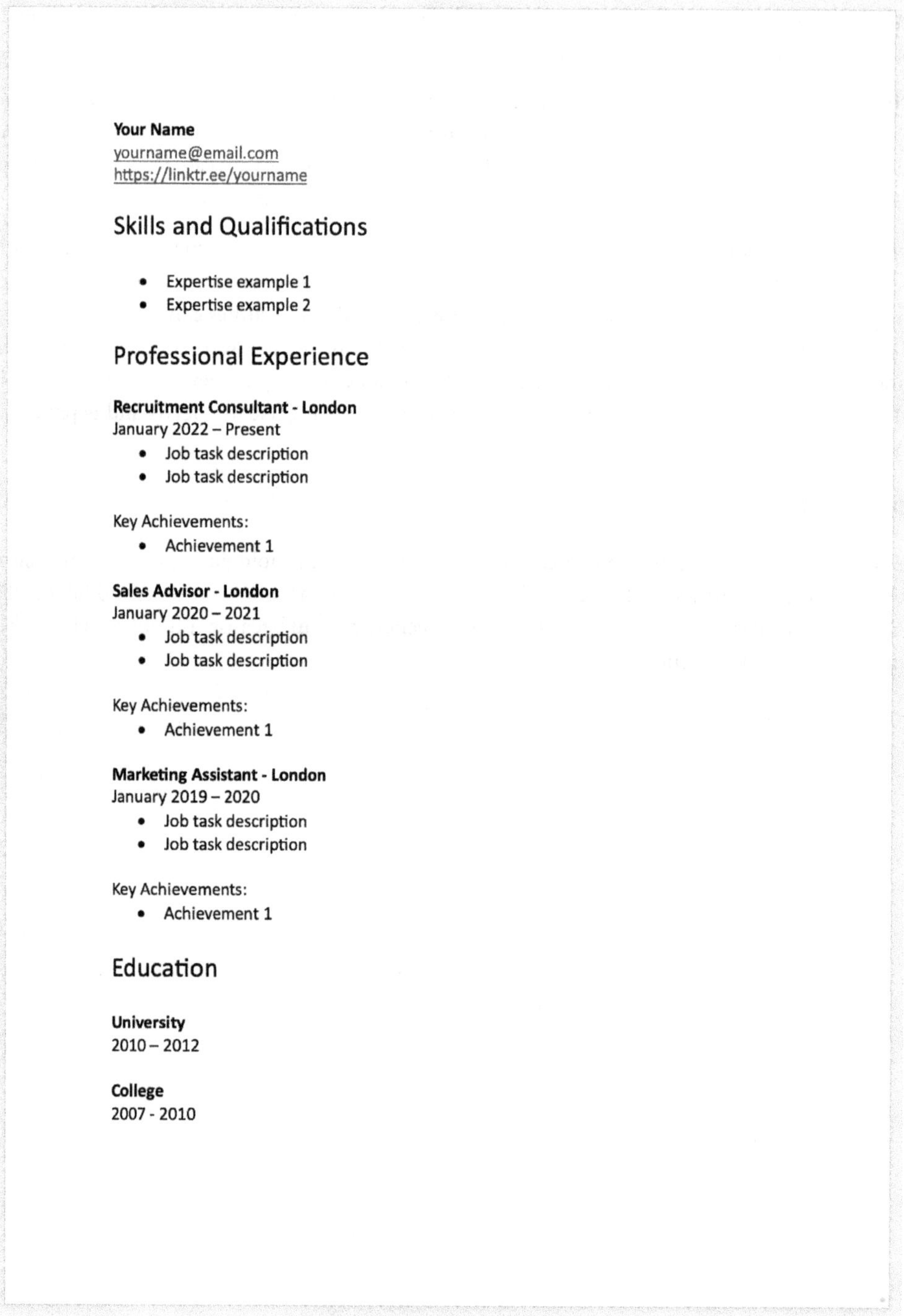

Your Name
yourname@email.com
https://linktr.ee/yourname

Skills and Qualifications

- Expertise example 1
- Expertise example 2

Professional Experience

Recruitment Consultant - London
January 2022 – Present
- Job task description
- Job task description

Key Achievements:
- Achievement 1

Sales Advisor - London
January 2020 – 2021
- Job task description
- Job task description

Key Achievements:
- Achievement 1

Marketing Assistant - London
January 2019 – 2020
- Job task description
- Job task description

Key Achievements:
- Achievement 1

Education

University
2010 – 2012

College
2007 - 2010

Figure 1.4: Combination resume

With a combination resume, the candidate's employment history is stated in reverse chronological order, but a summary of their most significant accomplishments and duties is given in place of a thorough description of each position. This enables the applicant to present their qualifications without going into too much detail.

A skills section is included after the work history section when the candidate outlines their main talents and accomplishments in a particular skill category. Technical ability, language ability, project management skills, and other talents can be included in this area, which is grouped in a way that is related to the position for which an application is being made.

A combination resume may also start with a summary or objective statement that highlights the applicant's significant accomplishments and career objectives, and it may finish with information about the applicant's schooling and other relevant credentials.

Targeted resume

A targeted resume is a kind of resume that is customized for a particular position or sector. It places emphasis on the knowledge and expertise that are most relevant to the position for which you are applying.

We can see an example of this type of resume in *Figure 1.5*:

Your Name
yourname@email.com
https://linktr.ee/yourname

Skills

- Expertise in data structures
- Strong knowledge of database architecture
- Mobile application experience with iOS and Android
- Next.js and React Native exposure

Professional Experience

React Developer - Remote
January 2022 – Present
- Job task description
- Job task description
- Job task description
- Job task description

React Developer - Remote
January 2020 – 2021
- Job task description
- Job task description
- Job task description
- Job task description

React Developer - Remote
January 2019 – 2020
- Job task description
- Job task description
- Job task description
- Job task description

Education

University
2010 – 2012

College
2007 - 2010

Figure 1.5: Targeted resume

An applicant for a targeted position would often thoroughly read the job description before tailoring their resume to the position's unique criteria. To highlight the applicant's relevant experience and talents and to show how they fulfill the particular job criteria, it is necessary to make changes to the content and keywords in the resume.

A targeted resume style could start with an overview or objective statement that highlights the applicant's strong education, training, and experience, as well as accomplishments that prove their suitability for the position. Although the candidate's employment history and educational background will also be included, the emphasis will be on highlighting their most pertinent qualifications that match the job description.

In general, a targeted resume can be a good method to highlight a candidate's skills and raise their chances of getting called in for an interview. It displays the applicant's interest in the position and their capacity to customize their application to the requirements of the job, which hiring managers may view as a favorable indicator.

Creative resume

The advantage of using a creative resume is that it is intended to highlight your individuality and inventiveness. To stand out, it could use unconventional forms or incorporate visual design components. Creative resumes tend to be the most expressive forms of resumes as you can use your design skills to truly make you unique. These can be created using design tools such as Photoshop, Illustrator, Figma, and Canva, to name a few. There are also many online and template websites that can let us create these types of creative resumes.

Infographics, charts, photographs, and other design elements are all possibly included in creative resumes in a variety of formats. Candidates frequently utilize them in creative professions where a visual portfolio is crucial, such as graphic design, marketing, or advertising.

It is also possible to submit a creative resume in addition to a regular resume in order to give a more thorough and aesthetically appealing summary of the applicant's experience and credentials. Ultimately, a creative resume can be a powerful tool for showcasing a candidate's design prowess and originality, as well as for leaving a lasting impression on prospective employers. But it's crucial to make sure the resume is still formal and simple to read and that it accurately and concisely conveys the candidate's credentials and expertise.

Moving on, in the next section, let's figure out some key elements of a good resume. It's one thing knowing how to create a resume, but if we really want it to stand out from the crowd, then it's important that we make it effective for our needs.

Key elements of a good resume

No resume is ever created equally, and although it can be common for resumes to be similar, it is well within our means to create a resume that can give us an advantage. We will now learn about some key elements that can help us make them less generic.

Firstly, it's important that our resumes are well formatted and easy on the eye. Obviously, you should not have any spelling or grammatical errors because this can damage your image and credibility. It has to look professional. Bullet points tend to be the most effective way to describe each job role. Just break them down into points, and describe what you did in the role and how it had a positive effect on the business. Avoid writing paragraphs because they will make your resume too long, and hiring managers are more likely to avoid them because it slows down their shortlisting process. This is advice I received after talking to lots of hiring managers and recruiters. Overall, three to four bullet points tend to perform the best in this situation.

In most scenarios, we will be listing our work experiences in reverse chronological order. So, the most recent roles are at the top, and past roles are lower down. Keeping our resume updated and with as few gaps as possible is going to help us in the long run. To demonstrate our talents and abilities, it is a good idea to give particular examples of our successes. To measure our accomplishments, a possible solution would be to use figures and percentages to show the gains that we managed to achieve during our time working there. Putting in content that is related to React is essential because we are applying for React roles, after all. So, the more React-related experience that you can put in the experience section, the better. In one example, you could show how your experience has advanced. Let's say that you worked on a code base that used the legacy class syntax, and then you updated it to use the latest Hooks syntax. That shows that you can work with legacy code bases and are familiar with the latest syntax too, and these are great traits for a programmer to have: problem-solving and being able to adapt to different situations.

The section on education should show our qualifications. So, any college or university degrees that we hold should be presented there. Mentioning any certifications, courses, and training can add further weight to our profile. When it comes to the skills section, it's best to include both hard and soft skills. Hard skills include programming-related areas such as JavaScript, React, and Node.js. Soft skills, on the other hand, include areas such as communication, teamwork, proactiveness, and so on.

Lastly, ensure that your resume is effectively tailored for the job and use keywords that highlight your skills and experiences in relation to the job that you are applying for. Many companies use **applicant tracking system (ATS)** resume scanner tools for finding candidates. So, if you can put in keywords such as HTML, CSS, and JavaScript, which could also be on their job description, then you have a good chance of getting a message from a hiring manager. I try to have as many keywords as possible in mine because you never know—it could make all the difference and determine if you are one of the candidates who gets shortlisted.

So, we just learned about the key elements of a good resume. The next step will be to do the same for cover letters as well.

Key elements of a good cover letter

Cover letters let us express ourselves in a more informal way, which is usually not a possibility on a resume, which has to be more formal. Let's explore some areas for writing good cover letters. The aim here should be to have good engagement, so have a strong fun introduction that briefly explains who you are, what you can do, and why you are applying for the role at that company. Don't forget to mention the company name and the job title on the job description you saw.

Start strong and highlight your best skills and experiences. Use as much charisma as possible to engage with the person who is going to be reading it, and try to write in a relaxed manner. All of this will show that you are a good fit for the role. Use this time to make it as personal as possible. Through this, we can show how well we have researched the company by showing lots of passion and motivation for the work.

With all of that out of the way, we should be ready to end the cover letter by requesting an interview or indicating your readiness to share more details. With these points, we can produce a strong and successful cover letter by adding these important aspects. When I write cover letters, my aim is to make them intriguing, engaging, and social. I work toward trying to captivate the reader so that they can imagine what it would be like to work with me. You can have the best programming skills in the world, but at some point, you will have to interact with people, so it's an area that needs to be worked on as well. A good combination of hard and soft skills is most desirable.

Cover letters give us significantly more creative freedom when compared to resumes, which are far stricter in terms of the structure that we use for them. Broadly speaking, it is like writing a letter or an email and selling our skills, brand, and personality to a potential new company that is looking for new hires.

Typically, we could be covering topics such as the following:

- An introduction
- How our skills are compatible with the job description
- What we know about the company from our own research
- A **call to action** (CTA) on how we are keen to get interviewed and looking forward to a response

These are some examples of content recommended to be included when writing a cover letter. A quick Google search for cover letter templates provides many examples and different ways to write one. Essentially, all you are doing is writing a letter on why you are a good candidate for this role, and this does not usually require a template; we can pretty much just make do with a good piece of writing. However, if you want to use a template, then feel free to do so if you think it will work for you.

We are making really good progress, so let's continue our journey. Our job search can be improved further, and all it takes is for us to have an in-depth look at the job descriptions we see out there. In this next section, we will learn why it's a good idea to examine job descriptions thoroughly.

Examining job descriptions

The better we get at reading job descriptions, the more likely we are to apply for the most suitable roles. In this section, we will walk through some key steps that are going to make our lives so much easier when it comes to looking for our next role.

When you search and find a job description, take your time and read through the whole thing from top to bottom. A job description is like a brief for a project. Go through it to ensure that you know exactly what is needed and don't miss anything. Look for areas that mention qualifications, education, skills, experience, and so on. You don't always need to meet all the specifications. In fact, it's quite common for people to get hired even when they don't possess all of the skills and experience, which has happened to me many times. Job descriptions are like guidelines; oftentimes, the winning candidate does not have everything required but is more than capable of learning on the job or in their free time. Keep a look out for those ATS keywords because the more of them that you find, the better your chances of getting to an interview.

Other areas of interest that we have to pay close attention to are the work, location, and salary. These factors are related to work-life balance, and if we want to have a healthy mental state, then they need serious consideration. The better these are, the higher the likelihood that we can perform well on the job. You can maximize your chances of receiving an interview call and eventually being hired by carefully reviewing job descriptions and adapting your application to the individual position and organization.

We have to use every asset at our disposal to find work, which is why there has to be an emphasis on identifying our key skills and accomplishments. Let's now see how this can be a great way to boost our profile.

Identifying key skills and accomplishments

We should create a list of the jobs we have held under a titled section of *Work History*, *Work Experience*, or something similar. This section should include volunteer work completed and the degrees we've earned. The aim is to determine the abilities we applied and the impact we had in each position. There are questions that we can ask ourselves, such as how we improved productivity or performance and if we completed the project on time and within budget. It's crucial that we list these achievements and any others that we can think of on our resume. Anything that makes us credible and an ideal candidate is well worth mentioning. In my early days, I listed all the experiences I could think of because this might have had some relevance to the job I applied for, such as—for example—if you had a job in customer service in retail, which might be a completely different job role from the one you're applying for now, but it is evidence that you can negotiate and talk to clients.

Creating a resume is not that difficult; however, it can be all too easy to make mistakes that you might not even realize unless someone points them out. We will now learn about some common resume mistakes to avoid.

Common resume mistakes to avoid

Probably the top concern that we have to be aware of is spelling and grammatical mistakes. Always proofread your resume a couple of times because giving it multiple pass-throughs improves the chances of you not missing something important. Use a spellchecker, and it is even better if you can use a tool such as Grammarly, which is a very effective and professional copywriting tool.

Removing non-essential information is going to work well in our favor too, such as with an introduction paragraph that explains who we are and what we are looking for. This belongs on the cover letter, not the resume. And any section that talks about our personal hobbies can be removed too because it is not required for the job. If they want to know what you do in your spare time, they can ask you at an interview, and in this situation, it becomes more appropriate, especially if it's a culture-fit interview.

I know it's probably obvious, but still, people skip this step or don't take it seriously at all. I am talking about researching the company you have sent your resume to. We like to focus on answering interview questions because, let's be honest, we can do hundreds of job applications, and nobody is going to learn about every company. Our main goal is to find a job, and that's why we send our resume out everywhere. Nonetheless, if that company invites us for an interview, at the very least, we should know something about them.

Let's see why this is essential in the next section.

Researching the company

Always research the company by going to their website. Don't make the mistake of going to an interview with only generic interview questions and knowledge at hand. It is not uncommon for interviewers to ask you what you know about the company, so don't expect it to be all coding questions related to React because you never know on the day.

Learn about the work they do, their clients, their technical stack, and their history—basically, everything—and you can use search engines such as Google to learn even more about them. I have made this mistake so many times over the years. I can recall one interview where one of the interviewers asked me what I knew about the company, and I tried to avoid answering because I knew nothing. I was super prepared for any programming-related questions because that was a weakness that I wanted to fix. I did not think that it was worth the time to gain deep insights into the company because—let's be honest here—the first-stage interview might not go anywhere, and then you will feel like you wasted your time. However, it has to be done on the off chance that you do get asked, and your failure to come up with an answer gets you removed from the shortlist.

We have covered resume mistakes, so now, we will do the same for cover letters too because these are equally important. So, on to the next section.

Common cover letter mistakes to avoid

Putting together a great cover letter is an excellent way to take our job profile to another level, yet it is also an area that many people tend to let themselves down in by not taking the time to do it properly. It should not be seen as an optional addition to a resume but as a document that should be submitted alongside it. They are like two sides of the same coin and complement each other.

By far one of the biggest mistakes we can make is using a generic template. Utilizing a generic cover letter template can give the impression that we didn't take the time to customize our application for the particular position. Instead, adjust your cover letter to the position you're seeking; this is how it should always be done.

Another area to be concerned about is duplication. Our cover letters should supplement, not rehash, our resume. Utilize your cover letter to showcase your unique examples and talents that make you the strongest applicant for the position. Put emphasis on how you can benefit the company, not on what you want in return. It is far better to be a giver than a taker because givers provide value, and that is a quality worth having in someone. Figuring out which tone of voice to use when you write can be challenging as well. Work on matching the way the company comes across; striking the right balance between formal and informal is important.

We are learning so much about resumes and cover letters, which is going to help us a great deal when it comes to applying for those React roles. It's time to tackle the subject of GitHub and portfolios. Our resumes and cover letters can get us in front of hiring managers, but ultimately, it is the projects and skills that we possess that are highly likely to get us interviews. In this upcoming section, we will learn about GitHub profiles and portfolios and why we should utilize them.

Building your GitHub profile or website portfolio

We will go through what it's like to build a GitHub profile and how this can make you stand out in the interview screening process. Likewise, it is just as important to have a website portfolio because this is truly an area that gives you the ability to make yourself unique and a stand-out candidate worthy of being hired. You need to realize that the job market is incredibly competitive, which means we are going to have to do everything we can possibly do to give ourselves the best chance of being the candidate who the company believes is the best fit for the role.

Throughout the years, I have managed to get interviews solely based on my portfolio website, through its design, content and details of work I have done over the years. Our resumes and cover letters can look almost identical to a hiring manager's eyes after they have gone through a dozen of them. However, having a custom portfolio and GitHub home page can become eye candy. It has worked for me, and it can work for you in the same way.

Benefits of building a GitHub profile or website portfolio for finding work

Creating a website portfolio or GitHub profile might help you find work and stand out throughout the hiring process. These not only highlight your abilities, but they also show that you can cooperate with others, use tools effectively, and handle challenging situations. Also, they provide potential employers with a more thorough picture of your coding experience and skills. Making an eye-catching profile or portfolio might be crucial in differentiating oneself from the competition.

How to make your GitHub profile or website portfolio stand out from the rest

When applying for employment, making a website portfolio or GitHub profile is an excellent approach to separate oneself from the competition. Although it may take some time, the effort will be worthwhile in the end. You can demonstrate to potential employers that you're serious about joining the team by investing the time to expand your skill set, share projects you've been working on, and establish contacts with other developers. Also, you may use these sites to highlight your greatest work and offer convincing arguments for why they should hire you. Show them what you've got since there's no denying that in today's employment market, an internet presence has a significant influence.

We learned some tips on how to make your GitHub profile and website portfolio stand out, and now, the next topic will help us dive into the type of content we should be putting on there.

What kind of content you should include in your portfolio

One of the most crucial things you can do to set yourself apart when looking for employment is to build a portfolio. But what sort of material should we include? Include your qualifications and any prior job experience that makes you the best candidate before anything else. Add any projects or websites you've created to demonstrate your technical expertise and sector understanding. Take it a step further and provide a synopsis of each project so that future employers can see your contribution to its completion right away. For instance, did you create any graphics or JavaScript apps? It's also a good idea to present documentation that demonstrates your familiarity with certain tools and technologies, such as software licenses or certificates. Include these items in your profile and website.

Examples of innovative portfolio pieces and how they can help you land a job

A solid GitHub profile and website portfolio might be a terrific approach to stand out to interviewers while trying to secure your ideal job. So, why not make your application stand out from the competition with an inventive portfolio? We can set ourselves apart from the competition by providing instances of how we push the envelope with our code. Interviewers can see that we have unique ideas, even from initiatives that were abandoned or never used. We should not undervalue the impact of demonstrating unconventional solutions, even if they weren't used. Employers will be impressed by our diligence and inventiveness.

For example, it is a well-known fact that everyone tries to build a to do app when trying to showcase their skills. It has become so generic because it does not make us any different from each other. It's hard to choose between candidates when they are almost all carbon copies of each other. In my opinion, a better solution would be to have projects on your GitHub or portfolio that show progression.

So, you could start with a basic React application that has some simple business logic of some sort—so, perhaps, a calculator—and then, you could create a more advanced React application that could have multiple features that do different things, such as having some CRUD functionality, or a store if we are building an e-commerce application. Afterward, we could take it a step further, maybe adding an authentication layer with login and logout, GraphQL, and various microservices all interacting with each other. This shows a clear progression as your skills continue to evolve and the projects become even more complex.

Now, with this understanding under our belt, let's take a look at some of the pros and cons of using third-party tools for building our websites when compared to the DIY approach.

Pros and cons of using a third-party portfolio building website versus DIY

It might be challenging to choose between creating content yourself and using a third-party website when creating an online portfolio. The ability to exhibit your work without having to worry about coding or design abilities is one benefit of using a third-party website. Several third-party websites such as Wix, Squarespace, and WordPress also let users display their skills and expertise while giving them advice on how to optimize their profiles. Yet, since users have total control over the layout and functionality of their website, going down the DIY route gives us more freedom when building a portfolio. A slick style or customizability should ultimately be considered carefully when weighing your alternatives when creating your portfolio.

Let's now take a look at a summary of the pros and cons to see what the differences are.

Summarizing the pros and cons

First, we'll look at the pros and cons of third-party build tools. Let's begin.

Here are the pros:

- Pre-made custom templates are available
- No-code tools require little technical know-how
- Design experience is not required
- Fast deployment because it's ready-made

- Quick setup

- Easy to update because it uses a **content management system (CMS)**

- Technical support and services

Here are the cons:

- Lack of customization

- Might need to pay for hosting and services

- Using a third-party tool means that you don't showcase your programming skills

Now, we will look at the pros and cons of a DIY custom approach. Let's begin.

Here are the pros:

- Full customization

- Able to showcase your programming skills

- Free or paid hosting options

Here are the cons:

- Without a design background, it might not look as good as you want it to

- Depending on complexity, it could take longer to build

- No technical support—you are responsible for everything

OK—so, we learned a great deal about GitHub and creating portfolios. In this next section, we are going to learn more about finding jobs to apply for. There are numerous ways to go about this, so let's keep reading to see how we can do it.

Finding jobs to apply for

In this section, we will go into detail on the best methods for finding work on job boards and using networks such as LinkedIn to do so. You will realize that we already have all the tools needed in front of us, and we need to learn how to best implement them into our job search.

Understanding your career goals and targeting specific job postings

Finding a job is not the only factor to consider. You could narrow your search for the jobs that are best for you by knowing your career objectives and applying to particular job openings. This can save you a lot of time and ensure that your efforts are focused on tasks that will help you advance your career goals. LinkedIn is a fantastic resource for staying current on what's available and how to match it to your ambitions. In this respect, when the employment details are provided, you are fully aware of how well the job corresponds with your overall career goals. Being active on the platform and engaging with other job seekers and hiring managers leads to more success, in my experience. I have far more people reaching out to me as a result.

Utilizing job boards to search for relevant opportunities

Searching for job vacancies on online job boards is the best approach to start the job search process. There are several ways we can utilize these boards to uncover relevant possibilities that will move us closer to our professional objectives thanks to the large choice of postings, which vary from online internships to entry-level jobs in any area. Make sure you understand how to use job boards and all of their services before diving headfirst into the applications and recruitment world; this will help to ensure that pursuing a particular job market won't be too overwhelming as you explore job opportunities and hone in on what you want. I like to set email alerts for job search parameters so that I get the latest roles in my inbox.

Networking offline and online

The good thing is that you have both offline and online networking alternatives accessible, which is essential when it comes to obtaining a job. Attending job fairs and workshops or conversing with people in your industry are examples of offline networking. By using social media sites such as LinkedIn, we can also do online networking. Joining job networks is a great way to network with people in your sector, including recruiters and possible employers. By effectively using these tools, you can network with the appropriate individuals and get access to the newest jobs in your industry. In order to improve your chances of success, don't be afraid to seek out new contacts and widen your professional network. I go to events to expand my network, and now there are so many meetups that we can go to. I have found that being open to online and offline opportunities has the most benefits.

Job fairs and professional gatherings are excellent places to get your job search going or learn more about the kinds of occupations that could be ideal for you. By taking advantage of these possibilities, you can meet hiring managers, influential people, and other people who can help you network effectively. You can learn about various career pathways and expand your expertise in your chosen sector, and they also provide you access to companies and updated information about industry trends. Also, going to job fairs and seminars may provide you with conference-like experiences where you can pick up practical skills to make yourself more competitive—a fantastic way to stand out. Use all opportunities to attend job fairs or professional gatherings that are nearby.

Researching companies and learning about their current job openings

Finding possible employment requires doing some research on potential employers. Once you've created a list of potential companies, you could research more information about company cultures, job vacancies, and other factors. LinkedIn is a fantastic tool for conducting company research as well; in addition to finding comprehensive company information, you can connect with hiring managers and current workers in the business. You can choose the employer you want to concentrate your time and attention on while submitting job applications by conducting research.

Using online resources such as Indeed to research salaries and more

Seeking employment need not be a guessing game. You can get crucial information about a possible employment opportunity, such as the typical wage for a role, and crucial corporate information with the help of job boards such as Glassdoor. You can gain the upper hand in negotiations and ensure that you are being paid competitively by being aware of what similar salaries are in your field. You could receive a genuine perspective of the good, the terrible, and everything in between by researching the company's history and evaluations from previous employees. Once you are informed, there is no reason why you cannot leave with the position or pay that you desire.

We learned about the significance of networking in this section. Let's go a bit further in the next section as we try to understand the role of meetups and referrals and how they can help us.

Understanding the role of meetups and referrals

We will go into the topic of meetups and referrals and how knowing the right people can get you through the front door to a new role. You are as powerful as your network, and it is so important to form bonds and connections with people whenever you can because one day, they could help you in ways you could never imagine. Network with fellow developers, hiring managers, CEOs, job seekers, accountants, and recruiters. All of these people are potential gateways to getting you into the industry. Let's now learn even more about this subject. First, let's begin with meetups.

What meetups are and why they are important for job seekers

Meetups are planned events that bring together individuals who have similar interests, such as job searchers, business owners, or academics. These gatherings give participants fantastic chances to network, learn from one another, and share concepts and tactics. They also offer a priceless chance to make beneficial contacts and gain insight from knowledgeable experts in the subject. Meetups can be a priceless resource for us when looking for referrals that could lead to our next position. Despite this immediate advantage, meetings provide a way to hone professional abilities, boost self-assurance, and get insights that could not otherwise be obtained through conventional job search channels.

Tips on how to find the right meetup group for you

A fantastic way to start looking for your ideal career is to locate a suitable meeting group for you. You could save time and stress by doing some research and planning beforehand. Find out which clubs in your region are focused on the topics that interest you or the abilities you wish to improve on first. Be sure the group's aims are in line with your own, and any feedback from former participants can also assist in simplifying the decision. You don't want to be in a predicament where you become bogged down in the middle of the event. Make an effort to ask friends or acquaintances for recommendations so that you can join the meetups that are ideal for your needs.

Benefits of attending meetups

It might be difficult to get a job, but by going to meetups and using references, you can make it simpler. Meetups offer excellent chances for networking with experts in your area and creating meaningful connections that might result in recommendations for job openings. This not only aids in the development of lasting relationships but also broadens your personal network and raises your chances of landing the ideal employment. Meeting individuals in your business who share your interests or hobbies through meetings is a quick and easy approach to give yourself an edge in the job search.

Another part that has helped in my career is actually participating in these meetups. Suppose you're skilled in one part of React; it helps your image if you can contribute to the meetup and even teach others. Potential recruiters and future colleagues may be in the meetup.

How to get the most out of a meetup

While looking for a career, meetups might be a great method to get your foot in the door. You could meet people who can introduce you to others or provide you access to employers. Take the initiative and be proactive in developing relationships with people to get the most out of every encounter. Engage in meaningful conversations and project the image of a lively, enthusiastic crowd member. Also, don't be afraid to engage with industry leaders you like on social media; by doing so, you might gain insight into the kinds of positions they could be hiring for and how you can help.

I have done this countless times, and unintentionally, too. All I was doing was engaging with like-minded people on social media, and it's this tenacity that has led to me getting DMs on X, formerly known as Twitter, from CEOs at companies who wanted to interview me for roles they had. Never waste time when it comes to networking professionally; take advantage of any chance that presents itself.

Now that we have enough information about meetups and their importance, let's take a look at referrals.

The importance of referrals in getting a job

In the modern world, recommendations are one of the most crucial resources for finding employment. This is due to the fact that a recommendation from an existing worker or friend can provide you access to a company's internal operations, including new job listings and career development chances. You can ensure that your name is put up for any opportunities that come up both inside and outside of your sector by participating in meetings and other networking events. This offers you an advantage over rivals who don't have as many testimonials praising them and gives you more possibilities. When it comes to taking charge of your own professional trajectory, taking advantage of references ought to be a top priority.

Tips on how to get referrals

A wonderful strategy to obtain your ideal job is to ask for recommendations. Even while it could seem frightening, it does not need to be. Look at the individuals who are already a part of your network, such as friends or acquaintances, to start. It's crucial that you pick a person who is knowledgeable about your qualifications and network. Then, ask them if they are aware of any openings or employment that match your qualifications. Consider attending local professional meetings as another opportunity to network and learn about available employment in your area. Take the chance to meet some lifelong, meaningful contacts at these events since you never know whom you could run into. Above all, be persistent when asking for references, be focused, and be enthusiastic.

OK—we are doing great, and everything we have learned so far has improved our profile as a React developer. In the next section, I want to cover some very useful interview tips that can elevate us even more. Read on to see what else we can do to enhance our presence.

Exploring interview tips

In this section, we will talk about some great interview tips and how we can incorporate them into our job search routine. It is crucial that we have good planning set up well in advance so that we can take advantage of job opportunities that are eventually going to come our way.

Applying for a job can be a nerve-racking affair, especially if you have no idea what to expect. The greatest approach to ensure success is to arrive prepared with the correct attitude and understanding of optimal interviewing methods. Let's go through some pointers to help us ace our next job interview.

Preparing for a potential technical interview

This is without a doubt the most important step and can be the difference between you getting close to a job offer or getting rejected and removed from the shortlist of potential candidates who make it to the next stage of interviews. The technical interview stage is where you are ultimately going to show your new prospective company what you can do and whether or not you are a good programmer. Typically, technical interviews can be in different formats.

For example, they could be any of the following:

- Conversations between yourself and another developer on programming topics
- Paired-programming code exercises with other developers

- Take-home code assignments that you need to complete in a few days

- Data structures and algorithms online exam

- Multiple-choice online questionnaire on programming

Personally, I have encountered all of these throughout my career. If you are extremely lucky, you might not have to do anything extremely technical because maybe the company that is hiring you does not believe in doing these types of code assessments. That's a possibility, and I have interviewed with companies who thought that way, but it's not always a guarantee. So, always be prepared no matter what. In terms of preparation, what I would do is work on my technical stack as much as possible—so, essentially, write as much code as I can and build apps.

For example, you might be applying for frontend or full stack jobs. So, what I have done in these situations is just practice building **create, read, update, delete (CRUD)** applications that connect to a database with a React frontend, and then taking it a step further and integrating third-party libraries such as Day.js, which is used for converting dates, or a chart library such as recharts.js, which is used for data visualization. These are tools that get used in real-world projects, so learning them now makes you better prepared for those take-home code challenges that could require you to use them.

Doing this step will give you more confidence in your programming skills for your technical stack. The other area that you should work on is data structures and algorithms. There are courses that you can do on Udemy, or you can study this subject elsewhere. Next, you have to find the time to practice online on coding platforms such as LeetCode. It can be tedious, but unfortunately, we need to be prepared for anything. On some job boards, I have seen forms that ask you how prepared you are for a code test, which is part of the application process when you are submitting your resume. And I can imagine that if you say that you are not that prepared, then you might not even make the shortlist. So, the moral of the story: get yourself to a place where you feel you are confident enough to at least attempt doing a code test. It's impossible to be 100% ready because there are so many different variables to take into account. At the very least, we should be prepared enough to give it a good go.

Researching the company

It is critical to conduct research about the organization and position we are looking for prior to our interview. Browse the company's website and read any relevant news releases or articles. Prepare a list of questions related to the material you discover ahead of time. This can assist potential employers in seeing our interest and expertise in the industry.

As job seekers, we can exhibit genuine interest in the organization and the position we are seeking by studying it. It demonstrates that they are taking the interview seriously and are prepared to put in the time and effort to prepare. I have found that I can adjust my replies to the individual job and business culture by researching the company. It enabled me to comprehend the company's beliefs, goals, and mission, as well as to tailor my replies accordingly.

Another important area that we should pay attention to is seeing how a company we want to work for is doing overall and what its employees think about the company in general. I'm sure that we have all at some point in our careers experienced what it's like to work for a bad company that has a toxic work environment. Not all companies are going to give you that dream experience, which is why it is worth investing some time to do research. It is normal to use websites such as Glassdoor when researching a company so that we can see what the feedback and reviews are like. It always fills you with hope and excitement when you read positive reviews; however, the same isnt true of the negative ones. Even though we all want to find that perfect job and are sometimes willing to compromise just to get a job offer, we all deserve to be happy in our jobs too. So, do your research beforehand.

Practicing your questions and answers

An excellent interview tip is to practice answering questions ahead of time so that you feel more at ease and confident while replying during the interview. Consider probable questions, and practice your replies with a friend or family member. These days, it's normal to have video interviews as well as phone calls. So, find a way to get some practice with this too. If you don't have anyone to practice with, you can always record yourself, watch it back, and work on improvements.

I did an internship course, and it taught me how to communicate better. We were taught to refrain from using filler words and other language flaws such as *umms* and *errs* that could take attention away from our message and degrade our language. More practice gives us opportunities to identify any potential areas of weakness we may have.

Dressing appropriately

When it comes to interviewing attire, it is critical to look tidy, professional, and well groomed. Make sure your clothing is clean and ironed and that it is appropriate for the job you're looking for. This is true even for video interviews. Even if the role is remote, you should still dress like a professional. At the very least, dress smart casual just to be safe.

Dressing adequately gives a sense of professionalism that might assist us in establishing a solid first impression. In my case, at the very least I shave or trim my beard before an interview so that I don't look unkempt. Getting a haircut or a trim is advisable too. These days, we are fortunate because if it's a video interview or phone call, then it's not too bad. You can get away with looking a bit rough. Personally, I would not take that risk with a face-to-face, though; wear aftershave or perfume, but not so much that it becomes overwhelming.

Being confident

Attitude is everything when it comes to interviewing. I try to work toward having a good attitude and excitement for the position I'm looking for. While responding to queries from possible employers, make sure to create good eye contact, smile frequently, and offer clear concise responses. This shows that we are self-assured and capable. Confidence may positively influence the interviewer and boost our chances of getting the job. Also, it is a great method to improve conversation during the interview. My interviews have had much better conversations when I was feeling confident and prepared. It does not always happen straight away, although confidence can be increased during the interview. I have found this to be especially true when I was able to correctly answer questions and had good responses to other ones.

Following up after the interview

Remember to express your appreciation to the interviewer for their time when the interview is over. I make sure that I do it as soon as possible, and send an email expressing my thanks and repeating my interest in the role. This can help distinguish you from other possible candidates and demonstrate how committed you are to the position. It shows that we as candidates are interested in the position and are prepared to make the effort to get in touch with the employer to follow up after an interview. This will impress the company and distinguish us from other applicants who may not have followed up.

This also gives us the chance to highlight our qualifications and enthusiasm for the position. We can reaffirm our qualifications and experience and remind the employer of the potential benefit we might bring to the business. The next stages in the employment process can be made clearer as a result of following up. It enables us to show our continuous interest in the position and inquire about the timetable for decision-making.

Summary

In this chapter, we discussed several important topics on interview preparation to assist you in getting ready for job interviews. We began by talking about how crucial it is to create a solid resume and cover letter that shows your experiences and talents. We then discussed the importance of developing your website portfolio or GitHub page to highlight your work and technical expertise. After that, we looked at several methods for locating employment, such as utilizing LinkedIn, going to meetings, and seeking recommendations.

Lastly, we provided some advice on how to ace the interview process, including studying the business, preparing your responses to typical questions, and being ready to pose your own inquiries. You will definitely improve your chances of getting the job of your dreams by taking time and following these steps to prepare.

All right—we did great! Let's keep going. In the upcoming chapter, we are going to learn about understanding ReactJS fundamentals and its major features. So, we can expect to gain knowledge of JSX, the virtual DOM, state, class, and functional components, and many more concepts related to the React API. Take a breather and get ready to learn about some more advanced topics next.

Part 2: Mastering the Core React Technical Interview

In this part, you will learn about the core concepts of React.js and its features to establish a strong foundation in React.js fundamentals. We will also take a look at Hooks to use state and other React.js features in function components. Then, we will handle routing to navigate between the screens in an application and internationalization to support various locales across regions. Finally, we will learn some advanced concepts, such as portals, error boundaries, and concurrent rendering, and how they can be used in React applications.

This part has the following chapters:

- *Chapter 2, Understanding React.js Fundamentals and Its Features*
- *Chapter 3, Hooks - Bring State and Other Features into Function Components*
- *Chapter 4, Handling Routing and Internationalization*
- *Chapter 5, Advanced Concepts of React.js*

2
Understanding ReactJS Fundamentals and Its Features

Web development is a critical requirement for today's modern businesses to generate long-term customer relationships because it provides a platform to interact with your customers. However, it is challenging to build scalable and optimized web applications for large enterprises that have heavy user interactions.

JavaScript is a popular programming language for web development. It has become more popular over the past few years, and it is used to create a wide variety of applications, including web-based apps, mobile apps, desktop apps, and games. As part of JavaScript's evolution, a few libraries were created while keeping its reusable **user interface** (**UI**) in mind to speed up development, but they failed to improve its performance by re-rendering the whole UI even for any small change. This situation has been overcome by the introduction of the ReactJS library, which is based on composable components and it only re-renders specific parts of the application wherever the screen updates are required. Before we deep dive into ReactJS's features, it is important to understand the fundamentals of React so that you can face interviews with confidence and have a strong foundation for the React developer role.

This chapter will give you complete knowledge of React fundamentals such as class components, functional components, state, props, and JSX as a starting point. You must understand important features such as virtual DOM unidirectional data flow, refs, the context API, and **server-side rendering** (**SSR**) to be able to answer most questions asked by interviewers.

In this chapter, we're going to cover the following main topics:

- Prerequisites to ReactJS
- Introduction to ReactJS
- Understanding JSX
- Building views with elements and components
- Controlling the component data using props and state

- Understanding the importance of key prop

- Learning about event handling

- Understanding the virtual DOM

- Difference between unidirectional data flow and bidirectional data flow

- Accessing DOM elements in React

- Managing state globally using the context API

- Understanding server-side rendering

Prerequisites to ReactJS

For this chapter, you need to know about the following web technologies and topics before you can learn about ReactJS's fundamentals and its features. These technologies will act as a strong foundation for learning ReactJS:

- Basic knowledge of HTML, CSS, and JavaScript

- The fundamentals of ES6 features such as `let`, `const`, arrow functions, classes, imports and exports, the spread operator, promises and destructing, and more

- A basic understanding of package managers such as npm

By understanding these prerequisites, you will have a clear understanding of the core building blocks of web development and commonly used ECMAScript features in the React ecosystem.

Introduction to ReactJS

ReactJS's popularity in the JavaScript community stems from its ability to build large-scale applications where the data changes repeatedly over time. At the beginning of the interview process, an interviewer expects you to discuss an introduction to ReactJS, its features, your reason for choosing it for programming, JSX and its purpose in React development, and more. So, let's answer some introductory questions.

What is React?

React (also known as **React.js** or **ReactJS**) is an open source frontend JavaScript library that is used for building UIs, especially for single-page and mobile apps. It is used for handling the view layer of web and mobile apps.

React was created by Jordan Walke, a software engineer working for Facebook, and later maintained by the Facebook team. React was first deployed on Facebook's newsfeed in 2011 and on Instagram in 2012.

What are the reasons for choosing React for programming?

React is a popular choice among frontend libraries nowadays for web development and there are multiple reasons for that. Here are some of the most notable reasons:

- **Fast**: React can handle complex updates while maintaining a fast and responsive UI.

- **Declarative**: It follows a declarative approach in which you write all the code you need. Thereafter, React is going to be in charge of taking your declared code and performing all the JavaScript/DOM steps for the desired output.

- **High performance**: React has better performance compared to other JavaScript languages due to its less expensive DOM manipulation calls by using the virtual DOM strategy.

- **SEO-friendly**: React allows you to create web applications that are **search engine optimization (SEO)**-friendly via SSR features. This feature makes apps faster with lower page load times and quicker rendering times, which, in turn, leads to better search engine ranking compared to **client-side rendering (CSR)**.

- **Cross-platform**: The library supports building web applications, cross-platform desktop apps, and even mobile apps using React Native.

- **Easy to test**: The library provides a comprehensive set of testing utilities to test the components easily by simulating user behavior in tests.

- **Strong community support**: It has very strong community support with millions of developers across the globe who can access or share resources such as tutorials, articles, blogs, and YouTube videos and discuss them in various forums and communities.

The preceeding reasons justify why ReactJS is a popular library compared to other frameworks or libraries. ReactJS also has some notable features that bring several benefits to businesses.

What are the major features of React?

React has some outstanding features that make it a superior choice among modern frontend technologies. Some of its major features are as follows:

- It uses the **JavaScript XML (JSX)** syntax, a syntax extension of JavaScript that allows developers to write HTML in their JavaScript code, which makes the code easy and understandable.

- It uses a virtual DOM instead of Real DOM since Real DOM manipulations are expensive. The legacy JavaScript frameworks update the whole DOM at once, which makes web applications quite slow.

- It supports SSR, which offers quick initial page load times and SEO-friendly applications compared to CSR.

- It follows a **unidirectional data flow** or one-way data binding in which the data flows from parent to child but not vice versa. This helps make the application less error-prone and easier to debug and provides more control over the data.

- It uses reusable or composable UI components to develop the view at a fast pace and follows the **Don't Repeat Yourself (DRY)** principle, which states that duplication in logic should be eliminated.

React can be written either in **JSX** or JavaScript code, but most developers use JSX in their code since the benefits are worth the learning curve. The next section will provide answers to the most common questions you'll be asked at the beginning of the interview.

Understanding JSX

It is recommended that you use JSX with React to describe what the UI should look like in a web application. Even though JSX is not mandatory to use in React, it comes with several advantages, all of which we'll cover here.

What is JSX?

JSX is an XML-like syntax extension of the JavaScript language that's based on ES6, which means you can structure component rendering using syntax such as HTML. This means it is just syntactic sugar that allows you to write HTML inside JavaScript and place it in the DOM without using any `createElement()` or `appendChild()` methods.

Let's look at an example of a simple JSX code snippet to better understand how it works:

```
const myElement = <h1>This is my first JSX code</h1>
ReactDOM.render(myElement, document.getElementById
    ('root'));
```

After rendering the code, React outputs the content inside the `<h1>` tag to your DOM.

The plain JavaScript code snippet without the preceding JSX code would look as follows:

```
const myElement = React.createElement('h1', {},
    'This is my React element without JSX code!');
ReactDOM.render(myElement, document.getElementById
    ('root'));
```

> **Note**
> JSX is stricter than HTML, so all the elements should have a closing tag.

Why can't browsers understand JSX?

Web browsers can only read JavaScript objects but not JSX because there is no inherent implementation for the browser engines to read and understand the syntax. To use JSX, you need to use transpilers or compilers such as Babel to convert JSX code into its respective plain JavaScript code at runtime:

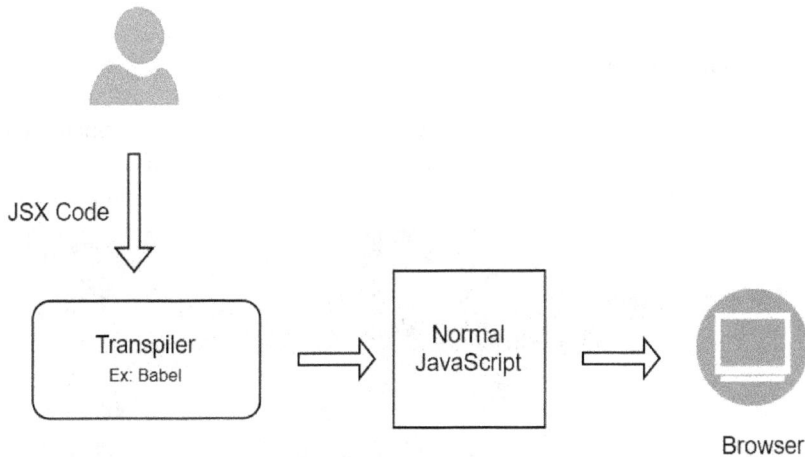

Figure 2.1: JSX transpilation

The preceding diagram explains how the transpilation works in JSX code.

What are the advantages of JSX?

JSX is not mandatory for writing React applications, but it offers many benefits:

- JSX makes it easier to read and understand the structure of a component just by seeing its layout in code

- Most developers find it helpful as a visual aid while writing the template code for the UI

- It allows you to create reusable components that can be reused throughout your application

- It can show useful errors and warning messages in React applications

- JSX makes optimizations while translating the code into regular JavaScript, so it improves performance compared to writing normal JavaScript

Once you are familiar with JSX code, it is easy to build views with elements and components.

Building views with elements and components

Both elements and components are basic building blocks for creating React views or apps. It is easy to build a UI with isolated, customizable, and reusable components. The following questions and the content they cover will help you answer the basics of ReactJS and will act as a foundation for the next set of questions in this book.

What are components?

A component is an independent, reusable code block that divides the UI into smaller pieces. For example, while building the UI part of a web application using the React library, you can break its UI into small pieces for reusability purposes, highlighted with blue boxes in the following figure:

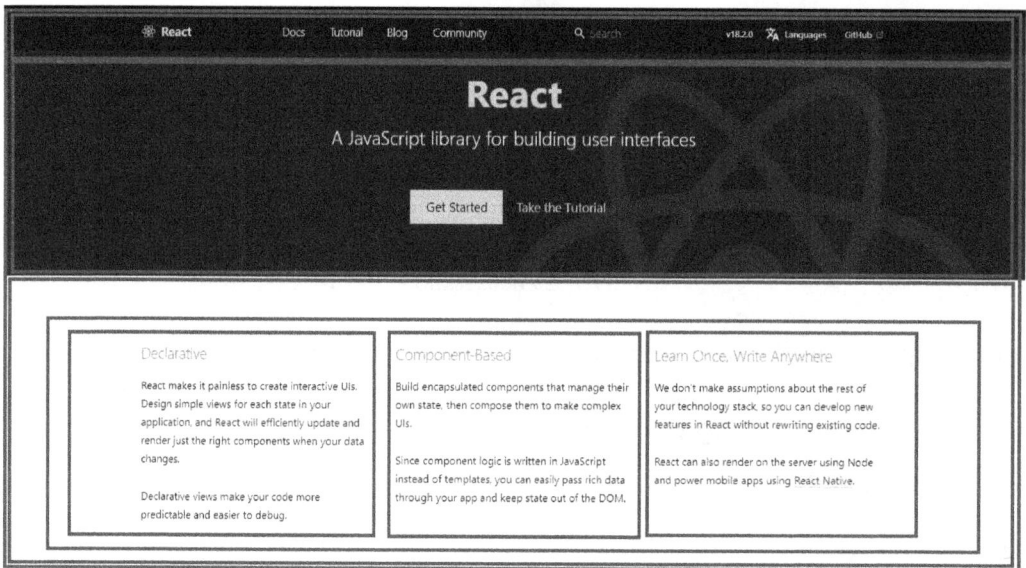

Figure 2.2: React components

Each piece can be considered a component and is represented in a separate file instead of the UI being built in a single file. These components can be reused across the application wherever they are applicable.

> **Note**
> Each component returns some HTML code, but you can only return a single HTML element. Otherwise, JSX will throw an error saying *JSX expressions must have one parent element.*

What are the different ways to create components?

There are two possible ways to create a component in ReactJS. Let's look at them:

- **Function components**: This is the simplest approach to creating components, and these are just JavaScript functions. In other words, these components are pure JavaScript functions that accept a `props` object as the first parameter and return React elements to render the output:

```
function User({ message }) {
    return <h1>{`Hello, ${message}`}</h1>;
}
export default User;
```

> **Note**
>
> It is also possible to use local state in function components after the introduction of the React Hooks feature.

- **Class components**: Class components can be created using ES6 classes, extending `React.Component`.

    The preceding function component can be written as follows:

```
class User extends React.Component {
  render() {
    return <h1>{`Hello, ${this.props.message}`} </h1>;
  }
}
export default User;
```

    The `render()` method in the preceding code is the only mandatory method that needs to be implemented in every class component.

What is the difference between an element and a component?

An element is a plain object that describes a component instance or DOM node with its desired properties to represent the UI at a certain point in time. It contains information such as the component's type, its properties, and any child elements under it. It is cheaper to create React elements compared to DOM elements.

The syntactical representation of any React element is as follows:

```
React.createElement(type, {props}, children);
```

Here is an example of creating a simple `SignOut` React element where an element contains another element:

```
const element = React.createElement("div",
  { id: "signout-container" },
React.createElement("button", {id: "signout-btn"},
  "Sign Out")
);
```

The preceding `React.createElement` method returns an object, as shown here:

```
{
  type: 'div',
  props: {
  children: {
    type: 'button',
    props: {
      children: 'SignOut'
      id: 'signout-btn'
    }
  },
    id: 'signout-container'
  }
}
```

Finally, it is rendered to the DOM using `ReactDOM.render()`.

The same React element can be simplified and represented in JSX in a short notation:

```
const signoutElement = <div id="signout-container">
  <button id="signout-btn">SignOut</button>
    <div>;
```

> **Note**
>
> React elements are immutable – that is, once you create an element, you can't modify its children or attributes further.

A component, on the other hand, is composed of React elements. In other words, a component is a factory for creating elements. This component can be one of two types – a class or a function type that optionally takes input and returns an element tree as output.

Let's understand this concept by looking at an example that uses the preceding `SignOut` React element to create a React component:

```
const SignOut = ({handleSignOut}) => (
  <div id="signout-container">
    <button id="signout-btn" onClick={ handleSignOut}>
      SignOut
    </button>
  <div>
)
```

The following figure represents how elements and components are structured inside the React view:

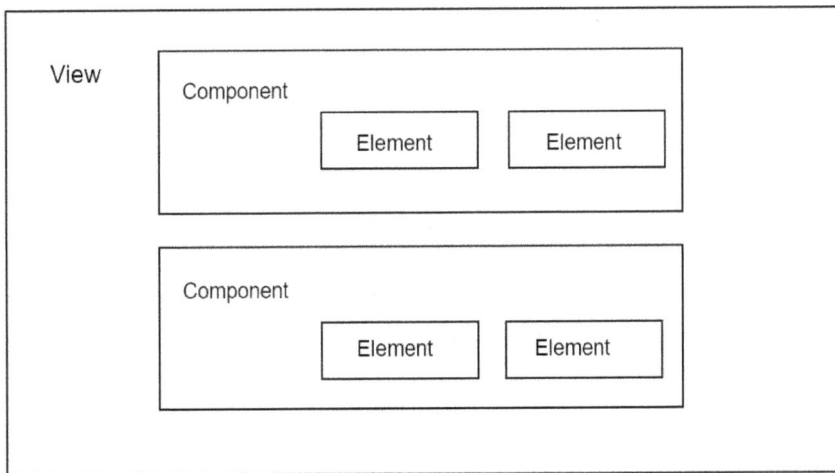

Figure 2.3: Components versus elements

These components can be further categorized into pure components, **higher-order components** (**HOCs**), and more, alongside their specific functionality. You will learn more about them in the upcoming questions.

What are pure components?

Pure components are components that render the same output for the same state and props. It is possible to achieve pure functionality within function components with the help of the Memoize API (that is, `React.memo()`), which you can wrap around the component. This API is mainly useful for performance optimizations.

The Memoize API prevents unnecessary updates from being rendered using shallow comparisons of props. This means it doesn't compare the previous state with the new state. This is because the function component itself prevents re-rendering by default when you set (that is, using the setter function) the same state again.

Let's understand this memoization concept using an example. First, create a parent `UserEnquiryForm` component to enter the user input and then create another component to display the same information called `UserProfile`; this is the child component. The child component has been wrapped with the Memoize API to prevent the same prop details from being passed down from the parent component:

```
import { memo, useState } from 'react';

const UserProfile = memo(function UserProfile
   ({ name, age }) {
   return (<>
            <p>Name:{name}</p>
            <p>Age: {age}</p>
         </>);
});
export default function UserEnquiryForm() {
   const [name, setName] = useState('');
   const [age, setAge] = useState(0);
   const [email, setEmail] = useState('');
   return (
     <>
       <label>
         Name: <input value={name} onChange=
           {e => setName(e.target.value)} />
       </label>
       <label>
         Age: <input value={age} onChange=
           {e => setAge(e.target.value)} />
       </label>
         <label>
         Email: <input value={email} onChange=
           {e => setEmail(e.target.value)} />
       </label>
       <hr/>
       <UserProfile name={name} age={age}/>
     </>
   );
}
```

In the preceding code, the `email` property has not been passed down to the child component. So, there won't be any re-rendering for the changes on email input.

However, in class components, the component will become a pure component since we extended it with `PureComponent` instead of `Component`. Internally, a pure component implements the `shouldComponentUpdate()` life cycle method with shallow comparison.

> **Note**
>
> It is recommended that all React components act like pure functions concerning their props. This guideline helps improve performance as it prevents unnecessary re-renders and avoids unexpected bugs in the application.

Apart from pure components, another special type of component is also created as a pattern in the React ecosystem. It works as a pure function with zero side effects, similar to a pure component's behavior.

What is a higher-order component?

An HOC is a function that takes a component and returns a new component. HOCs are not part of the React API but they are an advanced technique for reusing component logic. You can share props and states between components using HOCs.

An HOC can be represented with the following syntax:

```
const withHigherOrderComponent = (OriginalComponent) => (props) =>
<OriginalComponent {...props} />;
```

Third-party libraries such as Redux's `connect` and Relay's `createFragmentContainer` have been created based on the HOC concept.

What are fragments and where do you use them?

A React fragment is a syntax that allows you to wrap or group a list of child elements to a React component without the need to add an extra node to the DOM. You can use either `<Fragment>` or a shorter syntax with an empty tag (`<></>`).

For example, let's take an `Author` component to represent an author who has posted several blog posts. This component loops through the author's blog posts and displays them without adding an extra DOM node such as `<div>` or `<span>`:

```
function Author() {
        return posts.map(post =>
                <Fragment key={ post.id}>
                        <Post title={post.text} body={post.body} />
                        <Date date= {post.date} />
                </Fragment>
    );
}
```

In the preceding code snippet, the `<Fragment>` tag is used to support the key prop while iterating the list items. The alternative `<></>` syntax doesn't support key attributes. Hence, it is preferred to use `<Fragment>` over `<></>` if you're iterating the list items.

There are a few more benefits of using fragments:

- Fragments are faster and use less memory on very large or deep DOM trees
- CSS frameworks or libraries such as **Flexbox** and **CSS Grid** require a direct parent-child relationship and adding an extra `<div>` element will disturb the desired layout
- The DOM inspector is less clustered since it doesn't contain any additional DOM nodes

Now that you understand the various building blocks of a component, you can easily learn how to control the data in a component or between components. Data management is crucial for any web application.

Controlling component data using props and state

The data inside a component is controlled by props and state. All kinds of React applications are based on these two concepts, and they are important core topics that help with creating efficient and robust applications. These topics are not only useful in interviews, as you will also encounter their usage in everyday jobs.

What are props in React?

Props, which stands for properties, are arguments that appear in the form of either individual values or an object holding a set of values that are passed into components. Their naming convention is similar to that of HTML attributes. They help pass data from the parent component to the child component and are used to render the child component dynamically on the screen. This means that props act as a channel for components to communicate inside the component tree.

The main purpose of props in React is to achieve the following component functionality:

- Pass the custom data to your component based on business needs.
- Trigger state changes in a component based on the prop's value.
- Access props via `props.propName` for a function component or `this.props.reactProp` for a class component inside the component's rendering code. This data is helpful for conditionally rendering the UI.

The following is an example of how props are passed from a parent component to a child component (in this case, `Employee`):

```
import React from 'react';
function App() {
return (
    < >
        <Employee name="John" age="30" department="Manufacturing"></
          Employee>
        <Employee name="Malcolm" age="35" department="Engineering" ></
```

```
        Employee>
        <Employee name="Luther" department="Finance"></Employee>
    </ >
);
}

function Employee(props) {
return (
    < >
        <span>Name: {props.name} </span>
        <span>Age: {props.age} </span>
        <span>Department: {props.department} </span>
    </ >
)
}

Employee.defaultProps = {
    name: "Jack",
    age: "45",
    department: "HR"
}

export default App;
```

In the preceding code, the defaultProps property has been used to assign the default values of props. These will be used if no explicit props are passed.

The better alternative to access the properties of a props object is by using destructuring from ES6 (ECMAScript 2015).

With the help of destructuring, the preceding child component can be rewritten like so:

```
function Employee({name, age, department}) {
return (
    <>
        <span>Name: {name} </span>
        <span>Age: {age} </span>
        <span>Department: {department} </span>
    </>
)
}
```

> **Important note**
> Props are immutable (read-only) in nature and trying to modify these values will throw an error. If you still need to modify the data in a component, then state is the right choice for managing your data.

Can you describe state in React?

State is an in-built JavaScript object where you store property values that belong to the component. In other words, state is private and fully controlled by the component. The crucial part of state is that whenever the state object changes, the component re-renders.

The scope of state is always inside the component, as shown in the following diagram:

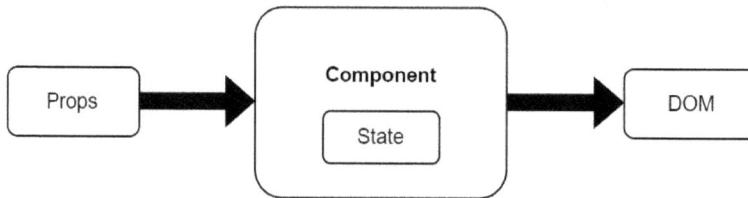

Figure 2.4: Scope of state inside a component

Here is an example of a User functional component with a welcome message as the state to explain more about its usage:

```
import React, { useState } from "react";

function User() {
  const [message, setMessage] = useState
    ("Welcome to React world");
  return (
    <>
      <h1>{message}</h1>
    </>
  );
}
```

In the preceding code, the useState Hook was used to add state to the User component. It returns an array which contains the current state and the setter function to update the state.

Compared to the functional component, the class component holds the state properties inside a built-in state object and accesses it through `this.state.message` inside the `User` component:

```
class User extends React.Component {
  constructor(props) {
    super(props);
    this.state = {
      message: "Welcome to React world",
    };
  }

  render() {
    return (
      <>
        <h1>{this.state.message}</h1>
      </>
    );
  }
}
```

The built-in `setState` function is used to update the state of the preceding class component.

> **Note**
> It is recommended to make the state variable as simple as possible for readability purposes and minimize the stateful components to achieve a single source of truth.

What are the main differences between props and state?

Both props and state are plain JavaScript objects that are used to manage the data of a component, but they are used in different ways and have different characteristics:

Props	State
Read-only and immutable	Mutable and changes asynchronously
Props are passed from the parent component to the child component	Managed by the component itself
Accessed by child components	Cannot be accessed by child components
Props make components reusable	State cannot make components reusable
Used for communication between components	Used for rendering dynamic changes

Table 2.1: Props versus state

Unlike props, state can be updated in different ways. Let's learn more about batching multiple state updates.

How does React batch multiple state updates?

React prevents components from re-rendering for each state update. React makes this possible by optimizing application performance using group updates within event handlers with the help of built-in Hooks. This entire process is known as **batching**. React version 17 only supports batching for browser events, whereas React version 18 supports an improved version of batching known as **automatic batching**.

Automatic batching supports state updates that are invoked from any location instead of just browser events. In other words, it supports native event handlers, asynchronous operations, timeouts, and intervals.

Let's look at an example demonstrating automatic batching:

```
import { useState } from 'react';

export default function MultiState() {
  const [count, setCount] = useState(0);
  const [message, setMessage] = useState('Batching');

  console.log('Application re-rendered');
  const handleAsyncFetch = () => {
    fetch(https://jsonplaceholder.typicode.com/todos/1
    ).then(() => {
      // trigger only one(1) re-render due to
        Automatic Batching
      setCount(count +1);
      setMessage('Automatic batching');
    });
  }

  return (
    <>
      <h1>{count}</h1>
      <button onClick={handleAsyncFetch}>
        Click Me!</button>
    </>
  )
}
```

Even though the preceding code updates two state variables using an event handler, React will batch them automatically by default and the component will only re-render once.

Can you prevent automatic batching?

Automatic batching is a great feature of the React library that optimizes rendering performance. However, there are situations where you need to re-render your component for each state update or update one state depending on another updated state value. React introduced the `flushSync` API function from ReactDOM to stop automatic batching whenever necessary. This function is also useful for use cases where you need to flush updates immediately to the DOM in case you're integrating with third-party code such as browser APIs and UI libraries.

For example, let's say you want to update the scroll position on a web page after adding a new to do or task to a simple to do list app. This behavior is helpful if you wish to have a direct focus on the new to do content. In this scenario, the latest to do state needs to be updated immediately for you to get the correct scroll position:

```
const handleAddTodo = (todoName) => {
  flushSync(() => {
    setTodos([...todos, { id: uuid(), task: todoName }]);
  });
  todoListRef.current.scrollTop = todoListRef.
    current.scrollHeight;
};
```

The usage of this function is not common and using it can often impact application performance badly.

How do you update objects inside the state?

You shouldn't update React's state object directly. Instead, you need to create a new object or make a copy of the existing object and then set the state with the newly created object. So, while updating the state object, you always need to treat objects inside the state as read-only, even though JavaScript objects are mutable.

Let's see this comparison in action and show the results of these two updating processes. As an example, the `WeatherReport` component has been created, along with its properties, including `temperature` and `city`. After that, component properties are mutated directly inside the event handler:

```
function WeatherReport() {
  const [weather, setWeather] = useState({
    temperature: 26,
    city: "Singapore",
  });

  const handleWeatherChange = (e) => {
    if (e.target.name === "temperature") {
      weather.temperature = e.target.value;
    }
```

```
    if (e.target.name === "city") {
      weather.city = e.target.value;
    }
  };
  return (
    <>
      <label>
        Temparature:
        <input value={weather.temperature} onChange=
          {handleWeatherChange} />
      </label>
      <label>
        City:
        <input value={weather.city} onChange={handleWeatherChange} />
      </label>
      <div>
        Report:
        <span>{weather.temperature}</span>
        <span>{weather.city}</span>
      </div>
    </>
  );
}
```

Once the preceding code has been deployed, try to enter the new weather details in the UI. You will see that the input fields won't get updated.

You can fix this by creating a new copy of the `weather` object and then setting the state. To do that, let's update the preceding event handler:

```
handleWeatherChange(e) {
    setWeather({
        ...weather,
        [e.target.name]: e.target.value
    })
}
```

The preceding code updates the weather details in the UI as intended.

Sometimes, only one field needs to be modified in the state object. In this case, it is recommended to use object spread syntax to get the benefit of reusing the previous state object property values instead of setting each field in the state.

How do you update nested state objects?

It is quite easy to update top-level state objects with the spread syntax. But when it comes to nested state objects, you cannot update the required nested property directly like you can in regular JavaScript objects.

This can be explained further with an example: we'll take a nested state object and modify the nested property inside it. To demonstrate this behavior, let's consider the `User` state object with nested address details as a property:

```
{
    name: 'Tom',
    age: 35,
    address: {
        country: 'United States',
        state: 'Texas',
        postalCode: 73301
    }
}
```

Now, you can try to update the `postalCode` property using an expression like `user.address.postalCode = 75015` in your React components, similar to how you do in plain JavaScript. The screen won't be updated with the latest value.

If it is not possible to flatten the nested `User` object as a workaround, then there are two possible approaches to update the state properly:

- **Create separate nested objects**:

  In this approach, first, create a separate new copy of the nested object (`updatedAddress`) using the spread syntax. After that, create a new top-level object (`updatedUser`) that points to the newly created nested object:

  ```
  const updatedAddress = { ...user.address,
    postalCode: 75015 };
  const updatedUser = { ...user, address:
    updatedAddress };
  setUser(updatedUser);
  ```

- **Update nested object with a single function call**:

  It is also possible to update the nested object together with a top-level object by using the spread syntax within a single state setter function:

  ```
  setUser({
    ...user,
    address: {
      ...user.address,
      postalCode: 75015
    }
  });
  ```

If you would like to go beyond the traditional approach, third-party libraries such as **Immer** provide a convenient way to update the deeply nested state objects. This library enables direct nested object updates just like regular JavaScript updates the properties.

Mutating nested objects using Immer looks like this:

```
setUser(user => {
  user.address.postalCode = 75015;
});
```

The component's state can be an array of items as well, not just a primitive value or an object type. However, you need to supply the additional key prop, as detailed in the upcoming questions.

Understanding the importance of key props

Keys help you control component or element instances. They play a major role in deciding whether the element needs to be re-rendered or not in a list of elements. Hence, every developer should have an idea about the importance of a key prop.

What is a key prop and what is the purpose of it?

A **key** is a special attribute that you need to include when creating a list of elements in a component. This key prop helps React identify which elements have changed and been added or removed. In other words, it helps you retain a unique identity of the elements or among the siblings in the list even after the elements have been modified.

Even if you don't supply a key prop, the list can render the content to the browser successfully, but with a warning message logged in the console, as shown here:

```
Warning: Each child in an array or iterator
         should have a unique "key" prop
```

It is recommended to use a unique ID value from the data as a key prop. This value can be a string or number.

Let's understand this key prop concept in a better way by implementing the to do list of a programmer. Here, you are assigning a key to the `TodoItem` component while iterating from the list and not to the extracted `<li>` tag:

```
import React from "react";
import ReactDOM from "react-dom";

function TodoItem(props) {
    const { item: todo } = props;
    return <li>{todo.id}: {todo.message}</li>;
}

function TodoList(props) {
    const { todos: list } = props;
    const updatedTodos = list.map((todo) => {
        return <TodoItem key={todo.id} item={todo} />;
    });
    return <ul>{updatedTodos}</ul>;
}
const devTodoItems = [{id: 1, message:"Write a component"}, {id:2,
message:"Test it"}, {id:3, message:"Publish the component"}];

ReactDOM.render(
    <TodoList todos={ devTodoItems } />,
    document.getElementById("root")
);
```

It is discouraged to assign indexes (received from iterating the list of elements) as keys because if the elements of the list get reordered in the future, then the keys of the elements will also change.

Learning about event handling

Event handling is essential for interacting with a web page in an application. React has its own event handling ecosystem. The event handler determines what action has to be taken whenever a particular event is fired. This section will give you a good understanding of event handling in the React library.

What are synthetic events?

A synthetic event is a cross-browser wrapper around a browser's actual native event object. It provides a unified API that prevents browser inconsistencies and ensures that the event works across multiple platforms.

There are some similarities between synthetic events and native events if you use the same `preventDefault` and `stopPropogation` methods in those two events. It is also possible to access native events directly by using the `nativeEvent` attribute on the `syntheticEvent` instance. As an example, the following search component is still able to access the native input event and other properties or methods inside the handler:

```
function Search() {
  handleInputChange(e) {
      // 'e' represents synthetic event
      const nativeEvent = e.nativeEvent;
      e.stopPropogation();
      e.preventDefault();
      // Code goes here..
  }
  return <input onChange={handleInputChange} />
}
```

The event handling in React has a few differences compared to HTML event handling, which we will discuss in the next section.

How do you differentiate between React event handling and HTML event handling?

React event handling is similar to event handling DOM elements in HTML. However, there are some notable differences between them:

- **Naming convention**: In HTML, the name of the event is represented in lowercase as a convention:

  ```
  <button onclick="handleSingUp()">SingUp</button>
  ```

  However, in React, the name should be in camelCase:

  ```
  <button onClick={handleSignUp}>SingUp</button>
  ```

- **Avoiding default behavior**: In HTML, you can avoid the default behavior of the event by returning `false` inside the event handler.

  As an example, let's take a simple login form that contains a username and a password field to input the data. After submitting the form, you need to restrict the default behavior of an `onsubmit` event, and the enclosing form must not be refreshed:

  ```
  <form onsubmit="console.log('The form has been
    submitted.'); return false">
        <input type="text" name="name" />
        <input type="password" name="password" />
        <button type="submit">Login</button>
  </form>
  ```

However, in React, the default behavior can be prevented by calling the `event.preventDefault()` method:

```
function Login() {

    function handleSubmit(e) {
        e.preventDefault();
        console.log('You submitted Login form.');
    }

    return (
        <form onsubmit="handleSubmit">
            <input type="text" name="name" />
            <input type="password" name="password" />
            <button type="submit">Login</button>
        </form>
    )
}
```

- **Invoking function**: In HTML, either you need to invoke the function by inserting parentheses (that is, `()`) after the function name or use `addEventListener()` to attach events and listeners.

The following example shows a button `onclick` event and invoking the respective handler. This can be done in two ways.

For the first approach, you can insert parentheses for the `handleSiginUp` function's name:

```
<button onclick="handleSingUp()">
```

As an alternative approach, you can use the `addEventListener()` method:

```
<p id="signup">
    Please SignUp
</p>

<button id="myBtn" />

<script>
    const element = document.getElementById("myBtn");
    element.addEventListener('click', handleSignUp);

    function handleSignUp() {
        document.getElementById("signup").innerHTML +=
            'SignUp completed';
    }
</script>
```

However, in React, you just need to specify the method name inside the curly braces ({ }) of the event attribute's value.

How do you bind event handlers in class components?

There are several ways to bind event handlers in React class components:

- **Binding event handlers in the constructor:**

  In JavaScript, classes are not bound by default; the same applies to React when you are defining the event handlers as a class. However, it is possible to bind the event handlers to an instance using the this keyword in a constructor function.

  As an example, let's add a handleUserDetails() binding inside the constructor:

  ```
  class User extends Component {

      constructor(props) {
        super(props);
        this.handleUserDetails = this.handleUserDetails.
          bind(this);
      }

      handleUserDetails() {
        console.log("Show User details");
      }

      render() {
        return <button onClick={this.handleUserDetails}>Profile</
          button>;
      }

  }
  ```

  If you forget to bind the handler, the this keyword will be undefined when the function is invoked.

- **Public class fields syntax:**

  If you are not interested in binding handlers in the constructor, the public class fields approach is much better for readability and ease of use. This syntax is enabled by default in the **Create React App (CRA)** tool.

  The previous binding approach can be rewritten and simplified using public class fields syntax, as shown here:

  ```
  class User extends Component {
    handleUserDetails = () => {
  ```

```
        console.log("Show User details");
      }
      render() {
        return <button onClick={this.handleUserDetails}>Profile</
          button>;


      }
    }
```

- **Use arrow functions**:

  Arrow functions can be passed in the callbacks directly without the need to bind with the `this` keyword explicitly.

  The arrow function is passed in the `User` component callback, like so:

```
    handleUserDetails() {
        console.log("Show User details");
    }


    render() {
        return <button onClick={() => this.handleUserDetails()}>
            Profile</button>;
    }
```

  The main problem with this arrow function approach is that a different callback is created every time the component renders, and the child component might do extra re-rendering if the callbacks are passed as props to child components. Hence, it is recommended to use either a binding in a constructor or the public class fields syntax approach.

The magic behind the React library, including syncing the component data with the UI, DOM updates, and more, is taken care of by the virtual DOM. In the next section, you will learn about virtual DOM, its importance, and its processes behind the scenes.

Understanding virtual DOM

DOM stands for **Document Object Model** and it represents the entire UI of a web page (HTML) in a tree data format. virtual DOM was not invented by React, but it uses it as its core feature. Its main purpose is to minimize the number of DOM operations when re-rendering the UI. React uses this feature to enhance its performance. There's a high chance you'll get questions related to this topic in an interview.

What is virtual DOM?

virtual DOM is an in-memory, lightweight virtual representation of Real DOM that's generated by React components. The virtual representation of a UI is stored in memory and synced with Real DOM to align with the latest state updates. This is possible through a library known as **ReactDOM**, and this step happens in between the render function being called and elements being displayed on the screen. This entire process is known as **reconciliation**.

How does virtual DOM work?

React and Vue.js technologies use virtual DOM under the hood to abstract the manual DOM operations away from developers. This programming mechanism works in four major steps.

As an example, let's take a simple search form with an inputfield inside the `CitySearch` component and see how the virtual DOM works. We'll provide diagrams for ease of understanding:

```
function CitySearch() {
    return (
        <div>
          <h2>Find city:</h2>
          <form>
              <span>
                  City:
              </span>
              <input onChange={handleCitySearch} />
          </form>
        </div>
    )
}
```

The preceeding city search works internally with the following steps of virtual DOM mechanism:

1. When the application is rendered for the first time, React creates a virtual DOM representing the UI and stores the same in memory:

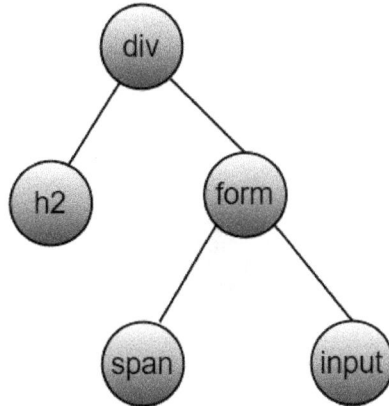

Figure 2.5: Initial vrtual DOM

2. Whenever the underlying state changes, it will automatically create a new virtual DOM for the update. Since virtual DOM is just an object representing the UI, there won't be any changes (such as repainting) in the UI at this point:

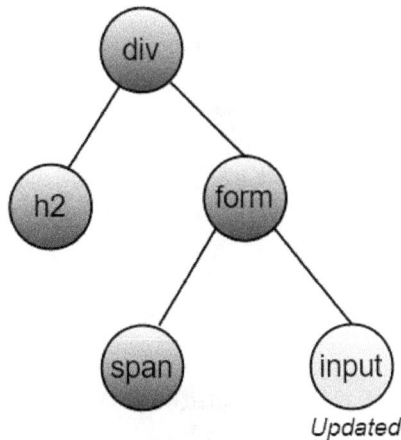

Figure 2.6: Updated virtual DOM

3. Once the new virtual DOM has been created, React compares it to a pre-updated version or snapshot of virtual DOM. React uses the **diffing** algorithm to compare the changes; this process is known as **reconciliation**:

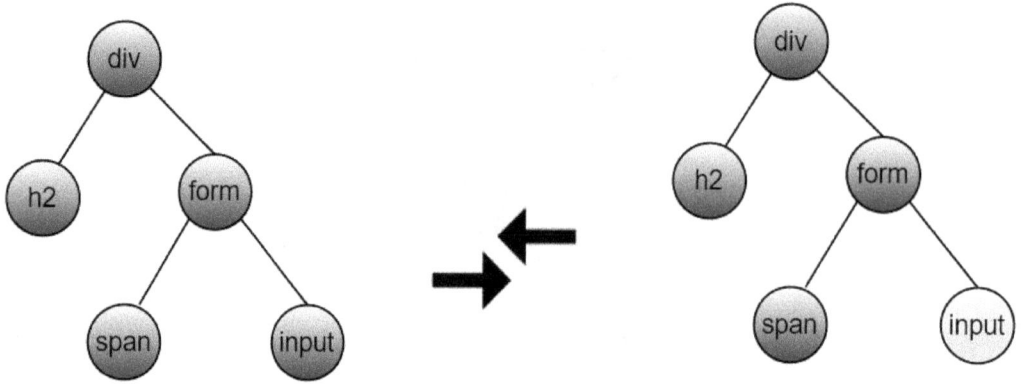

Figure 2.7: Comparing virtual DOM snapshots

4.   After the reconciliation process, React uses a render library such as ReactDOM, which takes the changes and updates that in Real DOM:

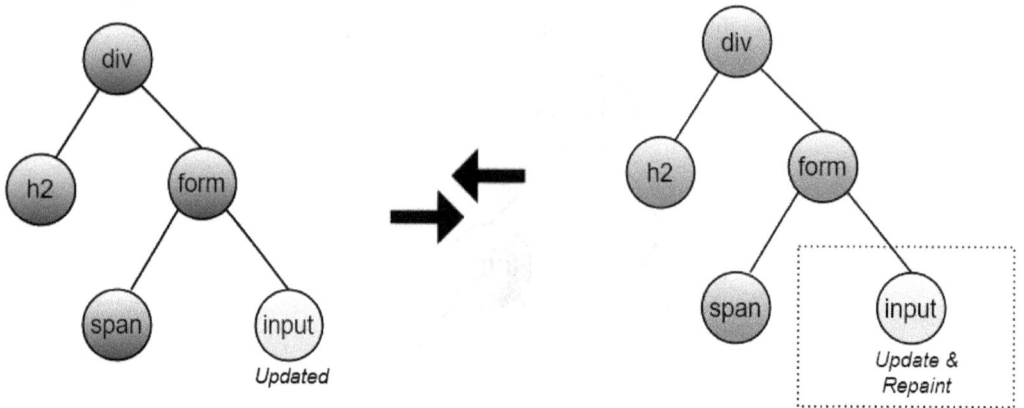

Figure 2.8: Updated Real DOM

What is Shadow DOM?

Shadow DOM is a web component technology that's designed primarily for scoping variables and CSS. This is useful when CSS styles defined in a parent component don't affect or apply to a child component.

What is the difference between Real DOM, virtual DOM, and Shadow DOM?

In modern web development, virtual DOM and shadow DOM have been introduced to improve performance and encapsulation as add-ons to real DOM.

Some of the notable differences among these three DOMs are listed here:

Real DOM	Virtual DOM	Shadow DOM
It creates a single DOM for the entire screen	It creates a copy of the entire real DOM in memory and keeps track of changes	It creates small copies of Real DOM with its isolated scope (that is, scoped CSS styles and JavaScript)
Any change will involve re-rendering the whole screen	The state change will involve re-rendering the specific part of the page	The changes apply to its own web component
Implemented in web browsers, such as via the Solid.js library	Implemented in JavaScript libraries such as React, Vue, and others	Implemented in web components, such as Lit and Vaadin libraries
Suitable for small to medium scale applications without complex interactivity	Suitable for large-scale applications with complex interactivity	Suitable for small to medium scale applications with less complex interactivity
Uses less CPU and memory compared to virtual DOM	Uses more CPU and memory compared to Real DOM	Uses less CPU and memory compared to virtual DOM
Doesn't support encapsulation because components can be modified outside	Supports encapsulation because components cannot be modified outside	Supports encapsulation because components cannot be modified outside

Table 2.2: Real DOM versus irtual DOM versus Shadow DOM

What is React Fiber?

Fiber is a new reconciliation engine that was introduced in React version 16 to enable in-built scheduling and incremental rendering of virtual DOM. Incremental rendering means having the ability to split rendering work into chunks and spread it out over multiple frames. So, with the help of incremental rendering, Fiber improves application performance in areas such as animation, layout, and gestures.

This reconciler is a complete rewrite of an old reconciliation algorithm called **stack reconciler**.

Data flow and communication in React applications

The unidirectional data flow feature of React makes the UI simple and predictable for data changes in small to large-scale applications. It is quite important to know the benefits of data flow and communication between components to better understand the relevant React concepts.

Can you describe unidirectional data flow in React?

Unidirectional data flow is also known as one-way data binding and is where the data flows one way only while being transferred between different parts of an application. This technique or feature already exists in functional reactive programming.

React follows unidirectional data flow, where the data is transferred from parent to child using props but not vice versa. Moreover, the child components can't update data that comes from the parent component. React doesn't encourage bidirectional or two-way binding to make sure you are following a clean data flow architecture.

The following figure gives a clearer idea of the data flow in React:

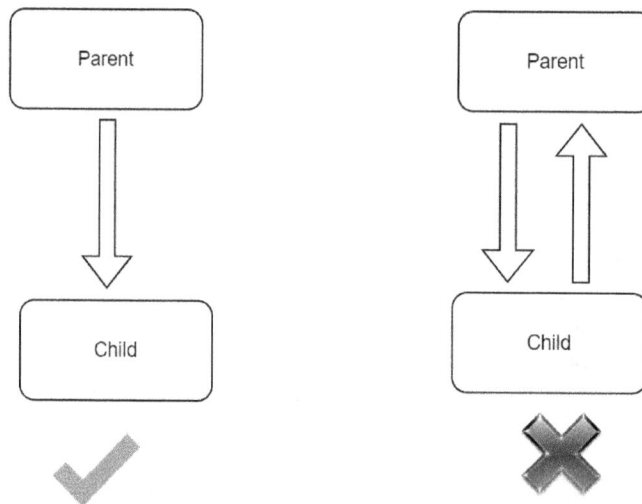

Figure 2.9: Unidirectional versus bidirectional data flow

The only way to update the data in the parent component is by triggering the events from the child component.

> **Note**
>
> In contrast to React, Vue.js follows two-way data binding or bidirectional data flow between the components.

What are the advantages of unidirectional data flow?

The main advantage of unidirectional data flow is having a single source of truth for your data. There are many other advantages of the unidirectional data flow feature. Some of the key benefits are listed here:

- **Debugging**: Since the developers know where the data comes from and where it goes, it is much easier to debug problems

- **Less error-prone**: The data flows in one direction, which makes the programs less error-prone and gives the developers better control

- **Efficiency**: No extra resources are wasted with the known boundaries of unidirectional data flow in the application

You cannot always depend on the state, props, and data flow concepts to control the view layer. Irrespective of the JavaScript library, you may need access to DOM elements, and accessing elements through conventional approaches such as `document.getElementById` becomes cumbersome. In the next section, you will find a better alternative to access DOM.

How do you access DOM?

DOM manipulation is taken care of by the React library under the hood, without the need for any manual DOM updates. But sometimes, you might encounter use cases (focusing, scrolling to specific elements, and so on) to have DOM element access managed by React. As a solution to these use cases, refs have been introduced to access the DOM nodes.

A React interviewer might expect a good knowledge of DOM access and possible use cases, both of which cannot be handled through a traditional declarative approach.

What are refs? How do you create refs?

Ref is the shorthand for a reference to an element or a component. Refs are used to access DOM nodes or React elements that are created in the render method. The reference to the DOM element is available in the `current` attribute of the ref. In other words, refs are plain JavaScript objects with additional current property. To understand this ref concept in a better way, let's look at an example of implementing auto-focus behavior for an input element using a ref. To do that, we'll follow the following instructions::

1. Import the `useRef` Hook from the React library.
2. Declare `inputRef` inside the `SignUpForm` component with the return value of the Hook.
3. Pass `inputRef` to the `<input>` element, which connects the input's DOM node to the `inputRef.current` property.
4. While loading the component instance, apply focus to an input element programmatically by calling `focus()` on the DOM node within the `useEffect` Hook.

After following all the preceding steps, the final component that's using refs should look like this:

```
import {useRef, useEffimport {useRef, useEffect} from 'react';

export default function SignUpForm() {

  const inputRef = useRef(null);
  useEffect(() => {
    inputRef.current.focus();
  }, [])

  return (
    <>
      <input type="email" ref={inputRef} />
      <button>
        Verify Email
      </button>
    </>
  );
}
```

Similar to how the `useRef` Hook is used in function components, `createRef` is typically used when creating a ref in a class component.

What is the main purpose of refs?

The main purpose of refs is to imperatively modify a child outside of the typical one-way data flow. A few common use cases that can be handled through refs as an escape hatch are discussed here:

- For the first use case, let's talk about how UI elements are modified through certain events or actions. This use case category includes scenarios such as managing input field focus, text selection, and media control (or playback).

  As an example, let's look at the aforementioned text selection and audio scenarios controlled through external button clicks:

  ```
  //Text selection
  const hasInputText = inputRef.current.value.length > 0;

  if (hasInputText) {
  ```

```
        inputRef.current.select();
    }

    // Audio controls
    const playAudio = () => {
        audioRef.current.play();
    };

    const pauseAudio = () => {
        audioRef.current.pause();
    };
```

- For the second use case, let's talk about triggering imperative animations in the UI without writing any explicit animations either through CSS or JavaScript.

  Here is an example of accessing the div element and finding its position based on the scroll event to perform certain actions in the layout:

  ```
  function handleScroll() {
      const block = blockRef.current;
      const { y } = block.getBoundingClientRect();
      const blockBackgroundColor = y <= 0 ?
         'white' : 'black';
      setBackground(blockBackgroundColor);
  }
  ```

- For the third use case, let's discuss integrating with third-party DOM libraries in a React application.

  It is easy to integrate an existing application with some of the JavaScript plugins or libraries using refs. For example, third-party plugins such as DataTable.js and select2 can easily be accessed inside React applications without recreating them from scratch.

> **Note**
> It is recommended to avoid refs if you can implement the task declaratively.

How do you compare refs with state?

Both refs and state are used to persist the component data between renders. However, there are many differences between them:

Ref	State
Created by the `useRef(initialValue)` Hook, which returns the `{current: initialValue}` JavaScript object	Created by the `useState(initialValue)` Hook, which returns the current state value and the setter function to update the state– that is, `[value, setValue]`
Doesn't trigger a re-render for any changes that are made to it	Triggers a re-render for any change in state
It is often used to communicate with external APIs	It is frequently used within a component to change its appearance
It is possible to update the `current` attribute value outside the rendering process – that is, ref is mutable	You should not update the state variables directly; a setter function should be used to modify the value – that is, state is immutable
React cannot track ref changes	React can track state changes
You shouldn't read or write refs during the rendering process	You can read state at any time
Avoid using refs unless declarative views based on state can't be implemented, since changes to the DOM structure may conflict with React's `diff` and `update` approach	It's always recommended to use state for UI updates

Table 2.3: Ref versus state

Even though refs are less strict (in terms of mutation) than state, most of the time, you will be using state over refs because refs are an escape hatch for accessing the DOM, which you don't need that often.

> **Note**
> If you are storing the information across the re-renders without rendering on the screen, then you should use refs. Otherwise, you always need to use state to store data.

What are forward refs?

Nowadays, components are more complex and barely use plain HTML elements directly. This leads to a parent and child component hierarchy with composable views. If you just try to pass down the ref to the child component as a prop, the child component won't receive the actual DOM element that needs to be accessed. Instead, it returns { current: null }.

React's forwardRef is a method that allows a parent component to pass down refs to its children. In the following example, the child component receivesa ref from its parent component by wrapping it with the forwardRef method. This, in turn, forwards it to the <button/> DOM element:

```
import { forwardRef } from 'react';

const MySignInButton = forwardRef(function  MySignInButton(props, ref)
{
  const { label, ...otherProps } = props;
  return (
    <label>
      {label}
      <button {...otherProps} ref={ref} />
    </label>
  );
});
```

The preceding child component receives a ref as a second argument, whereas the first argument refers to props.

> **Note**
> You can limit the information you expose about your DOM node instead of passing the entire DOM node using the userImperativeHandle Hook. You will learn more about this Hook in *Chapter 3*.

Managing state globally using the context API

Context helps you share global data with the child components, even though those components exist at a deeper level in the component tree. You can perform state management for large-scale applications by using the context API and Hooks. There's a high chance you'll get interview questions related to context implementation to solve common use cases regarding maintaining data globally in React applications.

What is prop drilling?

Prop drilling refers to the process of sending props from a higher-level component to a lower-level component in a component tree by going through several other components in the middle that don't need the data but only help in passing it around. This prop drilling term doesn't exist in ReactJS officially, but it is frequently used to represent the situation.

Can you describe context?

Context is used to solve the prop drilling issue. It provides a way to pass data from parent-level components to child components by storing the data in a central location without the need to pass the data manually at each level of the component tree.

You can use context in React by following three simple steps:

1. **Create the context**: The built-in `createContext(defaultValue)` factory function from the React library is used to create the context object. It only accepts one argument to provide the default value. Let's create a user context with the default username:

    ```
    // userContext.js
    import { createContext } from 'react';
    export const UserContext = createContext('Jonathan');
    ```

2. **Provide the context**: The `Context.Provider` component needs to be applied to the parent component with the context changes that were supplied to its child components. The `value` prop on this component is used to set the context value.

    In this step, the `username` field is going to be updated with current user details as context for the provider component:

    ```
    import { UserContext } from './userContext';

    function App() {
      const value = 'Michael';

      return (
        <Context.Provider value={value}>
          <MyParentComponent />
        </Context.Provider>
      );
    }
    ```

    The child components that need to consume the context should be wrapped inside the provider component.

3. **Consume the context**: The child components can consume the context using the `useContext` Hook. This Hook returns the value of the context:

```
import { useContext } from 'react';
import { UserContext } from './context';

function MyChildComponent() {
  const currentUser = useContext(UserContext);
  return <span>{currentUser}</span>;
}
```

You will learn more about the `useContext` Hook in *Chapter 3*.

These steps have been represented with a diagram to help you understand context in action:

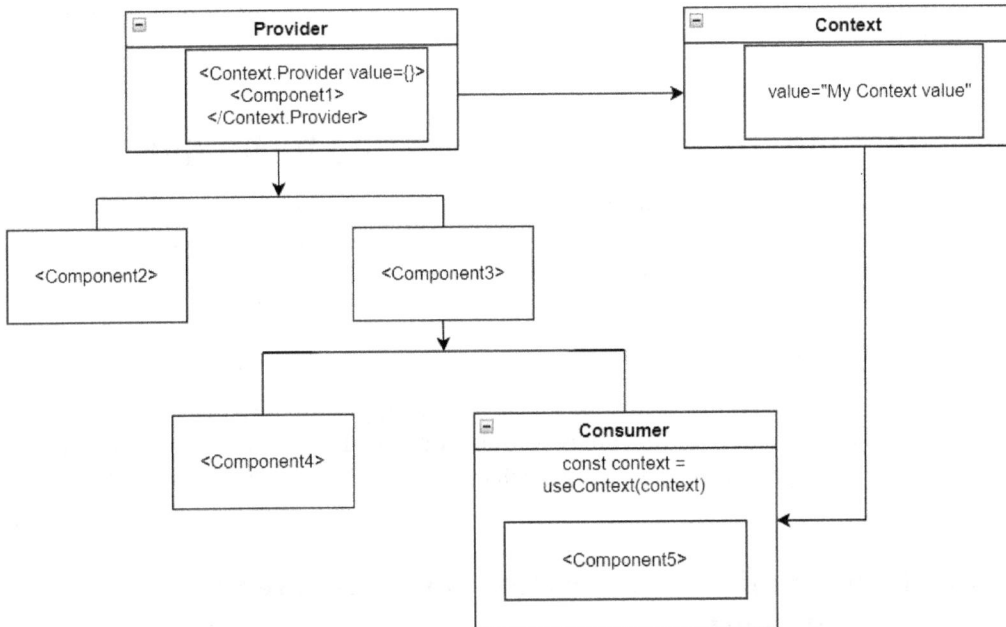

Figure 2.10: Context in action

What is the purpose of context?

The main purpose of context is to allow your components to access global data without you facing any prop drilling problems and re-render the components when the global data has been changed.

Here are some of the common use cases of context:

- Theme information for applying branding to the entire application
- Authenticated user profile information
- User settings
- Preferred language settings
- Application configuration

So far, we've learned how to render the React application on the client side. In the next section, you will learn how to render web content on the server side to improve page loading speed, along with a few other benefits.

Understanding the server-side rendering technique

SSR is rapidly becoming a more prominent feature in JavaScript libraries and frameworks. React-based frameworks such as Next.js, Gatsby, and others make creating SSR much easier. Nowadays, interviewers expect a good knowledge of SSR, along with regular **CSR**.

What is server-side rendering?

SSR is a popular alternative rendering method for **single-page applications** (**SPAs**). This technique renders a client-side SPA on the server and then sends a fully rendered HTML page to the client. This is helpful for SEO purposes because search engines can easily find the content first before they send the page to the users.

What is the main difference between server-side rendering and client-side rendering?

CSR is the rendering mode in which the browser downloads a minimal HTML page and it renders using JavaScript. The data fetching, templating, and routing processes are handled on the client side – that is, by the browser.

SSR, on the other hand, converts HTML files on the server into a fully rendered HTML page that includes the data for the client.

When do you need to use server-side rendering?

Which rendering method is used depends on the requirements of the business. But here, we have mentioned a few situations where you can consider using SSR:

- If you are prioritizing SEO and building a blog site, it is recommended to use SSR
- If your website needs a faster initial page load time
- If the application has a simple UI with less interactivity with a smaller number of features and pages
- If the application contains less dynamic data
- If the user traffic on the website is less

A few other pre-rendering techniques are also available, such as **static site generation (SSG)** and **incremental static regeneration (ISR)**, both of which will be discussed in *Chapter 9*.

We have now answered a lot of fundamental questions about React. This knowledge also acts as a foundation for answering the next stage of questions in the upcoming chapters.

Summary

In this chapter, we discussed a lot of fundamental concepts that are frequently asked about in React interviews. We started by introducing ReactJS and JSX and discussing their advantages in building robust web applications. Then, we went on to talk about the core building blocks of ReactJS, such as elements, components, props, and state, and how the virtual DOM and one-way data flow work behind the scenes.

Lastly, we covered questions related to an application's interaction through event handling and how to share data globally using context and SSR in the React ecosystem. In the next chapter, we will consider questions related to Hooks, their importance, and how Hooks make React so much better by implementing functionalities faster and more effectively.

3

Hooks: Bring State and Other Features into Function Components

Hooks were introduced in function components to reap the benefits of React features without writing any classes and life cycle methods. Most developers use Redux, Recoil, Mobx, and other third-party libraries to manage the global state in large-scale applications. But when you use React Hooks such as `useContext` and `useReducer` together, it becomes a better alternative for external state management. Hooks are much easier to use than complex external libraries that involve excessive amounts of boilerplate code, repetitive files, and folders across the application. React also provides numerous other built-in Hooks that can be useful for various use cases in React applications. If there is no specific built-in Hook available to handle your use case, you can create your own Hook to fulfill your business needs. Some common use cases (or cross-cutting concerns) for Hooks are authentication, logging, caching, data fetching, and error handling.

In this chapter, you will be introduced to React Hooks, their benefits, and various built-in Hooks that add React features to function components. The built-in Hooks will be explained in depth through examples to understand their usage in React applications. Additionally, you will gain the knowledge and confidence to answer questions related to third-party Hooks, create your own Hooks, and troubleshoot Hooks.

In this chapter, we're going to cover the following main topics:

- Introduction to Hooks and their purpose
- Local state management using Hooks
- Global state management using Hooks
- Performing side effects in React applications
- Accessing DOM nodes using Ref Hooks

- Optimizing the application performance
- Learning about popular third-party Hooks
- Building your own Hooks
- Troubleshooting and debugging Hooks

Introduction to Hooks and their purpose

Initially, React was mainly used with class components, but over the years the components became complex with the usage of various patterns to reuse the component logic. Subsequently, Hooks were introduced to simplify the code without writing any patterns, such as render props and **higher-order components (HOCs)**. Since Hooks play an important role in building React applications nowadays, you can expect a couple of questions on Hooks in a React interview. This section will give you detailed answers about what Hooks are and what their purpose is.

What are Hooks?

Hooks are simple JavaScript functions that allow components to use the local state and execute side effects (or cross-cutting concerns) and other React features without writing classes. The Hooks API has been introduced in React 16.8 to isolate the stateful logic from the components.

In a nutshell, the Hooks feature is a way for your function components to *Hook* into React's life cycle and state.

What is the motivation behind Hooks?

Hooks can solve a wide variety of problems.

Here are a few:

- *Difficulty in reusing stateful logic between components*: By default, React didn't provide a way to reuse the component logic. Programming patterns such as **render props** and **HOCs** tried to solve this problem. But those patterns require modifying the structure of the component hierarchy, which makes the application cumbersome with the several layers of wrappers and makes it harder to follow the code.

  As a result, Hooks were introduced to separate stateful logic from the components without modifying the component hierarchy.

- *Difficulty in understanding the complex components*: As an application grows, the components become much more complex with a full set of stateful logic and side effects. The life cycle methods become occupied with a mix of unrelated logic such as data fetching, adding event listeners, or removing event listeners in one place. For example, the componentDidMount life cycle method can perform data fetching for the component and add the event listeners too. At the same time, the related event listener logic, such as cleanup, needs to be added in the componentWillUnmount life cycle method. Ultimately, it becomes difficult to split the larger components into small components and, at the same time, difficult to test them.

Hooks can split the larger components into smaller functions with the related piece of code rather than splitting the code based on the life cycle methods.

- *Confusion created by classes*: Classes are not specific to React, but they belong to JavaScript. If you would like to work on class components, first you should have a clear idea about **the** keyword behavior called **this**, which is different from that in other languages. Also, if you are not familiar with using ES2022 public class fields syntax, you need to remember about binding event listeners in the constructor. All these concepts created a lot of confusion among the developers about the proper usage.

Hooks are helpful for creating React features without writing the classes and to avoid confusion within the developer community.

Can you describe the rules of Hook usage?

There are two main rules to be followed while using Hooks:

- **Call Hooks at the top level only**: You shouldn't invoke Hooks inside loops, conditions, or nested functions that are part of React's component logic. Instead, it is highly recommended to follow the rule of using Hooks at the top level of your React function components before any early returns.

  This guideline will ensure that Hooks have been called in the same order irrespective of the component logic each time a component is rendered. In other words, it preserves the state of Hooks between multiple useState and useEffect Hooks.

- **Call Hooks from React functions only**: You shouldn't call Hooks from regular JavaScript functions. Instead, you can call them from either React function components or custom Hooks.

> **Note**
> The eslint plugin named eslint-plugin-react-Hooks (https://www.npmjs.com/package/eslint-plugin-react-hooks) can be used to enforce the two rules described in the *Can you describe the rules of Hook usage?* section.

Can I use Hooks inside class components?

You cannot write Hooks inside class components. In other words, Hooks have been created for the function components only. However, you can mix class components, and function components with Hooks in a single component tree without causing any problems.

React components hold the data and keep track of data changes using an updatable structure called the **state**. In real-world applications, most components use the state to process and display the data in their UI. In the next section, we will be covering questions and their answers related to local state management using state Hooks.

Local state management using Hooks

There are two Hooks to achieve local state management inside React applications. The first Hook, named useState, can be used for simple state transformations, and the other Hook, useReducer, is used for complex state logic. Basically, useState uses useReducer internally. This means that the entire component state can be managed through the useReducer Hook itself. Since the state is a core building block of a React component, every developer should have a clear idea about managing the state using Hooks.

What is the useState Hook?

The useState Hook is used to add the state to a function component. This is one of the most used built-in Hooks from React. This Hook takes the initial state as an argument and the same initial state can be either a value or a function type (i.e., initializer function). If the initial state is derived from an expensive computation, it is suggested to use the initializer function, which will be executed only on the initial render. The useState Hook returns an array that contains two values: the state variable and the setter function to update the state.

The syntactic representation of useState looks as follows:

```
const [state, setState] = useState(initialState)
```

Let's take an example of a counter component that preserves the state of a counter using the useState Hook. The setter function is used to update the count state variable and re-render the UI for any changes:

```
import { useState } from "react";

function Counter() {
  const [count, setCount] = useState(0);

  return (
    <>
      <p>You clicked {count} times</p>
      <button onClick={() => setCount(count + 1)}>
        Click me</button>
    </>
  );
}
```

Upon clicking the counter button each time, the count state variable will be incremented by one and the respective UI updated with the latest state variable's value.

> **Note**
>
> The state setter function doesn't update the current state in the already executing code. It will be available only in the next render.

Is it always recommended to use an updater function?

You might hear about the recommendation from the developer community to always use an updater function to update the state if the new state is calculated from the previous state. This rule is helpful to avoid an unpredictable state after doing some state calculation logic. Even though there is no harm in following this rule, it is not always necessary. In most cases, React will update the state variable before the next event happens. That is, there is no risk of stale data for the state in the beginning of the event handler.

But if you are doing multiple state updates in the same event handler, then it is suggested to use an updater function to receive the expected data result. The usage of an updater function inside an event handler is coded as follows:

```
function handleClick() {
   setCounter(a => a + 1);
   setCounter(a => a + 1);
   setCounter(a => a + 1);
}
```

In this code, a => a + 1 is an updater function. React puts your updater functions in a queue and as a result, updates on same state variables are batched. During the next render, React will call them in the same order.

What is a useReducer Hook? How do you use it?

The useReducer Hook is an alternative to the useState Hook. It is used to separate the custom state logic (e.g., add, update, and delete items of a state) from the rendering logic. In other words, it is helpful for extracting the state management out of the component.

This Hook accepts three arguments. The first argument is a reducer function that specifies how to update the state, the second argument is for the initial state, and the third argument is an optional initializer function to determine the initial state. In contrast, useState just accepts the initial state.

The useReducer Hook returns an array with two values, current state and dispatch function, which is used to modify the state and trigger re-renders.

Let's understand the usage of this Hook with a counter example. Here, you can update the counter state value with increment, decrement, and reset actions using a reducer function:

```
ffunction reducer(state, action) {
  switch (action.type) {
    case "increment":
      return { count: state.count + 1 };

    case "decrement":
      return { count: state.count - 1 };

    case "reset":
      return { count: action.payload };

    default:
      throw new Error();
  }
}

function init(initialCount) {
  return { count: initialCount };
}

function Counter() {
  const initialCount = 0;

  const [state, dispatch] = useReducer(reducer, initialCount, init);

  return (
    <>
      Count: {state.count}
      <button
        onClick={() => dispatch({ type: "reset", payload: initialCount
})}
      >
        Reset
      </button>
      <button onClick={() => dispatch({ type: "decrement"
      })}>decrement</button>
      <button onClick={() => dispatch({ type: "increment"
      })}>increment</button>
    </>
  );
}
```

React will save the initial state once and ignore it for the next renders. So, you need to avoid recreating the initial state for each render if you are deriving the state through a function call. Instead, you can use an initializer function as a third argument for the reducer function.

In the third argument in the preceding code, the `init` function has been used to process the initial state based on a default value mentioned as the second argument within the Hook.

The important phases of the preceding code are described in the following steps:

1. When any of the button-click events are triggered, the respective event handler will be dispatched with an action to the reducer function.

2. Thereafter, the reducer function will update the state to a new state based on the requirement.

3. The state update will trigger the component to re-render to update the UI.

The flow diagram in *Figure 3.1* depicts the `useReducer` Hook's behavior in a step-by-step manner:

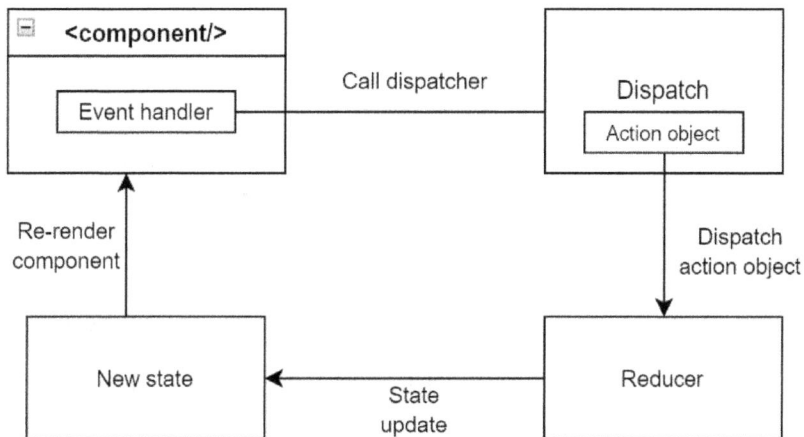

Figure 3.1: Behavior of the useReducer Hook

Note

The `useReducer` Hook won't re-render the children if there is no change in state compared to the previous state.

When should you use the useReducer Hook over the useState Hook?

Both the useReducer and useState Hooks are helpful in managing the application state, but the useReducer Hook provides a well-controlled and powerful state management solution for the following reasons:

- The useReducer Hook is preferred over useState when you need to manage complex state logic. For example, when the state contains multiple nested values or the next state depends on the previous one, the useReducer Hook is a better choice.

- The useReducer Hook can handle multiple actions in a single function rather than creating separate functions for each action using the useState Hook.

- The useReducer Hook is also helpful in optimizing the performance of components that trigger deep or nested updates, because you can pass down a dispatch function of the useReducer Hook at any nested level via context instead of passing callbacks to every level of a component tree. In other words, it helps in avoiding the prop drilling issue mentioned in *Chapter 2*. Moreover, the dispatch function won't change between re-renders.

> **Note**
>
> Since useState itself is derived from the useReducer Hook under the hood, you can cover all the state use cases with useReducer.

If you need to share the component state with multiple child components that exist in the deeper level of a component tree, it is preferred to use the in-built context Hook from React. This Hook is mainly used to maintain application-wide data, which is known as global state management.

Global state management using Hooks

The useContext Hook is commonly used along with the useState Hook for global state management. The major advantage of the useContext Hook is that it solves the prop drilling issue.

Detailed common use cases of the useContext Hook were already explained in *Chapter 2*. Hence, this section will mainly focus on specific use case questions related to global state management using the useContext Hook.

How do you override context for a specific part of the component tree?

Sometimes, you may need to override the context with a different value for a certain part of the component tree. It is possible to override the context value by wrapping that part in a provider with a different value.

As an example, the following code applies a blue background to all the pages except for the contact page, where a white background will be applied using a context provider:

```
<ColorContext.Provider value="blue">
  <About />
  <Services />
  <Clients />
  <ColorContext.Provider value="white">
    <Contact />
  </ColorContext.Provider>
</ColorContext.Provider>
```

There is no restriction on the nesting level or number of times you override the context using a provider.

What would the context value be for no matching provider?

If there is no matching provider above the calling component of the `useContext` Hook, the default value mentioned in the context creation will be returned – that is, the default value used in `createContext(defaultValue)`.

If you specify a default value, you can avoid unexpected errors on the page for any missing providers in the component tree.

In class components, the side effects are handled in different life cycle methods such as `componentDidMount`, `componentDidUpdate`, and `componentWillUnmount` based on the requirement. On the other hand, in function components, effect Hooks simplify the handling of side effects based on rendering in a single place. The next section will cover frequently asked questions about performing side effects in React applications.

Performing side effects in React applications

Effects are an escape hatch in React programming. React provides a few effect Hooks that are used to implement side effects such as data fetching, subscriptions, timers, logging, DOM manipulations, and so on within function components. These Hooks should be used only when you are synchronizing with external systems. There are three types of Hooks available:

- **useEffect**: This is a frequently used Hook to connect a component to an external system.

- **useLayoutEffect**: This Hook is the same as the useEffect Hook except that it fires before the browser repaints the screen to measure the layout.

- **useInsertionEffect**: This Hook fires before React makes changes to the DOM, such as adding dynamic CSS.

Let's thoroughly discuss the various effect Hooks and their features to answer the questions asked in the interview.

How do reactive dependencies impact the logic inside the useEffect Hook?

The useEffect Hook accepts an optional dependencies argument that accepts an array of reactive values. You cannot choose dependencies for your effect and every reactive value should be declared as a dependency to avoid any kinds of bugs. There are different scenarios for passing the reactive dependencies.

Passing the dependency array

If you pass the reactive values in a dependency array, the effect should run the logic after the initial render and also after each re-render with the changed dependencies.

The following is an example of passing name and status reactive dependencies to understand the syntax of useEffect with an array of dependencies:

```
useEffect(() => {
  // Runs after first render and every re-render with
    dependency change
}, [name, status]);
```

Passing the empty dependency array

If your effect doesn't use any reactive values, it only runs after the initial render. In this case, the effect Hook looks as follows:

```
useEffect(() => {
  // Runs after initial render only
}, []);
```

Not passing the dependency array

If you skip passing the dependency array, itself the effect runs after every re-render of your component, as follows:

```
useEffect(() => {
  // Runs after every re-render
});
```

React will compare each reactive value from the dependency array with its previous value using `Object.is` comparison to verify the changes.

How often are setup and cleanup functions invoked inside the useEffect Hook?

In most cases, effects should have a cleanup function to clear or undo the changes created by their respective setup code. React invokes setup and cleanup functions in the following different phases of the component life cycle:

- **Mounting**: The logic inside the setup function runs whenever the component is added to the DOM or view.

- **Re-rendering**: After every re-rendering of a component along with its dependency change, the cleanup (if it is defined) and setup functions will be invoked in an order. Here, the cleanup function runs with the old props and state, and the setup code runs with the latest props and state thereafter.

- **Unmounting**: The cleanup code runs one final time after the component is removed from the DOM or view. This cleanup function helps to avoid unwanted behaviors such as memory leaks and to improve performance.

If strict mode is turned on in your React application, there will be an extra development-only **setup and cleanup cycle** before the first actual setup call. This is to ensure the cleanup logic mirrors the setup logic to avoid any discrepancies with the setup code.

When should you remove an object or a function from dependencies?

There might be a situation where your effect might re-run more frequently than necessary if that effect depends on an object or a function created during rendering. This is because the object or function created is different for every render.

Let's understand this concept in a better way using an example. The following is an example of fetching a list of users inside the useEffect Hook based on the Url and name query parameter dependencies. Here, the query object has been created during rendering to build the absolute URL path:

```
const userUrl = "https://jsonplaceholder.typicode.com/users";

export default function Users() {
  const [users, setUsers] = useState([]);
  const [name, setName] = useState("John");
  const [message, setMessage] = useState("");

  const userQueryOptions = {
    url: userUrl,
    name,
  };

  useEffect(() => {
    const userUrl = buildUserURL(userQueryOptions); //buildUserURL is
      excluded from code snippet
    fetch(userUrl)
      .then((res) => res.json())
      .then((users) => setUsers(users));
  }, [userQueryOptions]);

  return (
    <>
      Users: {message}
      <input value={message} onChange={(e) => setMessage(e.target.
        value)} />
      <input value={name} onChange={(e) => setName(e.target.value)} />
      {users &&
        users.map((user) => (
          <div>
            Name: {user.name}
            Email: {user.email}
          </div>
        ))}
    </>
  );
}
```

In the preceding code, the userQueryOptions object has been recreated for every re-rendering due to the message state changes. Also, this message data is not related to reactive elements inside the effect.

This issue can be fixed by moving the object inside the effect and replacing the object dependency with a name string, because name is the only reactive value the effect depends on:

```
useEffect(() => {
  const userOptions = {
    url: userUrl,
    name,
  };

  const userUrl = buildUserURL(userOptions);
  fetch(userUrl)
     .then((res) => res.json())
     .then((users) => setUsers(users));
}, [name]);
```

In the same way, you can avoid creating the function during the rendering phase by moving it inside the effect Hook. After that, you can replace the function dependency with the direct reactive dependency value.

What is the useLayoutEffect Hook? How does it work?

The useLayoutEffect Hook is a special type of effect Hook that is invoked before the browser repaints the screen. This Hook is mainly used for scenarios where the component flickers when the state is updated. Imagine a pop-over component on the web page. The component first needs to determine the position of the element in the viewport before rendering it correctly on the screen.

The main purpose of the useLayoutEffect Hook is to provide the layout information to the component for rendering. It works in three simple steps:

1. Render the initial content without layout information.
2. Calculate the layout size before the browser repaints the screen.
3. Re-render the component using the correct layout information.

> **Caution**
> The component is going to be rendered twice and will block the browser before it repaints the screen. This impacts the application performance. Therefore, it is recommended to use the useLayoutEffect Hook only where it is required.

Since effects will run after every render, one of the major ways to improve performance in React applications is to avoid unnecessary re-renders. There are a few in-built Hooks created in React to optimize the performance. Let's dive deep into those details in the next section.

Optimizing the application performance

The performance optimizations have a massive impact on the customer experience. Even though React applications have a very fast UI by default, there might be performance issues when the size of the application increases. This section will focus on the questions related to performance optimization Hooks, which you could expect to be asked by interviewers to gauge your skill from a broader perspective.

What is memoization? How can it be implemented in React?

Memoization is an optimization technique for speeding up web applications by caching the results of expensive function calls. It returns the cached result when the same input arguments have been passed again.

In React, this optimization can be implemented through two Hooks: useMemo and useCallback. These Hooks improve the performance, skipping the unnecessary re-rendering by returning the cached result when the same input is given.

Can you describe the useMemo() Hook?

The useMemo() Hook is used to cache the result of an expensive calculation between re-renders. The syntax of this Hook looks as follows:

```
const cachedValue = useMemo(calculateValue, dependencies)
```

This Hook returns the value of the expensive calculation by accepting two arguments. The first argument is a function to do the expensive calculation, and the second is an array of dependencies that are reactive values used in the calculation. In other words, the cached result (or stored value from the last render) will be returned when there are no changes to the dependency values. Otherwise, the calculation will be performed again.

Let's understand this concept with an example. Consider a factorial calculation function of a number and apply the useMemo Hook around it. The component also performs an increment action that is independent of the calculation function:

```
import { useState, useMemo } from "react";

function factorial(number) {
  if (number <= 0) {
    return "Number should be positive value.";
  } else if (number === 1) {
    return 1;
  } else {
    return number * factorial(number - 1);
  }
```

```
}

export default function CounterFactorial() {
  const [count, setCount] = useState(0);
  const [number, setNumber] = useState(1);

  const factorial = useMemo(() => factorial(number), [number]);

  return (
    <>
      <h2>Counter: {count}</h2>
      <button onClick={() => setCount(count + 1)}>Increment</button>
      <h2>Factorial: {factorial}</h2>
      <input
        type="number"
        value={number}
        onClick={() => setNumber(number + 1)}
      />
    </>
  );
}
```

In the preceding code, if you increment the counter value, there won't be any re-rendering related to the factorial function because the respective reactive number was not updated. That is, the factorial function will only be called where there is a change in the input number, but not when the counter value is incremented.

What are the possible use cases of the useMemo() Hook?

Memoization is helpful in optimizing the application performance, and some of the developers even think that there is no harm in memoizing almost all the components as much as possible. However, this technique is unnecessary for simple calculations within the functions.

There are a few common cases where memoization is useful:

- When there are expensive calculations, such as sorting, filtering, changing the format, and so on while rendering the content

- When you are passing a prop to a component wrapped within the useMemo Hook and want to skip re-renderings when there is no change in the prop – that is, when pure components can be wrapped within useMemo

- When the value passing to the wrapped component has been used as a dependency of some other Hook

The **profiler** section of **React DevTools** will be helpful in identifying the components that are laggy and require memoization to add.

What are common mistakes with the usage of useMemo? How do you rectify them?

The usage of the useMemo Hook is quite straightforward, and this Hook might be used extensively to optimize the rendering performance. However, you need to be careful with some of the following common mistakes:

- If you try to return an object from the useMemo Hook, then either wrap it with parentheses or write an explicit return statement.

  For example, the following useMemo Hook returns an undefined value because the opening brace ({) is part of an arrow function but not the object:

  ```
  const findCity = useMemo(() => {
     country: 'USA',
     name: name
  }, [name]);
  ```

  This can be fixed by an explicit return statement for the object, as follows:

  ```
  const findCity = useMemo(() => {
    return {
      country: "USA",
      name: name,
    };
  }, [name]);
  ```

- If you forget to specify the dependencies, then the calculation will re-render every time:

  ```
  const filterCities = useMemo(() => filteredCities(city,
  country));
  ```

  The reactive values used in the calculation are to be passed in the dependencies array to avoid unnecessary renders:

  ```
  const filterCities = useMemo(
    () => filteredCities(city, country),
    [city, country]
  );
  ```

- You shouldn't call useMemo inside loops. Instead, wrap it or extract it under a new component:

  ```
  {
    products.map((product) => {
      const revenue = useMemo(() => calculateRevenue(product),
  ```

```
      [product]);

         return (
           <>
             <span>Product: {product.name}</span>
             <span>Revenue: {revenue}</span>
           </>
         );
       });
    }
```

This can be solved by extracting the useMemo calculation inside a child component:

```
    {
       products.map((product) => {
         return <Report product={product} />;
       });
    }
```

The aforementioned points can be treated as best practices while working with the useMemo Hook.

When should you use the useCallback Hook instead of the useMemo Hook?

When a top-level component re-renders, by default, React re-renders all its children recursively. This situation will impact the performance of the application if the child component has heavy calculation. In this case, the child component needs to be optimized using the Memo API or the useMemo Hook.

However, if you pass the callback function as a prop to the child component, React will always re-render the children because either the function definition or arrow function is treated as a new function every time re-rendering occurs. This defeats the purpose of memoization. In this case, useCallback is helpful in optimizing the performance.

The useCallback Hook is like the useMemo Hook, but it caches the callback function instead of a value. You can still use the useMemo Hook but the calculation function would have to return another function; that is, it requires an extra nested function.

Let's discuss this concept with an example that contains TaxCalculation as the parent component and TaxPayer as the child component. In the child component, you need to skip re-rendering considering when the same props are sent and re-rendering is slow.

To skip re-rendering, first, you need to wrap the child component (TaxPayer) with the memo function:

```
import { memo } from 'react';
const TaxPayer = memo(function TaxPayer({ onSubmit }) {
  // ...
});
```

If the parent component re-renders with a change in the income prop, then this change leads to the re-rendering of the child component as well. This won't be a big problem when the child component doesn't have any big calculations and changes from the income prop are minimal.

However, if you pass a callback function to a child component as a prop, it creates a new function every time. This specific case should be avoided all the time, irrespective of the performance impact.

To skip the re-render because of a new prop every time, let's apply the useCallback Hook for the handleSubmit callback function:

```
function TaxCalculation({ year, income}) {
  const handleSubmit = useCallback((taxPayerDetails) => {
    post('/tax/' + year, {
      taxPayerDetails,
      income
    });
  }, [year, income]);

  return (
    <div>
      <TaxPayer onSubmit={handleSubmit} />
    </div>
  );
}
```

In the preceding code, the callback function is going to be memoized until or unless there is a change in dependency reactive values.

Similar to the Ref API that exists in class components, some Hooks have been created in function components especially to interact with DOM nodes. The next section talks about important concepts related to accessing the DOM nodes using Hooks.

Accessing DOM nodes using ref Hooks

Refs are useful when you need to work with external systems (or non-React systems) such as built-in browser APIs. There are two built-in ref Hooks available in function components. The useRef Hook is used to declare a ref to hold any kind of value but is mainly used for DOM nodes. useImperativeHandle is used to expose the customized ref with only the required methods.

Please note that an introduction to refs has already been covered in *Chapter 2*. In this section, we will go beyond what we have already discussed about refs in *Chapter 2*.

How do you avoid recreating the Ref contents?

The useRef Hook accepts the initial value (or default value) as an argument, like the useState Hook. The declaration of this Hook should be placed at the top of the enclosed component.

React saves this initial value at the first render and ignores it for the next renders, but if you create an expensive object for the initial value of the ref, it might be called for every render unnecessarily. This will impact the performance of the application.

The declaration of the initial ref value and how the ref content is recreated can be explained in a better way with the use of the following example:

```
function CreateBlogArticle() {
  // This is an expensive object to create the article
}

function Blog() {
  const articleRef = useRef(new CreateBlogArticle());
  //...
}
```

In the preceding code, the CreateBlogArticle() function is always invoked to create the expensive object, even though React ignores this object from the second render onward.

This issue can be resolved by restricting the invocation of the CreateBlogArticle() function for the subsequent renders, as follows:

```
function Blog() {
  const articleRef = useRef(null);

  if (articleRef.current === null) {
    articleRef.current = new CreateBlogArticle();
  }
  //...
}
```

Now the blog article object is calculated only once during the initial rendering.

Is it possible to access a ref in the render method?

Yes, you can access the current value of a ref inside the render method, but it is not recommended to read or write the ref.current value during the render process. This is because the ref value appearing on the screen may not be updated for any events by knowing the fact that changing a ref doesn't trigger re-rendering, unlike the state variable.

How do you expose a subset of methods from a ref instance?

The useImperativeHandle Hook is used to expose customized methods or only a subset of existing methods of a DOM node from a child component to a parent component. This is useful to restrict a parent ref to access only certain functions or properties without giving access to the entire ref. The common use case is creating a component to share it under a library and consumers can access only the exposed API.

Let's say you are planning to create a dialog component and want to share some basic features of the dialog in some top-level parent component. In this case, you can expose open, close, and reset methods inside child component instead of giving access to the entire dialog DOM node:

```
useImperativeHandle(ref, () => ({
    open: () => ref.current.invokeDialog(),
    close: () => ref.current.closeDilaog(),
    reset: () => ref.current.clearData(),
}));
```

The component which uses the useImperativeHandle Hook needs to be wrapped with forwardRef and the ref received as a second argument from the forwardRef render function.

There are a few more built-in Hooks, such as useId, useDeferred, useTransition, and useSyncExternalStore, that are not covered because of their minimal usage. Let's learn about them quickly:

- useId: This Hook is used to generate unique IDs for the HTML accessibility attributes
- useDeferred: This Hook is used to defer updating a part of the UI until the latest data is available
- useTransition: This Hook is helpful to improve user responsiveness by marking some of the state modifications as low-priority
- useSyncExternalStore: This Hook is used to subscribe to an external data store that exists outside the React system

There are several built-in Hooks provided by React, but you can go beyond the usage of these Hooks and use third-party Hooks created by the React community to cover specific use cases based on your business needs. In the next section, we will cover questions related to third-party Hooks and their respective answers.

Learning about popular third-party Hooks

The Hooks API is quite popular among the developer community, and built-in Hooks have existed since 2019. The developers tried to create many third-party Hooks, such as useImmer, useFetch, useDebounce, useForm, useLocalStorage, Redux Hooks, and so on, to solve common use cases observed in web development. If you would like to master the Hooks concepts then you should have a good understanding of third-party Hooks and how they are useful to solve some common problems.

What is the useImmer Hook? What is its purpose?

The useImmer Hook is just like the useState Hook but it provides advantages while managing the complex state with nested levels of data. It updates the state as if it were directly mutable, similar to regular JavaScript. This Hook is based on the Immer library by creating a new copy of the state that can be mutated.

This Hook can be installed through the use-immer npm library. Like useState, it returns a tuple. The first value of the tuple is the current state, and the second is the updater function.

Let's see an example of the UserProfile component and update the address details directly, as follows:

```
import { useImmer } from "use-immer";

function UserProfile() {
  const [user, setUser] = useImmer({
    name: "Tom",
    address: {
      country: "United States",
      city: "Austin",
      postalCode: 73301,
    },
  });

  function updatePostalCode(code) {
    setUser((draft) => {
      draft.address.postalCode = code;
    });
  }

  return (
    <div className="profile">
      <h1>
        Hello {user.name}, your latest postal code is ({user.address.
          postalCode}
        )
```

```
      </h1>
      <input
        onChange={(e) => {
          updatePostalCode(e.target.value);
        }}
        value={user.address.postalCode}
      />
    </div>
  );
}
```

Under the hood, Immer creates a temporary draft object and all the changes are applied to it. Once all the mutations are completed, Immer will produce the next state object.

If your use case is not fulfilled by built-in Hooks or by any third-party Hook, then you can build your own Hook to provide the solution for your needs. After the next section, you will be in a position to answer questions related to custom Hooks.

Building your own Hooks

Even though React provides some built-in Hooks such as useState, useEffect, useContext, and so on for common use cases, you may sometimes need to use Hooks for specific requirements that cannot be solved by built-in Hooks or third-party libraries. By the end of this section, you will be able to answer questions related to custom Hooks and their purpose, and how to avoid traditional approaches to share the component logic.

What are custom Hooks? How do you create them?

React comes with several built-in Hooks, but it won't restrict you from using Hooks for limited scenarios. It is also possible to create your own Hooks by extracting the component logic into separate reusable functions known as **custom Hooks**. These Hooks are helpful in hiding the complex logic from the components. They cover a wide range of use cases such as data fetching, form handling, online or offline status subscriptions, connecting to a chat room, animations, and so on.

The creation of custom Hooks and their usage can be explained in a better way with the demonstration of a real-time example. Let's consider a blogging site application where you list all the posts of a particular user and at the same time display the comments on a particular post. Here, you need to create two components named **Posts** and **Comments**. Both of these components need to fetch the data from the server based on a given URL with an optional query parameter. Once the response is received, both the components display the data on the screen.

Instead of having duplicated logic related to data fetching, loading, error handling, and so on in both components, the code can be moved to a separate reusable custom Hook prefixed with the word use. The data fetching Hook can be created with the name useFetchData inside the useFetchData. js file, as follows:

```
import { useState, useEffect } from "react";

const useFetchData = (url, initialData) => {
  const [data, setData] = useState(initialData);
  const [loading, setLoading] = useState(false);

  useEffect(() => {
    setLoading(true);
    fetch(url)
      .then((res) => res.json())
      .then((data) => setData(data))
    .catch((err) => console.log(err))
    .finally(() => setLoading(false));
  }, [url]);

  return {data, loading};
};

export default useFetchData;
```

Thereafter, the above custom Hook can be used in consumer components created as a part of the Posts.jsx files and Comments.jsx. The usage in the **Posts** component would look as follows:

```
import useFetchData from './useFetchData.js';

export default function Posts() {
  const url = "https://jsonplaceholder.typicode.com/posts?userId=1";
  const { data, loading} = useFetchData(url, []);
  return (
    <>
      {loading && <p>Loading posts... </p>}
      {data && (
    data.map((item) =>
      <div key={item?.title}>
        <p>
          {item?.title}
              <br/>
          {item?.body}
        </p>
```

```
        </div>
      )
    )}
  </>
  );
}
```

In the same way, you can reuse `useFetchData` in the **Comments** component as well. After these changes, the **Posts** and **Comments** components' code became much simpler, more concise, and more readable.

What are the benefits of custom Hooks?

The main advantage of using custom Hooks is code reusability without writing the duplicated logic in many components. There are a few other advantages as well to considering custom Hooks:

- **Maintainability**: It is easier to maintain code with custom Hooks. In the future, if you need to change the logic of the Hook, you only need to change the code in one place without disturbing other parts of the code – that is, components or files.

- **Readability**: The application code becomes cleaner and more readable using custom Hooks instead of wrapping layers of HOCs, providers and consumers, and render props around the actual presentation components shown in the UI. Moreover, the component code becomes much cleaner by moving out specific component logic into separate Hooks.

- **Testability**: You need to write separate tests for test containers and presentation components in React applications. This is challenging especially for integration tests if your containers use many HOCs. The complexity increases because you need to test the containers and the components together to perform integration tests. This issue can be eliminated with custom Hooks as they allow you to combine containers and components into a single component.

  Moreover, it is easier to write unit tests and mock Hooks compared to HOCs.

- **Community-driven Hooks**: The React community is already popular and has created many Hooks for their specific use cases. The recommended approach is first to check whether the Hook you are looking for has already been created by someone or not before going to create your own Hook. Some community-driven Hooks are available at `https://usehooks.com/` and `https://github.com/imbhargav5/rooks`.

The advantages listed inspire many React developers to create custom Hooks for unique features encountered in their React applications. If any third-party open source library has already provided the Hook to cover your specific scenario, it is suggested to reuse the same Hook instead of reinventing the wheel by building a custom Hook.

Should you still consider using render props and HOCs?

Both render props and HOCs are traditional advanced patterns used in the React ecosystem to share the component state logic between components. However, Hooks are somewhat simpler and sufficient to cover use cases compared to these two traditional patterns. Moreover, using Hooks, you don't need to change the existing component structure and add more components to end up with a nested tree.

Do you recommend moving effects into custom Hooks?

Effect Hooks are used to perform application side effects when you need to interact with the world outside of React's scope. Some non-React systems can access web APIs, invoke external APIs, and so on. Over time, the number of effects in your code should be reduced by implementing specific solutions to your use cases. The standard guideline is to use effect Hooks when there are no built-in solutions available. This is because avoiding the effects makes your application simpler, faster to run, and less error-prone. By moving out your effects to custom Hooks, it becomes easier to upgrade the code related to effects when there are solutions available.

As your application grows with lots of custom Hooks to fulfill the business requirements, the application complexity increases and there is a high chance of encountering bugs in the application. The next section addresses how to debug React custom Hooks.

Troubleshooting and debugging Hooks

Traditional debugging methods, such as debuggers with an IDE and browser DevTools, are not effective for debugging custom Hooks. React provides the `useDebugValue` Hook to allow developers to debug custom Hooks by assigning custom formatted labels to them. By the end of this section, you will have an idea about debugging custom Hooks.

How do you debug custom Hooks?

The `useDebugValue` Hook is used to extend the visualization of data related to the internal logic of custom Hooks within **React DevTools**. This information appears inside the **Component Inspector** tab of the **React DevTools** extension.

The current debug information is limited to displaying the information about in-built Hooks used inside of our custom Hook. It is hard for developers to read the information by counting each line in the output and identifying which entry map corresponds to Hooks called inside the code. This difficulty can be rectified by adding additional entries to the **React DevTools** output for our custom Hook.

Let's understand this in a better way using an example. The required details can be logged in various places using the useDebugValue Hook inside the custom useFetchData Hook, as created in the *What are custom Hooks? How do you create them?* section:

```
const useFetchData = (url, initialData) => {
    useDebugValue(url);
    const [data, setData] = useState(initialData);
    const [loading, setLoading] = useState(false);
    const [error, setError] = useState(null);
    useDebugValue(error, (err) =>
      err ? `fetch is failed with ${err.message}` :
        "fetch is successful"
    );

    useEffect(() => {
      setLoading(true);
      fetch(url)
        .then((res) => res.json())
        .then((data) => setData(data))
        .catch((err) => setError(err))
        .finally(() => setLoading(false));
    }, [url]);

    useDebugValue(data, (items) =>
      items.length > 0 ? items.map((item) => item.title) :
        "No posts available"
    );

    return {data, loading};
};
```

In the preceding code, the second and third debug calls use an *optional second argument* to format the displayed value.

React DevTools will list all the additional entries under the label called **DebugValue** inside the FetchData custom Hook. For example, if you hover over the **Posts** component, the **Hooks** section on the right side looks as follows:

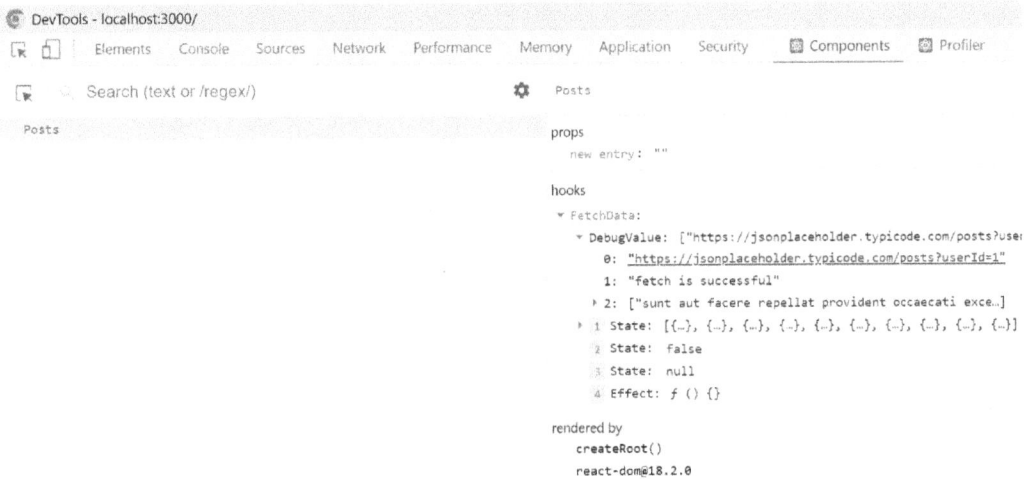

Figure 3.2: DebugValue label in DevTools

In the same way, when the API throws an error due to service unavailability, the respective root cause can be tracked through the **DebugValue** label.

So far, we have discussed several questions related to built-in Hooks, followed by topics related to third-party Hooks and custom Hooks. All these topics have been covered in a specific order to understand the connection between various types of Hooks.

Summary

This chapter offered a thorough understanding of Hooks in React applications. We began by providing an introduction to Hooks, which included the motivation behind Hooks and rules to be followed when using Hooks. We next looked at state management within components using the useState and useReducer Hooks, and global state management to share data across components using the useContext Hook. Thereafter, we covered how to perform side effects in applications with the help of effect Hooks.

Apart from the frequently used built-in Hooks, we discussed accessing DOM nodes using ref Hooks, doing performance optimizations through Hooks, using third-party Hooks, and creating your own custom Hooks for your business needs.

In the next chapter, we will cover an important navigation library known as React Router to navigate from one page to another, and learn about its rich features. Another important topic to be discussed in that chapter is supporting internationalization and creating dynamic localized messages by passing the arguments.

4
Handling Routing and Internationalization

Navigating the vast world of software development doesn't come without its difficulties. Our trip frequently necessitates expertly navigating various screens and language settings to ensure an excellent user experience. This chapter delves into the ideas of routing and internationalization, as well as the virtual environment and horizon of any modern React application.

This chapter will take us on an in-depth investigation of screen navigation and introduce us to React Router. It is the most important tool in web application navigation since it refreshes the browser URL as users go across your application without refreshing the page. We'll go over the many types of routes, such as basic and nested routes, learn how to add routes to our application, and even dive into the world of accessing URL parameters.

But our adventure does not end there. As we migrate into the realm of internationalization and localization, we will advance beyond the functional difficulties and chart our way throughout the globe. These aspects of development demonstrate our dedication to diversity, ensuring that our application speaks the language of its users, no matter where they are from.

We'll present a detailed approach for adding translations and formatted messages to our program, increasing its accessibility to a global audience. We'll also learn how to utilize placeholders and give parameters to these messages, allowing for dynamic translations. Consider this chapter to be your roadmap to a more user-friendly and worldwide application. We will utilize this knowledge to guide us through the realm of software development, avoiding any stumbling blocks and delivering a flawless user experience. Prepare to go on this fascinating adventure in the next few sections.

In the upcoming sections, we will cover the following topics as we aim to understand how to handle routing and how internationalization works:

- Navigating screens and an introduction to React Router
- Routes, types of routes, and links

- Adding routes

- Accessing URL parameters

- Nesting routes

- Introducing internationalization and localization

- Adding translations and formatted messages

- Passing arguments and placeholders

Technical requirements

Please ensure that you have the JavaScript build tool **Vite.js** set up and installed on your machine. You can find it here: `https://vitejs.dev/`. We will be using it for our upcoming React project.

Also, familiarize yourself with the React Router library: `https://reactrouter.com/en/main`.

We are now ready to begin. The next section will introduce us to React Router. Let's go for it!

Navigating screens and an introduction to React Router

Understanding navigation and the React Router library is critical for any coder. In this section, we will go through the fundamentals of traversing screens with React Router and why it is crucial. The aim of this section is to provide an overview of React Router along with simple descriptions of how navigation works via various web apps without becoming unduly technical. We are going to close the gap between what employers expect and your existing skill level in this part by offering useful recommendations on enhancing workflow efficiency while utilizing React Router.

Now, let's explore why we should be using the React Router library in the first place and what it can help us with. It's worth mentioning that Next.js already has the functionality for routing built in, but this is still knowledge worth learning. This is because routing is different in other React frameworks and the core principles of how it works are still valid and can be used anywhere.

What is the purpose of the React Router library?

Creating routing logic can prove time-consuming and difficult, which is where React Router comes in handy. Because of the library's extensive functionality, it can greatly ease our routing challenges. React Router is an open source web application routing module that allows you to move between different pages and components. It provides an easy-to-use interface for implementing dynamic routing in your web project. It supports numerous URLs and gives you complete control over your application's routing, resulting in a seamless and engaging user experience.

Now that we understand the purpose of using this library, we are going to learn how navigation works in the next section.

How does navigating between screens work in React Router?

Navigating between screens can seem daunting at first, but using React Router makes it considerably easier and more practical. With React Router, you can efficiently manage all of your routes within your app, making it a breeze to switch between different screens. Plus, it allows you to keep your UI in sync with the URL. So, even if you're not an expert, React Router means you can easily add the functionality you need to get your app running smoothly.

Client-side routing is enabled by React Router, and this is basically how routing is initiated. Essentially, the computer's browser requests a page from a website's server, which gets and determines the CSS and JavaScript files, and renders the HTML supplied from the server itself on a website. When a user clicks a link on the website, the process is restarted for a brand-new page.

Next.js already has a routing solution built in, so we will use another popular JavaScript build tool, Vite.js, to see the code in this chapter. Here is the link for the tool: `https://vitejs.dev/`.

The first step is to construct a `BrowserRouter` component and configure the primary route. This enables client-side routing for our web application. Our `main.jsx` file serves as the starting point, as shown here:

```
import * as React from 'react';
import * as ReactDOM from 'react-dom/client';
import { createBrowserRouter, RouterProvider } from 'react-router-
dom';
import './index.css';

const router = createBrowserRouter([
  {
    path: '/',
    element: <div>Hello world!</div>,
  },
]);

ReactDOM.createRoot(document.getElementById('root')).render(
  <React.StrictMode>
    <RouterProvider router={router} />
  </React.StrictMode>
);
```

This code defines our initial route. So, in this case, it would be our root route. The root route is known as the first page that loads and is displayed on a website – commonly known as our home page.

Before we jump into the next section, let's get a quick look at `BrowserRouter` and some of the subtopics surrounding it. Firstly, `BrowserRouter` is a router solution that keeps your UI in sync with the URL by using the HTML5 History API. This API utilizes events such as `popstate`, `replacestate`, and `pushstate`. We can use `BrowserRouter` to store the current location in the address bar using clean URLs and history. We can also use it to track changes in the URL in the cases of iframes.

React Router has many features that you can find in its documentation. Here's an overview of what's on offer:

Feature	Description
Routers	Although your apps will only utilize one router, several of them can be accessed, depending on the setting it is operating in. Some of the ones that are included are `createBrowserRouter`, `createMemoryRouter`, `createHashRouter`, and `createStaticRouter`.
Router components	The type of router component you will use for page routing in your app.
Route	The methods that will be used for creating and managing routes. These can include actions, lazy loading, and loaders.
Components	With this feature, we can use custom-made components to manage our data. For example, we can use the `Form` component, which emulates the browser for client-side routing and data mutations, or the `Await` component for automatic error handling. There's also the important `Link` component for navigating to other pages. These are a few of the ones available to us.
Hooks	These custom Hooks work just like any React Hook and give us new functionality. `useNavigation`, `useSearchParams`, `useOutlet`, and `useLocation` are all Hooks that have different purposes.
Fetch utilities	These are used for managing the data we receive from APIs. We can get the data and perform redirects.
Utilities	We can use utilities to perform different actions. For example, `matchPath` can be used to match a route path pattern and compare it to a URL path name, and the information about the match is returned.

Table 4.1: React Router features

This covers most of the main features of React Router. To learn more, read the official documentation: `https://reactrouter.com/en/main`.

In the next section, we will take this further and learn more about routing and links.

Routes, types of routes, and links

Routes are the most critical components of a React Router app. They link URL segments to components, as well as perform data loading and data modifications. Sophisticated project layouts, as well as information dependencies, become straightforward thanks to route nesting and the process becomes easier because routes are objects that are provided to router construction operations.

What types of routes can we use?

React Router gives us access to various forms of routing. The following table explains this:

Route Type	Description
path	The path pattern will be compared to the URL to see whether this route matches a URL, link href, or form action.
index	This determines whether or not the route is an index route. Index routes, such as default child routes, render into their parent's Outlet at their parent's URL.
children	Nested routes allow you to render many components on a single page while maintaining route integrity.
caseSensitive	This specifies whether the route should match the case or not.
loader	Before the route renders, the route loader is invoked and gives data for the element through useLoaderData.
action	When a submission is submitted to the route from a form, fetcher, or submission, the route action is called.

Table 4.2: Types of routes

Now that we have learned about some different route types, it's time to learn the code for creating a route and a link.

How do you create a route and a link?

We can create routes by using React Element and React Component.

The typical syntax for using element is as follows:

```
<Route path="/about" element={<About />} />
```

If you wanted to use Component instead, then the code would look like this:

```
<Route path="/about" Component={About} />
```

Links work slightly differently. Client-side routing enables our app to adjust the URL after a link click, rather than requesting another document from the server. Instead, the application can swiftly display a fresh UI and use `fetch` to execute data calls to update the content of the page with freshly obtained data. Since the web browser does not need to request a completely new page or revisit CSS and JavaScript content for the next page, this results in speedier loading times. It also allows for enhanced user interactions, such as scrolling.

The following example shows us how to use links for page navigation:

```
import { createRoot } from 'react-dom/client';
import { createBrowserRouter, RouterProvider, Link } from
  'react-router-dom';
const router = createBrowserRouter([
  {
    path: '/',
    element: (
      <div>
        <h1>Hello World</h1>
        <Link to="about">About Us</Link>
      </div>
    ),
  },
  {
    path: 'about',
    element: <div>About</div>,
  },
]);

createRoot(document.getElementById('root')).render(
  <RouterProvider router={router} />
);
```

This code block shows us how to create a home page that has a link that navigates us to an about us page.

Now that we know about routes and links, let's learn how to add routes.

Adding routes

Routes can be rendered throughout our application if we use the `<Routes>` component, which matches up with other child routes in our files. Routing searches through all of its child routes to find the best match, and if the location changes, then it renders that branch of the UI. To represent a nested UI, which also corresponds to nested URL pathways, `<Route>` components can also be nested. By rendering `<Outlet>`, parent routes render their child routes.

The following code example illustrates how to add routes to a file:

```
<Routes>
  <Route path="/" element={<Menu />}>
    <Route
      path="messages"
      element={<MenuItems />}
    />
    <Route path="actions" element={<MenuActions />} />
  </Route>
  <Route path="about" element={<About />} />
</Routes>
```

In this file, there are four routes:

- `"/"`
- `"/messages"`
- `"/actions"`
- `"/about"`

The routes for messages and actions are nested routes under the main route, which is `"/"`. The `"/about"` route is a top-level route because it is separate and not nested like the previous two. The component inside the property element will load when the page is on its defined route. Routes can also be declared with JSX and `createRoutesFromElements`.

Those are the basics out of the way. Now, let's move on to the next topic, which is accessing URL parameters. This is where we will learn how to navigate to a page that is determined by its ID. This gives us more customization options when we're doing our GET requests, which is the next step after we have learned how to navigate to a page using basic routing.

Accessing URL parameters

We can use the `useParams` Hook in React, which provides a key/value object of the dynamic parameters from the current URL that matches the specified route. All of the parameters are inherited by child routes from their parent routes. A working example is shown here:

```
import * as React from 'react';
import { Routes, Route, useParams } from 'react-router-dom';

function ProfilePage() {
  // Get the userId param from the URL.
  let { userId } = useParams();
  // ...
```

```
}

function App() {
  return (
    <Routes>
      <Route path="users">
        <Route path=":userId" element={<ProfilePage />} />
        <Route path="me" element={...} />
      </Route>
    </Routes>
  );
}
```

So, with this routing configuration, the application can render various components according to the URL's structure. Firstly, the page route of users/userId renders the ProfilePage component and provides the component with the userId portion as userId. The route for users/me is the one that renders the component that's supplied in the element attribute.

As you can see, URL parameters are powerful and give us another level of customization for our routes. In the next section, we will take a look at nesting routes, which is the natural progression now that we have learned how to create basic routes. With nested routes, we will be able to have multiple components rendered on the same page.

Nesting routes

In React Router, nesting routes were influenced by Ember.js's routing mechanism in 2014. The Ember.js team discovered that parts of the URL usually determine the method to render a page layout and how the data is connected with the layouts that are rendered. One method of creating a page with nested elements can be seen in our example here:

```
createBrowserRouter(
    createRoutesFromElements(
        <Route path="/" element={<Root />}>
          <Route path="connect" element={<ConnectPage />} />
          <Route
            path="admin"
            element={<Admin />}
            loader={({ request }) =>
              fetch("/data/api/admnin.json", {
                signal: request.signal,
              })
            }
          />
```

```
            <Route element={<AuthLayout />}>
              <Route
                path="login"
                element={<Login />}
                loader={redirectIfUser}
              />
              <Route path="logout" action={logoutUser} />
            </Route>
          </Route>
        )
      );
```

This code block is for a user-authenticated login flow. If the user is logged in, then the admin page loads. There is also a login and logout route. Now, let's look at dynamic routing, which is another useful feature.

Dynamic routes

When developing apps with several pages or views that have a basic structure but differ in information or behavior, dynamic routing becomes convenient. Dynamic routing, as opposed to establishing a predetermined number of routes in your application, allows you to construct routes on the spot based on the present state of the app as a whole.

We can see what that looks like here:

```
import { BrowserRouter, Route } from 'react-router-dom';

function App() {
  return (
    <BrowserRouter>
      <Route path="/users/:id" component={Profile} />
    </BrowserRouter>
  );
}
```

The :id property in the route structure indicates a dynamic value that can vary depending on the input provided by the user. React Router grabs the id parameter from the URL and provides it to the Profile component when the URL fits this pattern. Next, we'll look at error pages since it's a situation we need to be aware of when a user encounters a page that is broken.

Error pages

To address scenarios where users go to non-existent routes or face difficulties while traversing our application, we can create error pages or *not-found* pages in React Router. When anything goes wrong, this helps provide a better user experience by stopping users from encountering a blank page or an inconsistent layout.

The following code example shows how to create error pages.

Firstly, we must create the necessary components:

```
import React from 'react';

const NotFound = () => {
  return <div>404 - The page was not found</div>;
};

const ErrorPage = () => {
  return <div>An error occurred. :(</div>;
};

export { NotFound, ErrorPage };
```

This code creates two components - one for 404 error pages and the other for general error pages.

Now, let's set up the routes:

```
import React from 'react';
import { BrowserRouter as Router, Route, Switch } from
  'react-router-dom';
import { NotFound, ErrorPage } from './ErrorComponents';
import Home from './Home';

function App() {
  return (
    <Router>
      <Switch>
        <Route exact path="/" component={Home} />
        <Route path="/error" component={ErrorPage} />
        <Route component={NotFound} />
      </Switch>
    </Router>
  );
}

export default App;
```

This code creates a component that contains all of the page routes for our app.

With that, we've considered error pages and learned how to set up some routes.

Next, we will cover internationalization and localization. Knowing how to tailor your application to different regions is important because we all live in different countries. So, let's get right to it.

Internationalization and localization

Internationalization and localization are basic practices in software development that enable you to design and deploy systems that can be tailored to multiple languages and areas. Let's learn the difference between them.

What is internationalization?

Internationalization is the process of creating and preparing your application so that it can potentially be used in several languages. This frequently entails extracting all of your application's strings into distinct files that can potentially be translated into multiple languages. It also requires structuring your software to ensure that it can correctly manage and show these translations.

What is localization?

This involves translating your locally optimized application into specific native languages. Translating an application's text is only one aspect of localization. It might also include other regionally unique elements, such as text direction, number forms, and date and time formats, among other things.

React Router allows you to build localized routes. To manage language choice, you might, for instance, have several routes for various languages (such as `"/en/about"` and `"/fr/about"`) or you can utilize a context or state.

We have learned so much already and our knowledge has increased a lot. Next, we will move on to the penultimate section of this chapter, where we are going to learn all about adding translations and formatted messages in our React applications. We just learned about internationalization and localization, which is where we prepare our applications for different languages. Now, let's learn how to implement different languages in the code we write.

Adding translations and formatted messages

The process of translating text content in your application from one language into another and doing it in a style that follows regional customs and standards is referred to as translations and formatted messages. We can make use of a library such as **FormatJS** to add translations and formatted messages to a React application. React Router does not allow translations or localization by default; however, it can easily be used in tandem with FormatJS (or a comparable package) to build an internationalized routing system.

Let's look at a code example of what this could look like if we were to use the library:

```
import { IntlProvider, FormattedMessage } from
  'react-intl';
import English from './translations/en.json';
import French from './translations/fr.json';

const Home = () => (
  <div>
    <h2>
      <FormattedMessage id="home.title" />
    </h2>
    <p>
      <FormattedMessage id="home.welcome" />
    </p>
  </div>
);

// We can assume that we are able to get the user's preferred language
from somewhere like in user or browser settings...
const userLanguage = 'fr';
// This value can be dynamically created.
const messages = {
  en: English,
  fr: French,
};

const App = () => (
  <IntlProvider locale={userLanguage} messages=
    {messages[userLanguage]}>
    <Home />
  </IntlProvider>
);

export default App;
```

In this example, the application has been set up for English and French translations. The default language is hardcoded to be French; however, in a real-world application, it can be generated dynamically, depending on what language user settings someone has set up in their browser. The en and fr language codes are mapped to the translation files that are imported by the messages object.

Translations and formatted messages – what are they exactly? We are about to find out. So, keep reading.

What are translations?

This often refers to translating text from one language into another within your program. In software, we often keep many language files that contain the translated texts for each supported language (commonly in JSON or a similar format). This enables the app to show the appropriate language, depending on the user's preferences or locale, dynamically.

What are formatted messages?

Many applications require dynamic material to be shown within translated strings in addition to straightforward translations. Formatted communications have a role in this. With formatted messages, you can manage pluralization rules, add variables to your translated strings, format dates and numbers using regional standards, and much more.

We can develop apps that are readily adaptable to various languages and locations by combining translations with formatted messages, thus improving accessibility and user experience.

Our progress has been fantastic – there's just one more section to go and we will have completed this chapter. The last section will be about passing arguments and placeholders. So far, we've learned how to add data to one page; however, in real-world applications, we have multiple routes within our single-page applications. So, in the next section, we will learn how to pass arguments and placeholders so that we can have dynamic routing in our applications.

Passing arguments and placeholders

React and JavaScript in general, as well as React Router specifically, support passing placeholders and arguments. However, for dynamic routing and data transmission between routes, these work well when combined with React Router.

How do we pass arguments?

With the use of several techniques, such as URL parameters, query parameters, or the state object of the history prop, we can send data to components that are displayed by React Router. Usually, this is done to convey precise data from one route to another.

This example shows us the process of passing arguments when we are using the state object of the history prop:

```
import { Link } from "react-router-dom";

<Link
  to={{
    pathname: "/route",
    state: { myData: "Hello, World!" }
```

```
  }}
>
  My Link
</Link>
```

The receiving component reveals how we can access the data that we passed in:

```
import { useLocation } from "react-router-dom";

function MyComponent() {
  const location = useLocation();
  console.log(location.state.myData);
  // Outputs: "Hello, World!"

  // ...
}
```

Lastly, we shall learn how to use placeholders (URL parameters).

How do we use placeholders?

URL parameters, which are parts of the URL that can change depending on the content you would like to display but still render the same core component, are supported by React Router. These are regularly used to develop dynamic routes.

Here is an example of how to create a route and utilize a URL parameter in a component:

```
import { Route, useParams } from "react-router-dom";

function MyComponent() {
  let { id } = useParams();
  return <h2>My id is: {id}</h2>;
}

function App() {
  return (
    <Route path="/post/:id">
      <MyComponent />
    </Route>
  );
}
```

In this example, the `id` placeholder can depend on any value. When you go to `"/post/123"`, the `MyComponent` component renders, and `useParams()` returns an object with `{ id: "123" }` in it.

Building dynamic and responsive apps using React Router requires both arguments and placeholders.

Summary

As we come to the end of this chapter, it's evident that the journey through the environment of routing and internationalization in React apps has been both difficult and gratifying. We examined, probed, and unraveled the complexity of several critical themes, each of which contributed to the development of comprehensive, interactive, and internationally accessible apps.

We started by learning about React Router, our trusty navigator for the displays in our applications. We looked into routes, learned about their many types, and learned how to use them effectively in our applications. Our investigation of obtaining URL parameters and layering routes has broadened our expertise, allowing us to design sophisticated and complex pathways inside our apps.

Then, we shifted our focus to internationalization and localization, widening our horizons to ensure people all around the world can interact with our application. We recognized the significance of breaking down language barriers and the enormous impact this can have on user experience. Learning how to add translations and formatted messages has given us the ability to connect with users in their native language, allowing our application to become a worldwide entity. We also uncovered the power of creating dynamic and responsive translations by learning how to use placeholders and pass arguments to messages.

These abilities help us become efficient developers who are capable of creating programs that are not only useful but also ubiquitous. This path has given us the tools we need to design and build online apps that are not only responsive and resilient but also global and inclusive. As we finish this chapter, think about what you've learned, but keep in mind that this is just one stop on your larger trip. Continue to explore, learn, and, most importantly, continue your growth and follow the path that resonates with you most.

In the next chapter, we will learn about more advanced ReactJS concepts, such as error borders, portals, higher-order components, concurrent rendering, and forwarding refs. So, let's get ready for another adventure as we increase our knowledge.

5
Advanced Concepts of ReactJS

Every web developer should have in-depth knowledge of React fundamentals, core concepts, Hooks, and router navigations to build a successful career in the React technology stack. But if you want to elevate your React skills to the next level, you should be able to build production-level apps by applying advanced React concepts such as portals, error boundaries, concurrent rendering features, profilers, and more. While some of these concepts were introduced a long time ago and improved with new features in each major release, other advanced concepts have only been introduced in recent releases.

In this chapter, you will understand the advanced concepts of ReactJS so that you can use them in various real-time use cases. Advanced concepts such as error boundaries, portals, concurrent rendering, and suspense, as well as code quality and performance optimization-related features such as strict mode, static type checking, and profilers, will be discussed to cover the interview questions for mid-level to senior developer candidates. At the end, we will quickly explore some questions related to React Native that are meant for mobile environments such as iOS and Android.

In this chapter, we're going to cover the following main topics:

- Exploring portals
- Understanding error boundaries
- Managing asynchronous actions with the Suspense API
- Optimizing rendering performance using concurrent rendering
- Debugging React applications with the Profiler API
- Strict mode
- Static type checking
- React in mobile environments and its features

The main objective of this chapter is to give you a clear understanding of React's advanced concepts and tackle interview questions that are asked to test the advanced skill levels of any job aspirant.

Exploring portals

Nowadays, it is quite common to use model windows or popups on web pages to quickly grab the user's attention. They help notify the user of some important information or ask the user to enter their input. But the implementation of these widgets is challenging in large apps since it involves writing complex CSS code and handling the DOM hierarchy. Fortunately, React provides the portals feature to solve these kinds of use cases.

Portals were introduced in 2017 and were first seen in React version 16. They are used to render React components outside of the DOM hierarchy. The usage of portals is not typical, but they are helpful in specific use cases, as you will see in the following subsections.

What are portals? How do you create them?

React portals allow you to render children into a DOM node that exists outside of the parent DOM hierarchy. Even though you render a child component outside the parent, the parent-child relationship still exists between the components.

A React portal can be created by calling the `createPortal` function, which is imported from the `react-dom` package. This function accepts two mandatory arguments and one optional argument:

- `Children`: Any JSX code that can be rendered with React.

- `DOMNode`: The DOM node where you need to render the portal's content.

- `Key`: A unique identifier to distinguish the portal inside the component tree. This is optional.

The following example of a modal window shows how a portal is created at a particular DOM node outside the root tree hierarchy:

```
import { createPortal } from 'react-dom';

const ModalWindow =({ description, isOpen, onClose })=> {
  if (!isOpen) return null;
  return createPortal(
    <div className="modal">
      <span>{description}</span>
      <button onClick={onClose}>Close</button>
    </div>
    ,document.body);
}
```

In the preceding code, the portal returns a React node that can be rendered anywhere in the component tree. In this example, the returned node is going to be a modal widget. This modal has been appended to the document body and is available at the same level as the `root` node in the HTML.

> **Note**
>
> It is common practice to name the top-level node `root` because everything inside it will be managed by React. Applications built with React alone usually have a single root node. But if you are integrating React into an existing application, you might have many isolated root DOM nodes.

Any React component can use the preceding portal as a child component:

```
function ParentComponent() {
  const [open, setOpen] = useState(false);

  return (
    <div className="container">
      <button onClick={() => setOpen(true)}>Open Modal</button>
      <Modal
        message="This is a portal modal!"
        isOpen={open}
        onClose={() => setOpen(false)}
      />
    </div>
  );
}
```

There is no restriction on the number of portals that can be used in a particular component or an application. Using portals, you can also render React components into non-React server markup such as static or server-rendered pages and non-React DOM nodes that are managed outside of React.

What are the common use cases of portals?

In applications where you can see the child components visually breaking off of the parent container, portals can be useful. The most common use cases are listed here:

- **Modal windows or dialogue components**: Portals can be used to create large dialogues or modal windows that float over the rest of the web page without you having to worry about the parent component.

- **Tooltips**: Tooltip text can be placed outside of the DOM hierarchy without it affecting the page layout. For example, if the parent component has `overflow:hidden` or `z-index` styling, then tooltips created inside the portal won't be cut off from their parent container.

- **Loaders**: When a background task such as fetching data from a database is in progress, it is sensible to show a loading screen on the modern web. This helps block the user from interacting with the application until the background task has been completed.

- **Popovers**: Popovers are useful for quickly providing context information to the user. For example, profile cards can be used to display user profile information without the need to click and visit the profile itself. You can just read the details by hovering over the icon or button elements.

- **Cookie alerts**: It is possible to create cookie alerts (or banners) so that visitors can choose what cookies are allowed to track while they're visiting the website.

- **Drop-down menus**: If the drop-down menus are displayed inside a parent component that has hidden overflow styling, it can be created as a portal.

> **Note**
> By moving the child components outside the main component tree, the rendering performance will be optimized as the components aren't re-rendering for each state update. Moreover, it provides the flexibility of abstraction.

How does event bubbling work inside portals?

Even though a portal exists somewhere in the DOM tree, the portal retains its position in the React component tree by supporting all component features, such as accessing props, state, context, and event propagation. This means event bubbling also works with portals.

The behavior of event bubbling in portals is similar to how a React child component fires events inside the component tree. The events that are fired from a portal will propagate upwards to ancestors in the containing React tree, even though those elements are not ancestors in the DOM tree. For example, in the following HTML code, the parent component under the main root (#main-root) can catch an uncaught bubbling event from a sibling node (#dialog-root) that's been implemented using portals:

```
<html>
  <body>
    <div id="main-root"></div>
    <div id="dialog-root"></div>
  </body>
</html>
```

> **Note**
> Event bubbling in portals follows the React tree but not the DOM tree.

What accessibility precautions are taken care of in portals?

You need to ensure that React applications built with portals are accessible, even for people with disabilities. For example, keyboard focus should work naturally when you move the focus between the modal window and the parent web page. The modal dialogues that are created as part of portals should follow the WAI-ARIA modal authoring practices (`https://www.w3.org/WAI/ARIA/apg/patterns/dialog-modal/`).

Some of the guidelines for achieving keyboard accessibility are as follows:

- When the dialog or modal is open, the focus moves to an element inside the dialog.
- Tabbing the focusable elements should only cycle through the dialog elements. The focus should not skip the dialog that has been opened.
- After pressing the *Esc* key, the dialog should close.

If you are going to use a third-party library to create the modals, you need to make sure that the package follows the required accessibility guidelines.

You will always encounter unexpected errors while building applications. These errors can occur in several ways, such as via network requests, invoking third-party APIs, accessing nested object properties that don't exist, and so on. Error boundaries are mainly used in React applications to handle these kinds of errors.

Understanding error boundaries

In React applications, you can handle errors in two possible ways. The first approach is using a `try..catch` block to handle the errors in an imperative code block, similar to regular event handlers. The second approach is to use **error boundaries**. These are used to deal with declarative component code that will render on the screen.

The React team introduced error boundaries as part of React version 16. No official component has been created for error boundaries in the React library, so you need to create the error boundary component on your own.

What are error boundaries?

Error boundaries are just React components with a certain list of tasks. They are used to catch JavaScript errors that can occur in their child component tree, log those specific errors, and redirect the screen to the fallback UI to recover from the error state. This component helps prevent the entire component tree from crashing just because of an error that happened somewhere in the tree.

Error boundaries catch errors during rendering, in life cycle methods, and in the constructors of the entire component tree below them. An error boundary can be created with a class component by defining either or both of the following life cycle methods:

- `static getDerivedStateFromError`: This method is used to render a fallback UI after an error has been thrown
- `componentDidCatch`: This method is used to log error information

An error boundary can be created using these two methods to protect the application from crashing. This is how it is done:

```
class MyErrorBoundary extends Component {
  constructor(props) {
    super(props);
    this.state = { isErrorThrown: false };
  }

  static getDerivedStateFromError(error) {
    return { isErrorThrown: true };
  }

  componentDidCatch(error, errorInfo) {
    logErrorToReportingService(error, errorInfo);
  }

  render() {
    if (this.state.isErrorThrown) {
      return <h1>Oops, the application is unavaialble.</h1>;
    }
    return this.props.children;
  }
}
```

The `getDerivedStateFromError` method will be invoked if an error occurs in the rendering phase of any life cycle method. In this method, you can update the error state flag variable's value to reflect the fallback UI in the next render. Based on the error state variable, the `render` method will update the UI on the screen. At the same time, the same error can be reported to the logging service for debugging purposes using the `componentDidCatch` method.

Once the error boundary has been created, it can be used as a regular React component. The error boundary component needs to be wrapped around the top-level React component where you suspect any kind of possible bugs. The usage of the component looks as follows:

```
<MyErrorBoundary>
  <MyComponent />
</MyErrorBoundary>
```

The preceding error boundary catches any error thrown within the `MyComponent` component tree and prevents the application from crashing.

> **Note**
>
> You can also wrap error boundaries for individual components with a different set of error messages to prevent them from breaking other parts of the page. The decision of error boundary design depends on the business requirements and UX design.

If the enclosed error boundary failed to catch the error, the error will propagate to the next closest error boundary around it. This behavior is similar to a `catch()` block, which propagates an error to the next nearest catch block.

Popular testing frameworks such as Jest can be used to write unit tests for error boundaries similar to any other React component. The unit test should simulate the error in the React component (to which the error boundary is wrapped) and verify that the error boundary can catch errors and renders the fallback UI properly or not. It is also possible to verify the error boundary using React DevTools by forcing the selected component into an error (red button) state.

Is it possible to create an error boundary as a function component?

At the time of writing, it is not possible to create an error boundary as a function component using the latest React version – that is, you can only create an error boundary using a class component. Moreover, you can avoid writing an error boundary class altogether by reusing the `react-error-boundary` (`https://github.com/bvaughn/react-error-boundary`) package from the community.

When do error boundaries not work?

Error boundaries do not catch errors in the following scenarios:

- **Event handlers**: Since event handlers (such as `onClick`, `onChange`, and others) aren't used during the rendering phase, error boundaries won't be required to recover the UI from errors
- **Asynchronous code**: Error boundaries cannot catch errors inside asynchronous callbacks such as `setTimeout`, `requestAnimationFrame`, and others
- **Server-side rendering**: React doesn't support error boundaries on a server
- **When there's an error inside the error boundary**: React cannot catch errors thrown in the error boundary itself

You may need to opt for a regular JavaScript `try..catch` statement or `promise#catch()` block to handle errors for the aforementioned cases except for the last one, where you need to make sure no errors occur in the error boundary.

Just like error boundaries are used to display a fallback UI for any error caught in the application, the Suspense API is used to display a fallback UI until its children have finished loading.

Managing asynchronous actions with the Suspense API

The Suspense feature was introduced in React version 16, alongside error boundaries. Initially, it was only meant to be used with the `lazy` API for code splitting and could not be used for server-side rendering. React18 improved the Suspense API so that it can support many use cases, including server-side rendering and asynchronous operations such as data fetching.

What is the Suspense API? How do you use it?

The Suspense API is used to display a fallback UI such as a loading indicator until its children are ready to render. The suspense component accepts a `fallback` prop to render an alternative UI if its children have not finished rendering. You can wrap your application with a suspense component either at the top level or individual sections of the application.

Let's learn how to use the Suspense feature by looking at the following example.

Consider a simple use case of loading blog posts from a specific author. Here, the blog posts component (that is, `<Posts/>`) suspends while fetching the list of posts. Before the content is ready to be displayed, React switches to the closest suspense boundary to display the fallback loading indicator (that is, `<Loading />`) in place of displaying the list of posts:

```
import { Suspense } from "react";

import Posts from "./posts.js";

export default function Author({ author }) {
  return (
    <>
      <h1>{author.name}</h1>
      <span>{author.age}</span>
      <Suspense fallback={<Loading />}>
        <Posts authorId={author.id} />
      </Suspense>
    </>
  );
}

function Loading() {
  return <h2>Loading...</h2>;
}
```

Once the blog post data has been fetched, React switches back to displaying the actual blog post data.

You can also defer updating the list and display state content until the new results are ready. This alternative UI pattern is possible by passing a query to the `useDeferredValue` Hook:

```
const deferredAuthorDetails = useDeferredValue(author);
```

In traditional applications, you need to use the `isLoading` data flag variable to indicate whether data fetching has finished or not and display the respective content on the screen. However, if you use the Suspense feature, React automatically determines whether to display the fallback UI or component data, without depending on any additional flag.

> **Note**
> Only suspense-enabled frameworks have integrations with the Suspense feature to communicate loading states to React.

Can I use the suspense component for any kind of data fetching?

The suspense component cannot detect data fetching inside an effect or event handler. It can only be used for the following suspense-enabled data sources:

- Data fetching with suspense-enabled opinionated frameworks such as Relay, Next.js, Remix, and Hydrogen
- Lazy-loading component code with the `lazy` API

Using the Suspense feature without a framework is not supported at the time of writing. However, there is a plan from the React team to provide an official API to integrate data sources with the suspense component in future versions.

How do you prevent unnecessary fallbacks during an update?

If the visible UI is replaced with a fallback, there will be a flashing user experience. This is not a good UX experience. This situation happens when a state update causes a component to suspend, but the nearest suspense boundary is already showing some fallback content to the user. You can avoid these unnecessary fallbacks by marking the state updates as non-urgent using the `startTransition` API.

Consider an example of navigating pages in an application and applying a transition for the page update to prevent unnecessary fallbacks:

```
function navigate(url) {
  startTransition(() => {
    setPage(url);
  });
}
```

During the transition, React will wait for the content to be loaded without retriggering the suspense fallback UI to hide the already revealed content.

> **Note**
> React only prevents unnecessary fallbacks for non-urgent updates. It will not delay the render for any urgent updates.

In the past, React was only able to handle one task at a time and the render process was synchronous. Once the task had been started, it could not be interrupted. This is called blocking rendering. Later, this issue was fixed by introducing concurrent mode, which can interrupt the task if there is another urgent task. Concurrent mode was introduced as an experimental feature and replaced by the concurrent rendering feature in React version 18.

Optimizing rendering performance using concurrent rendering

React 18 introduced the concurrent renderer, which makes the rendering process asynchronous and ensures it can be interrupted, paused, resumed, and even abandoned. As a result, React can respond to user interactions quickly, even if it is in the middle of a heavy rendering task.

New features such as suspense, streaming server rendering, and transitions are powered by concurrent rendering.

How do you enable concurrent rendering in React?

First, you need to update both the `react` and `react-dom` packages to version 18. After that, you need to replace the deprecated `ReactDOM.render` method with the `ReactDOM.createRoot` method. Concurrent rendering will be enabled automatically in whichever parts of your application you use concurrent features such as suspense, streaming server rendering, and transitions.

As the application becomes complex, you need to spend a significant amount of time analyzing the application's performance. It is especially crucial to measure the application performance's characteristics before delivering it to customers. Even though you can use the browser's User Timing API (Web API) to measure the rendering cost of your components, there are better alternatives that have been created by the React team. The Profiler API, for example, helps identify performance bottlenecks in React applications.

Debugging React applications with the Profiler API

If you are benchmarking a React application's performance, then tracking how many times your components are re-rendered and the cost of each re-rendering will help you identify the defecting areas or parts in the application. React provides two different ways to measure the application's rendering performance: the **React Profiler API** and the **React DevTools** profiler tab. The React Profiler API is recommended considering that it supports the Suspense feature.

How do you measure rendering performance?

React provides the Profiler API to measure the rendering performance of a component tree programmatically. The component has two props: the `id` prop, which is used to identify the part of the UI being measured, and the `onRender` callback, which is called every time the tree updates.

The callback receives arguments such as `id`, `phase`, `actualDuration`, `baseDuration`, `startTime`, and `commitTime`, which are used to log the rendering time.

Imagine you are suspicious of the rendering performance of an author biography component that exists inside an online bookstore application, and you would like to profile the component. In this case, the `AuthorBio` component needs to be wrapped with the `Profiler` component, along with the `onRender` callback. This will look as follows:

```
<App>
  <Profiler id="bio" onRender={onRender}>
    <AuthorBio />
  </Profiler>
  <Posts />
</App>
```

You can also use multiple `Profiler` components to measure the different parts of your application.

JavaScript provided strict mode as a new feature in ECMAScript5 to enforce the restricted version of JavaScript. This feature brings stricter rules when you write code and throws errors if you violate them. Strict mode can be enabled by adding a `use strict` line at the top of your file. Similarly, React provides the `StrictMode` component as a development-only tool, which is used to enforce stricter warnings and checks while writing React code.

Strict mode

The React team introduced strict mode as a debugging tool to identify potential bugs or issues in a web application. This tool is available as the `StrictMode` component in the React API. It doesn't render any UI that is similar to the `Fragment` component. This feature is only applicable to development mode – it won't impact behavior in production. This section focuses on the important strict mode concepts and questions that might be asked in the interview.

How do you enable strict mode?

You can enable strict mode for an entire app by wrapping it around the root component, as follows:

```
import { StrictMode } from "react";
import { createRoot } from "react-dom/client";

const root = createRoot(document.getElementById("root"));
root.render(
  <StrictMode>
    <App />
  </StrictMode>
);
```

You can also only use strict mode in certain parts of the application (that is, not the entire application) where you think there is a high possibility of bugs. Consider strict mode for the main body of the page of an application. It should look something like this:

```
<>
  <Navigation>
    <Details>
      <StrictMode>
        <Services />
        <Support />
      </StrictMode>
    </Details>
    <Footer />
  </Navigation>
</>;
```

Most of the time, React developers face issues with improper logic in the rendering section, as well as issues with missing cleanup code inside effects Hooks. These types of bugs can easily be identified with strict mode.

Can you describe the list of development-only checks enabled by strict mode?

Strict mode enables the following list of development-only checks to find commonly occurring bugs during early development:

- Components will re-render one more time to find the bugs that were caused by impure rendering
- Components will rerun effects one more time to find the bugs that were caused by missing cleanup for the effect

- Components will be verified for the usage of deprecated APIs and will notify the users with warnings

These checks are applicable for development purposes only. They won't have any impact on the production builds.

What functions are called twice in the double rendering process of strict mode?

Strict mode calls the following list of functions twice in development mode:

- The function's component body, excluding code inside event handlers
- The functions that are passed to Hook, such as `useState`, `useReducer`, and `useMemo`
- State updater functions
- Class component methods such as `constructor`, `render`, `shouldComponentUpdate`, and `getDerivedStateFromProps`

If your function is impure, running it twice in development mode will impact the expected output. This result helps you identify any bugs in your code as early as possible.

Apart from strict mode, you can also use static type checking in React applications to avoid bugs and errors that appear at runtime. As your application grows, you can catch many bugs using type checking.

Static type checking

React is based on JavaScript and JavaScript is a loosely typed language. So, we don't get the default static type-checking feature in React.

In its older versions (<15.5), React had `PropTypes` validators so that it could perform simple type checking in applications. Post that, this library was moved out from React's core module and created as a separate library, `prop-types` (`https://www.npmjs.com/package/prop-types`). Nowadays, `PropTypes` are not commonly used in modern React applications. Even though static type checking is not mandatory in React, you might encounter some questions related to static type checking in the interview.

What are the benefits of static type checking?

There are many benefits of static type checking in JavaScript applications. Some of these are listed here:

- Can identify type errors before runtime (that is, errors at compile time)
- Can detect bugs and errors in the early stages
- Optimized and easy to read

- Better IDE support

- Can generate documentation

It is cheaper to fix bugs if you identify them as early as possible.

How do you implement static type checking in React applications?

In React, there are multiple ways to implement static type checking, but the following two ways are the best:

- TypeScript

- Flow

These two static type checkers help identify certain types of errors, even before you run your code. Since TypeScript is robust and has the most community support, let's see how it can be implemented in React.

TypeScript was created by Microsoft and is considered a typed superset of JavaScript. It comes with its own compiler and can catch errors and bugs at build time. It supports JSX and can use React hooks without any problems. Nowadays, TypeScript can be supported by major frameworks just by appending various options, as listed here:

- Next.js:

    ```
    npx create-next-app@latest --ts
    ```

- Remix:

    ```
    npx create-remix@latest
    ```

- Gatsby:

    ```
    npm init gatsby -ts
    ```

- Expo:

    ```
    npx create-expo-app -t expo-template-blank-typescript
    ```

If you are not using any of these frameworks, you need to follow the following manual steps to set up TypeScript in React applications:

1. **Add TypeScript as a dependency to your project**: You need to install the latest version of TypeScript using npm or the yarn package manager:

    ```
    npm install --save-dev typescript
    ```

This dependency will give you access to the `tsc` compiler (that is, the TypeScript compiler) so that you can build the application.

2. **Configure the TypeScript compiler's options**: A set of rules can be defined in `tsconfig.json` by generating the file using the following command:

```
npx tsc --init
```

The frequently used options are the source directory for TypeScript files and generated JavaScript files for the output folder. The configuration looks like this:

```
//tsconfig.json
{
  "compilerOptions": {
    // ...
    "rootDir": "src",
    "outDir": "dist"
    // ...
  },
}
```

You can add more configuration options, as described here: `https://www.typescriptlang.org/docs/handbook/tsconfig-json.html`. TypeScript's React starter provides this configuration file with a good set of rules.

3. **Choose the file extension**: You can use the default `.ts` extension or the `.tsx` extension for files that contain JSX code.

4. **Add type definitions for libraries**: It is possible to use external JavaScript packages in TypeScript by including either a bundled declaration file or getting one from the `DefinitelyTyped` (`https://github.com/DefinitelyTyped/DefinitelyTyped`) repository or creating a local declaration file.

Now, you can build your TypeScript project with the `tsc` command, which is available through the TypeScript package.

Initially, React was mainly used for web development. Nowadays, it can be used for mobile, desktop, and VR apps too. React Native is a separate library that was created to support mobile devices. It is based on the same concepts as React but uses native components instead of web components to render on the screen.

React in mobile environments and its features

When Facebook initially chose to make its services available on mobile devices, it decided to run mobile pages based on HTML5 instead of building native apps, which was preferred by many tech giants at that time. However, it ended up with UX and performance overhead issues.

In 2013, the Facebook team found a method of generating UI elements for iOS apps by using JavaScript. This idea was successful for mobile applications and later, React Native was supported for Android devices too.

This section will focus on React Native, so that we can go beyond ReactJS concepts and cover important topics related to architecture, navigation, and its differences from ReactJS, which might be expected in React interviews.

What is React Native?

React Native is a popular JavaScript-based mobile app framework for building natively rendered mobile applications for iOS, Android, and Windows. The main advantage of this library is that you can use one code base that runs on multiple platforms.

The Facebook team open sourced React Native in 2015. After only a few years, this library became one of the top solutions for mobile development and is now used in popular mobile apps such as Facebook, Instagram, Skype, Uber, and others.

What are the differences between React and React Native?

React Native is based on the React library and they share many concepts. But there are a few major differences, as shown here:

React	React Native
It is used to develop web applications	It is used to develop mobile applications
It uses the `react-router` library to navigate pages	It uses an in-built navigator library to navigate pages
A virtual DOM is used to render the web pages	A native API is used to render the pages
React uses HTML, CSS, and JavaScript to create a user interface	React Native uses native components and APIs to build apps
It uses JavaScript and CSS libraries for animation	It comes with built-in animation libraries

Table 5.1: React versus React Native

So, React Native is an additional library built on top of React library to create native apps and this native library has its own architecture.

Can you describe the React Native architecture based on the threading model?

Fabric is the new rendering architecture that was created by the Facebook team and even their app is backed by this renderer. The core principles of this architecture are unifying the renderer logic in C++ and optimizing the interoperability between host platforms. It is based on the threading model, similar to the old architecture, but it functions differently to optimize the user experience better than native apps.

In the old architecture, React Native bridge was used to communicate between JavaScript and native modules. But it has its limitations – for example, communication can only happen through asynchronous operations and it is required to serialize or deserialize the data as JSON. This bridge component was replaced with **JavaScript Interface (JSI)** in the new architecture.

Let's take a look at how the various components communicate in the new rendering architecture:

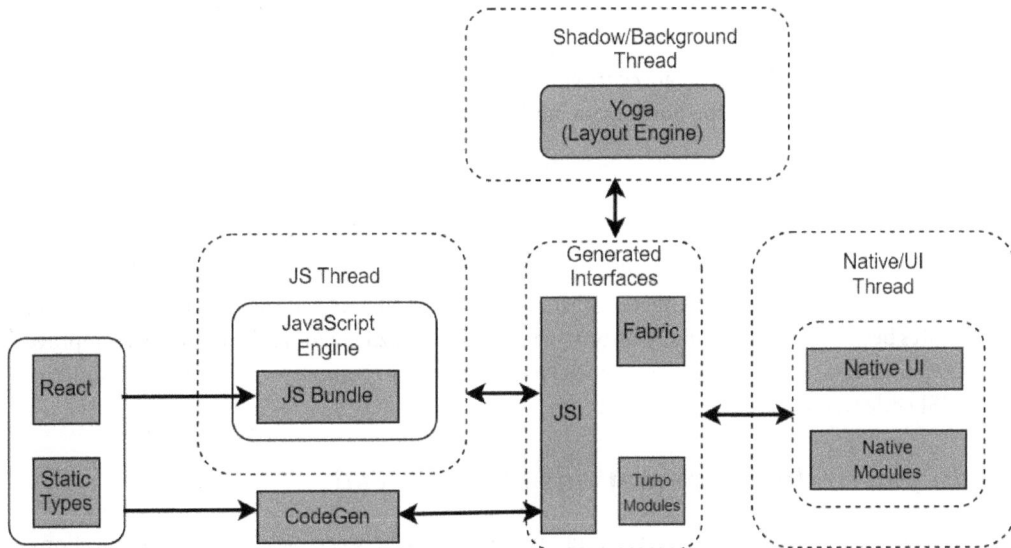

Figure 5.1: Fabric rendering architecture

Three parallel threads run in every React app, irrespective of whether the old or new renderer is used:

- **UI thread or main thread**: This thread is responsible for handling iOS and Android host views. It handles some native interactions, such as tapping on a button, user gesture events, scrolling, and others.

- **JS thread**: This thread is responsible for handling all the logic of your React Native application. It takes care of all the DOM hierarchy operations written in the code and executes them. After that, the code is sent to the native module thread for optimizations.

- **Shadow or background thread**: This thread is responsible for layout calculations such as positions and the height and width of elements and then transforming them into native elements.

In the old architecture, the bridge component was used to communicate between the JS thread and the UI thread asynchronously by serializing and deserializing the data. As a result, memory management and application performance became overloaded. In the new architecture, the bridge component has been replaced with JSI for efficient communication between native and JavaScript code. JSI is a lightweight layer where methods written in C++ can be used by the JavaScript engine, such as **JavaScript Core (JSC)** or Hermes, to directly invoke or call methods in the native code.

The workflow of the new architecture is as follows:

1. When the user clicks an app icon of a mobile application, the Fabric rendering system directly loads the native side instead of opening native modules.

2. The rendering system notifies the JS thread once it is ready. After that, the JS thread loads the final bundle, named `main.bundle.js`, which consists of JavaScript code, React logic, and its components.

3. The JS code is invoked through the ref native function, which has been exposed as an object using the JSI API to Fabric.

4. The yoga engine inside the shadow thread performs layout calculations, converting from the Flexbox-based style into the host layout, and so on.

5. Finally, the components are rendered on the screen.

Additionally, two new components have been added to the new architecture: `Turbo module` and `CodeGen`.

`Turbo module` is an improved version of the native module (it exists in the old architecture) that communicates between JavaScript and platform-native code by lazily loading the modules to improve the startup performance. The `CodeGen` static type checker helps communicate dynamic JavaScript code and JSI code written as statically typed C++.

How do you perform navigations in React Native?

React Native uses the `react-navigation` library to navigate between pages in native applications. The transition between multiple screens is managed by various kinds of navigators, such as stack navigators, drawer navigators, and tab navigators. While navigating between multiple screens, you can also pass data between them.

React Navigation is made up of core utilities that are used by navigators to create the navigation structure in your app. The package can be installed using the following command:

```
npm install @react-navigation/native
```

Each navigator in React Navigation lives in its own library. For example, if you want to use the `native-stack` navigator, it should be installed separately using the following command:

```
npm install @react-navigation/native-stack
```

The stack navigator provides a way for your app to transition between screens and manage navigation history. This behavior is similar to how a web browser handles navigation history. It also provides gestures and animations that you might expect in Android and iOS devices while navigating the pages within the stack.

Here is an example of an organization's website navigation menu items that have been created based on the stack navigator:

```
import * as React from "react";
import { View, Text } from "react-native";
import { NavigationContainer } from "@react-navigation/native";
import { createNativeStackNavigator } from "@react-navigation/native-stack";
import HomeScreen from "components/HomeScreen";
import ServicesScreen from "components/ServicesScreen";

const Stack = createNativeStackNavigator();

function App() {
  return (
    <NavigationContainer>
      <Stack.Navigator>
        <Stack.Screen name="Home" component={HomeScreen} />
        <Stack.Screen name="Services" component={ServicesScreen} />
      </Stack.Navigator>
    </NavigationContainer>
  );
}

export default App;
```

In the preceding code, we created a stacked navigation menu to redirect users to important screens of the website, such as the home and services pages.

Additionally, you can nest navigators using the Navigation API.

What are the benefits of the new architecture?

The new architecture of React Native brings several benefits in terms of user experience, code quality, performance, and extensibility. We have compiled a few of them here:

- **Better interoperability**: In the old architecture, there was a layout jump issue when you try to embed a React view into the host view. This was because the React Native layout was asynchronous. The new renderer provides improved interoperability by rendering React pages synchronously.

- **Better data fetching behavior**: The data fetching user experience has been improved with the integration of React's Suspense feature.

- **Type safety**: Code generation ensures type safety between the JS and platform layers. It uses JavaScript component declarations to generate C++ structs to hold the props. The code generated from the JS specification must be typed through Flow or TypeScript.

- **Synchronous execution**: This improves the user experience. Now, it is possible to execute the functions synchronously rather than asynchronously.

- **Concurrency**: JavaScript can invoke functions that are executed on different threads.

- **Shared C++ code**: The new renderer is implemented in C++. As a result, it is possible to write platform-agnostic code and share it between platforms.

- **Improved performance**: In the new rendering architecture, all the limitations of a particular platform can be identified, and solutions have been provided for working with both iOS and Android. Initially, the view flattening solution was only available on Android, but it is now available by default for both platforms.

- **Faster startup**: Since the host components are lazily initialized by default, there will be a faster startup time.

- **Consistency**: The component's behavior is consistent across platforms because the new render system is cross-platform.

- **Less overhead**: You don't need to perform serialization or deserialization between JavaScript and the UI layer anymore.

You cannot achieve these benefits with the old architecture.

What is view flattening?

The declarative and composition characteristics of the React API allow you to create deep React Element Trees, where most of the nodes only affect the layout of a screen instead of rendering on the screen. These nodes are called **layout-only** nodes. Large amounts of layout-only nodes lead to poor performance during rendering.

The renderer implements the view flattening algorithm to improve performance. View flattening is an optimization algorithm that's used by the React Native renderer to avoid deep layout trees. This mechanism merges or flattens these types of layout-only nodes and reduces the depth of the host view hierarchy displayed on the screen.

This process can be explained with `MyLogoComponent`, which contains view container components with margin and padding styling:

```
function MyLogoComponent() {
  return (
```

```
  <View>
    <View style={{margin: 10}} >
      <View style={{padding: 20}}>
        <Image {...} />
        <Text {...}>This is a caption</Text>
      </View>
    </View>
  </View>
);
}
```

In the preceding code, two host views (that is, `<View style={..}>`) have been added between the container and the actual content of the component to apply structural styling for the inner content.

The view flattening algorithm is integrated as a part of the **diffing** stage of the renderer and merges the styling of the second and third views into the first view. This way, it avoids the need to create and render two extra host views.

The following diagram shows how the native screen appeared without deep layout trees using this mechanism:

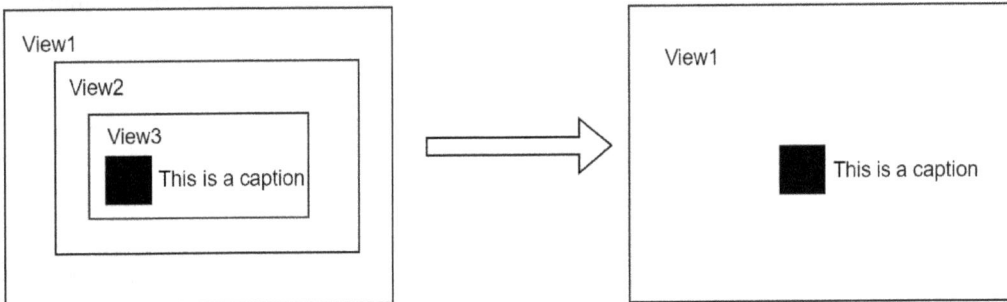

Figure 5.2: Native screen with merged views

There won't be any visible changes after this view flattening algorithm has been applied.

In this section, we covered some of the important fundamental concepts of React Native that you might encounter in React job interviews. You might be asked about these to test your knowledge of the React technology stack. This section also brings you to the end of this chapter, where we covered a wide range of advanced topics in the React ecosystem.

Summary

This chapter covered a list of advanced concepts that you might encounter in a ReactJS interview. We began by covering new features such as portals, which handle modal windows, error boundaries, which prevent the app from crashing due to errors, and the Suspense feature, which displays an alternative UI for heavily time-consuming background tasks. After that, we covered topics related to concurrent rendering, which supports features that improve the rendering performance, followed by the Profiler API, which can be used to detect the rendering cost of specific parts of an application.

Then, we discussed development-only features such as strict mode and static types, which help us avoid any possible bugs and errors encountered in the code. Finally, we introduced React in mobile environments and React Native and its differences with ReactJS, as well as its internals and rendering architecture.

Throughout this chapter, we have helped you learn advanced concepts, their significance, and their best practices in React development. As a result, this book will improve your React skill set so that you become an expert and stand out in the competitive job market.

In the next chapter, we will understand popular state management solutions in React. We will start by looking at Flux patterns and the Redux architecture so that you understand the foundation of Redux. After that, we will cover important topics such as core principles, various components, handling asynchronous requests, middleware, and debugging Redux applications.

Part 3:
Going Beyond React and Advanced Topics

In this part, you will learn about the popular React.js state library Redux and why having a global state store in our projects can be extremely beneficial, compared to using a local state. We will also take a look at the numerous ways to use CSS within a React.js application and how each method has its pros and cons.

Then, we will be testing and debugging as we learn of the different ways we can use testing to make our code more reliable. Finally, we will learn about the React.js libraries Next.js, Gatsby, and Remix, seeing how they can help us to build React.js applications.

This part has the following chapters:

- *Chapter 6, Redux: The Best State Management Solution*
- *Chapter 7, Different Approaches to Apply CSS in React.js*
- *Chapter 8, Testing and Debugging the React Application*
- *Chapter 9, Rapid Development with the Next.js, Gatsby, and Remix Frameworks*

Redux: The Best State Management Solution

As the requirements of your JavaScript single-page applications become more complicated, it will become challenging to maintain the application state. This application state can be created from server or API responses, the local component state, and the UI state such as pagination controls, active routes, and selected tabs. The state can be changed with the help of direct or indirect models or UI interactions in your application. At some point, you may lose control over when, why, and how the state has been changed. This issue has been resolved by state management design patterns and libraries such as Flux, Redux, MobX, Recoil, Rematch, Vuex, and so on.

Choosing the right state management solution is crucial for any medium- to large-scale React application. After reading this chapter, you will be able to answer questions fluently about the Flux pattern and Redux architecture, core principles, main components, handling asynchronous data flow, middleware such as Saga and Thunk, and Redux DevTools for debugging.

In this chapter, we're going to cover the following main topics:

- Understanding the Flux pattern and Redux
- Core principles of Redux, components, and APIs
- Redux middleware – Saga and Thunk
- Standardizing Redux logic using RTK
- Debugging applications using Redux DevTools

Redux was initially created for React applications and it is quite popular among all the state management libraries available. Let's learn more about the Flux pattern, Redux fundamentals, and core concepts in the next section for a better understanding of the Redux library.

Understanding the Flux pattern and Redux

Flux has been created as a design pattern to manage the data flow in React applications. This is a slight modification of the *Observer* pattern, which defines a subscription mechanism in which any state change to one object notifies all other objects (`https://en.wikipedia.org/wiki/Observer_pattern`).

In 2015, the Redux library was introduced. It was inspired by Flux architecture but implemented differently. The next couple of questions focus on Flux and Redux core concepts for the strong foundation of the Redux state management library.

What is the Flux pattern? Can you explain the data flow?

Flux is a pattern for managing the unidirectional data flow in your application and acts as a replacement for the traditional MVC pattern. It is neither a framework nor a library but a new kind of architecture to resolve the state management complexities in client-side web applications. It has been developed and used by Facebook internally while working with React applications.

Flux has four major components in its data flow: Action, Dispatcher, Store, and View. Here's a little more about them:

- **Action**: This represents a JavaScript object that is sent to the dispatcher to trigger the data flow.
- **Dispatcher**: This is a singleton registry of callbacks to update the store, and it works as a central hub of the data flow in the Flux application. It has no real intelligence and simply dispatches the payload from the action to the store.
- **Store**: This is the place where the application state and logic are maintained.
- **View**: This receives the data from the store and re-renders the app. The view is going to trigger the action for any user interactions.

The step-by-step data flow of the Flux architecture based on the preceding components looks like this:

1. If any user performs any UI interactions, an event will be generated, and the views will send actions to the dispatcher.
2. Dispatchers send those actions to the respective stores.
3. Stores update the state and notify the views to re-render.

The following diagram describes how the data flow happens in a Flux-based web application:

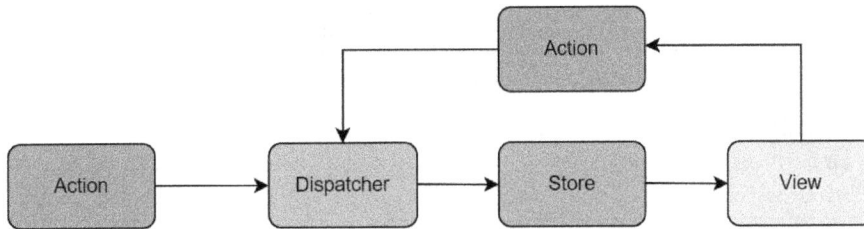

Figure 6.1: Flux data flow

In most applications, we will also create *action creators* as a library of helper methods that not only create action objects but also pass the action to the dispatcher.

What are the advantages of Flux?

The Flux architecture comes with the following advantages and is helpful to use in client-side web applications:

- It is easy to understand because of its unidirectional data flow
- The Flux components are decoupled, and each component has its own responsibility
- It is an open source architecture rather than a framework or a library
- Runtime errors will be reduced because of its design
- It is easy to maintain

The Flux architecture helps move the implementation of API communication, caching, and localization code out from the view or UI layer.

How do you differentiate Flux from MVC?

The **Model, View, Controller (MVC)** design pattern was introduced in 1976 in the Smalltalk programming language. As the application grows, this pattern becomes complex with its multi-data flow. The Facebook team solved this problem by introducing the Flux architecture. The major differences between MVC and Flux design patterns are listed in the following table.

MVC	Flux
The data flow direction is bi-directional	The data flow direction is unidirectional
The controller handles the logic	The store handles the logic
There is no store concept in MVC	There can be multiple stores in Flux

MVC	Flux
It is synchronous	It is asynchronous
Debugging is difficult due to the bi-directional data flow	Debugging is easier with the dispatcher
It is used for both client-side and server-side frameworks	It is used for client-side frameworks only

Table 6.1: MVC versus Flux

Flux is not totally a different approach from MVC, but it is an improved MVC pattern. If the application is complex and has a complicated data model, it's better to opt for Flux over MVC.

What is Redux?

Redux is a popular and predictable state container library designed to write JavaScript applications that behave consistently across client, server, and native environments, and at the same time, is easy to test. It is inspired by Facebook's Flux architecture. The unnecessary complexities that existed in the Flux pattern have been eliminated by it.

It is quite straightforward to use a component state when the application contains fewer components. As the number of components increases and the application becomes larger, it will be challenging to maintain the state of each component in your application. In this case, Redux comes to the rescue to manage the state of large applications by creating a global store, and all the needed components use this global store without passing down props from one component to the other.

> **Note**
> Redux is a lightweight library with a size of around 2 KB, including its dependencies.

What are the differences between Flux and Redux?

Even though Redux is inspired by the Flux architecture, there are a few major differences, as listed in the following table.

Flux	Redux
This was developed by Facebook	This was developed by Dan Abramov and Andrew Clark
It is an application architecture to manage the application state	It is an open source JavaScript library to manage the state

Flux	Redux
Flux provides multiple stores in the application	The intended pattern in Redux is to have only one store in the application
It consists of four major components: Action Dispatcher Store View	It consists of three major components: Action Reducer Store
The store manages the logic handling	Reducers manage the logic handling
It has a singleton dispatcher	It won't use any dispatcher
The store's state can be mutable	The store's state is immutable

Table 6.2: Flux versus Redux

Apart from the preceding differences, Redux reduces complexity via functional composition, unlike Flux, which uses callback registration.

When do you need to use Redux?

Redux is used to maintain and update the data across your application with a shared state for multiple components. But it may not be needed for all kinds of applications. It comes with a big learning curve and the need to write more code.

The following is a list of use cases where Redux is useful:

- You have large amounts of application state that needs to be shared by many components in the app

- You need to follow a single source of truth for your application state

- The application state needs to be updated frequently

- The logic of updating the application state is complex

- You need to monitor how the state update happens over a period

- The application code is not a small-scale code base and many team members need to work on it

Moreover, if you can manage state within React or any other frontend framework itself, then you don't need to use Redux.

Redux is not just a tiny library; it is also a pattern based on core principles, a working system with three major components, and provides several add-ons and vast APIs to cover common use cases in Redux applications. Let's dive deep into all these topics in the next section.

Core principles of Redux, components, and APIs

Even though Redux is inspired by the important qualities of Flux architecture, it has its own foundation principles and various components that make the Redux system handle state management in massive applications. As part of this section, you will get a clear understanding of Redux internals and their usage to answer medium- to advanced-level questions.

What are the core principles of Redux?

Redux is based on three core principles. These principles are helpful to understand the library in a better way:

- **Single source of truth**: The global state of your application is stored in a single store in the form of an object tree. Since all the states exist in a single place, it is called a single source of truth.

  The single tree makes it easier to debug and inspect the application. As a result, you can easily implement *Undo* or *Redo* functionalities, which were hard to implement previously. The entire state of the application is retrieved by using the getState() function, as follows:

  ```
  console.log(store.getState());
  ```

  This single tree is also helpful to persist the state in development for a faster development cycle.

> **Note**
>
> The one-store approach of Redux is one of the major differences from the multi-store approach of Flux.

- **The state is read-only**: The only possible way to modify the state is to emit an action, an object form that describes what happened. That means an application cannot change the state directly, but instead, expresses an intent to change the state by passing an action.

  The following is an example code snippet that adds a new city to cities state by dispatching an action:

  ```
  store.dispatch({
    type: 'ADD_CITY',
    payload: "London"
  })
  ```

  Since the preceding action is a plain JavaScript object, it can be serialized, stored, logged, and replayed for debugging purposes.

- **Changes are made with pure functions**: Reducers need to be written to specify how the state is transformed by actions. They are simply pure functions that take arguments such as the previous state and action and return a new state. You need to remember that the new state object has been returned instead of modifying the old state.

The following sample reducer adds a new city and updates the `cities` state variable:

```
function cities(cities = [], action) {
  switch (action.type) {
    case 'ADD_CITY':
      return [
        ...cities,
        {
          name: action.payload,
          position: 1
        }
      ]
    default:
      return cities;
  }
}
```

Initially, your application can start with a single reducer. Once your application grows, you can split the large reducer into multiple small reducers that manage specific parts of the state tree. Moreover, you can also control the order of reducers invoked, passing the additional data, and making them reusable in the application for common tasks.

How does Redux work? What are the main components of Redux?

The Redux system works by holding the entire state of the application in a central store. Each UI component that is a child of the Redux's provider can access this stored state instead of sending the props from one component to the other. The entire process of the Redux workflow is based on three main core components: **Actions**, **Reducers**, and **the Store**.

The workflow of Redux using the core components is explained with a simple todo example for better understanding in the following code. In the example, daily activities such as eating and running are considered as todos and added to the store using the Redux workflow:

- **Actions**: Actions are plain JavaScript objects that contain `type` fields that denote what kind of action to perform, and other data fields that are used to change the state. They are the only way to send the application data (for example, through form data, user interaction, or API calls) to the Redux store. All these actions are created via action creators, which are just functions that return actions.

The following code snippet is an example of adding a todo action creator named `addTodo` that returns a todo action:

```
function addTodo(todo) {
    return {
        type: 'ADD_TODO',
        payload: todo
    }
}
```

The preceding action also contains todo details as a payload. It will be executed by the `store.dispatch(addTodo)` method, which sends this action to the store.

- **Reducers**: Actions describe what to do but they don't tell us how to do it. So, reducers are used to handle how the store's state will change in response to an action. Reducers are similar to event listeners, which handle events based on the received action type.

The reducer has logic to add a new `todo`, which looks like the following code snippet:

```
const todoReducer = (state = initialState, action) => {
    switch (action.type) {
        case "ADD_TODO":
            const { name, priority } = action.payload;
            return [...state.todos, { name, priority }];

        default:
            return state;
    }
};
```

The preceding reducer takes the initial state and action as arguments. If the switch case matches with the ADD_TODO action type, it copies the existing todos from the state, updates the todos with a new `todo` value, and returns the todo new list. Otherwise, the existing state with unchanged todos will be returned. You can add more functional cases based on possible actions such as updating, deleting, and filtering todos in the application.

> **Note**
> It is not restricted to using switch-case code blocks only to decide what the new state should be. You can also use `if/else` loops or any other programming constructs.

- **Store**: The store is used to hold the application state and the same state modified by React components by dispatching actions to the store. Redux provides the following helper methods for creating the store, accessing it, and dispatching actions to the store:

  - `createStore` or `configureStore`

- `dispatch(action)`

- `getState()`

These helper methods are going to be used to create or update the todos state in the store, as shown here:

```
import { createStore } from "redux";
import todoReducer from "reducers/todoReducer";


const store = createStore(todoReducer); // Create a store
const firstTodo = addTodo({ name: "Running", priority: 2 });

console.log(firstTodo);
store.dispatch(firstTodo); // Dispatch a todo

const secondTodo = addTodo({ name: "Eating", priority: 1 });
console.log(secondTodo);
store.dispatch(secondTodo);
console.log(store.getState()); // Returns the todos list
```

In the preceding code, new todo actions have been created and dispatched to update the existing todo list in the store. The updated todos state is also accessible.

The `createStore` method has been deprecated and it is recommended to use the `configureStore` method from the RTK by the Redux team. The `configureStore` method provides additional defaults for the store setup and the inclusion of the Redux DevTools extension automatically. In the previous code snippet, we used `createStore` from plain Redux, and you will see the usage of the `configureStore` method when we introduce the RTK.

> **Note**
>
> As the application grows, the specific parts of the state information from the store's state can be accessed using functions known as *selectors*. The reselect library is popular for memoized selector functions.

It is also possible to extend the store functionality by adding store enhancers and middleware. These topics will be covered in the upcoming questions in this chapter.

Can I use Redux with non-React UI libraries?

Even though Redux is mostly used with React and React Native libraries, it can be used with any other UI library (i.e., Redux works as a data store for various UI libraries). But you need to use the UI binding library to integrate Redux with your UI framework or library. For example, React Redux is the official binding library to tie Redux together with the React library. There are bindings available for AngularJS, Angular, Vue, Mithril, Ember, and many other frameworks too. Redux provides a subscription mechanism that can be used by any other code, but it is mostly useful when you integrate with declarative views or UIs created via React or other similar libraries.

What are the rules followed by reducers?

In Redux, the reducer component should follow some specific rules. Those rules are listed here:

- Reducers should only derive the new state value based on the current state and action arguments.
- Reducers shouldn't modify the existing state. However, they can perform immutable updates by copying the existing state and making changes to the copied values instead.
- They are not allowed to perform any asynchronous logic, calculate random values, or any side effects.

The functions that follow the preceding rules are also known as **pure functions**. In other words, reducers are simply pure functions. By following these rules, reducers make Redux code and state predictable without any bugs.

What is the difference between the mapStateToProps() and mapDispatchToProps() methods?

The `mapStateToProps()` method is a utility function used to select the part of the data from the store that the connected component needs. The selected state is going to be passed as props to the component to which `connect()` is applied. In this way, this method is helpful to avoid passing the entire application state to the component.

The following example passes a `city` value as a prop to the `WeatherReport` component to find the weather information:

```
const mapStateToProps = (state) => {
  return {
    city: state.user.address.city,
  };
};
connect(mapStateToProps)(WeatherReport);
```

Now, the `WeatherReport` component only accepts `city` as a prop. You can easily use this component anywhere else in the application by decoupling Redux code from React components:

```
<WeatherReport city={city} />
```

The shorthand notation for this function is `mapState` and this function is called every time the store state changes.

The `mapDispatchToProps()` method is a utility function that is used to specify which actions your component might need to dispatch. This function provides action dispatching functions as props.

The following function specifies the actions required for the `WeatherReport` React component:

```
const mapDispatchToProps = (dispatch) => {
  return {
    changeCity: (city) => {
      dispatch(changeCity(city));
    },
  };
};
```

The preceding code snippet performs a city change action. This is done by invoking the `props.changeCity(city)` action directly in the component instead of calling the `props.dispatch(changeCity(city))` verbose expression.

There is a recommended object shorthand notation for the `mapDispatchToProps` function. In this approach, Redux wraps it in another function that looks like `(...args) => dispatch(changeCity(...args))` and passes that wrapper function as a prop to your component.

Now, the preceding code can be simplified as follows:

```
const mapDispatchToProps = {
    toggleCity
};
```

In summary, the `mapStateToProps` function is used to render the stored data to the component and `mapDispatchToProps` is used to provide the action creators as props to the component.

What is a store enhancer?

A store enhancer is a higher-order function that accepts a store creator function (i.e., `createStore`) and returns a new enhanced store creator function. This is helpful to customize the original Redux store, and it will override the store methods such as `dispatch`, `getState`, and `subscribe`.

Take a look at the following snippet to see how the store enhancer implementation looks:

```
const ourCustomEnhancer =
  (createStore) => (reducer, initialState, enhancer) => {
    const customReducer = (state, action) => {
      // Logic to return new state
    };
    const store = createStore(customReducer, initialState, enhancer);
    //Add enhancer logic
    return {
      ...store,
      //Override the some store properties or add new properties
    };
  };
```

Store enhancer is quite similar to the concept of **higher-order component (HOC)** in React. So you can also call the HOC as **component enhancer**.

> **Note**
>
> Middleware provides additional functionality to the Redux dispatch function and enhancers provide additional functionality to the Redux store.

Real-time applications contain logic that involves side effects such as external API calls, generating random values, saving files, and updating local storage. By default, Redux has no support for these kinds of side effects to be executed. However, Redux middleware makes it possible to intercept the dispatched actions and inject additional complex behavior, including side effects. Next, we will get a better idea about that.

Redux middleware – Saga and Thunk

The basic Redux store can only perform simple synchronous state updates by dispatching an action. Middleware such as **Redux Thunk** and **Redux Saga** help extend the store capabilities by writing the async logic to interact with the store. These middleware are helpful to avoid directly causing side effects in our actions, action creators, or components.

What is Redux middleware? How do you create middleware?

Redux middleware provides a third-party extension to intercept every action sent to the reducer by modifying the action or canceling the action. It is helpful for logging, error reporting, routing, and making asynchronous API calls. Although Redux middleware is like Node.js middleware (for example, Express and Koa), it solves different problems.

In the following example, let's demonstrate the creation of a custom middleware named `loggerMiddleware` to log the various actions in the console with step-by-step instructions:

1. As a first step, you need to import the `applyMiddleware` function from the Redux library as follows:

    ```
    import { applyMiddleware } from "redux";
    ```

2. Create a middleware named `loggerMiddleware` to intercept the action for logging purposes with the following structured syntax:

    ```
    const loggerMiddleware = (store) => (next) =>
      (action) => {
      console.log("action", action);
      return next(action);
    };
    ```

3.   After the `loggerMiddleware` function has been created, it needs to be passed to the `applyMiddleware` function:

```
const middleware = applyMiddleware(loggerMiddleware);
```

4.   Finally, we need to pass the custom middleware to the `createStore` function. Even though the middleware is assigned as a third argument to the store, the `createStore` function automatically identifies the middleware based on the type:

```
const store = createStore(reducer, middleware);
```

Before the action is dispatched to the store, the middleware gets executed by logging the action details in the console. Since the next function has been invoked inside the middleware, the reducer will also be executed to update the state in the store.

It is also possible to create multiple middleware by passing them to `applyMiddleware` function as follows:

```
const middleware = applyMiddleware(
  loggerMiddleware,
  firstMiddleware,
  secondMiddleware,
  thirdMiddleware
);
```

In the preceding code, all these middleware are executed one after the other.

How do you handle asynchronous tasks in Redux?

Most modern web applications need to deal with asynchronous tasks. In React, there are two popular libraries available to handle them: **Redux Thunk** and **Redux Saga**.

Redux Thunk middleware is used to write an action creator that returns a function instead of just an action object in the Redux application. The functions returned from the action creator are called thunk functions and are used to delay the computation. These functions accept two arguments – the `dispatch` and `getState` methods:

```
const thunkFunction = (dispatch, getState) => {
  // This is the place where you can write logic to
     dispatch other actions or read state
}
store.dispatch(thunkFunction);
```

All thunk functions are invoked through the store's `dispatch` method but not from the application code. The same behavior can be seen with the preceding code as well.

Similar to action creators generating actions for dispatching, you can use Thunk action creators to generate thunk functions. For example, the list of posts created by a specific user can be retrieved using the thunk action creator named getPostsByAuthor, which generates anonymous thunk functions:

```
export const getPostsByAuthor = (authorId) => async (dispatch) => {
  const response = await client.get(`/api/posts/${authorId}`);
  dispatch(postsLoaded(response.posts));
};
```

After that, you can access the action creator inside the UI component for any user interaction. The following AuthorComponent accesses the list of posts on the lazy loading event:

```
function AuthorComponent({ authorId }) {
  //...
  const onLazyLoading = () => {
    dispatch(getPostsByAuthor(authorId))
  }
}
```

The last important step is configuring the redux-thunk middleware to the Redux store to dispatch the thunk functions. There are two possible options available. Thunk middleware needs to be passed to the applyMiddleware() method to add thunk middleware to the store manually. But if you are using RTK, the configureStore API automatically adds the thunk middleware during the store creation (i.e., it doesn't require any additional configuration).

What are the use cases of Redux Thunk?

Redux Thunk can have any arbitrary logic and it can be used for a variety of purposes. The most common use cases of Redux Thunk are listed as follows:

- When you're trying to move complex logic out of React components
- When you are making async requests such as Ajax calls and other async logic
- When you need to create a logic that needs to dispatch multiple distinct actions in a row
- When you are planning to write a logic that needs to access getState or other state values to make decisions

In summary, the main use case of Redux Thunk middleware is for handling actions that are not synchronous.

What is Redux Saga?

Redux Saga is a popular competitor for Redux Thunk middleware for handling asynchronous side effects. Redux Saga uses an ES6 feature known as **generators** that helps in writing asynchronous code. These generators are functions that can be paused, resumed, exited in the middle of execution, and re-entered later during the operations.

The side effects will be generated using special helper functions from the `redux-saga` package. Some of those commonly used functions are listed here:

- `Call`: An effect description that instructs the middleware to call other functions in Saga

- `Put`: Used to dispatch an action to the store

- `Yield`: A built-in function that allows the use of generator functions sequentially

- `takeLatest`: Invokes the function handler only once at a time and cancels the previous tasks by running again with the latest data

- `takeEvery`: Invokes the function handler every time infinitely and concurrently whenever the action fires

The Saga functions listen for the actions that got dispatched and trigger side effects written in your code. For example, the following `postsSaga` function listens for the `GET_POSTS` action and invokes the Posts API to retrieve the author's posts:

```
import { takeLatest, put, call } from "redux-saga/effects";
import { GET_POSTS } from "./actionTypes";
import { getPostsSuccess, getPostsFail } from "./actions";
import { getPosts } from "../backend/api/posts ";

function* fetchAuthorPosts() {
  try {
    const response = yield call(getPosts);
    yield put(getPostsSuccess(response));
  } catch (error) {
    yield put(getPostsFail(error.response));
  }
}

function* postsSaga() {
  yield takeLatest(GET_POSTS, fetchAuthorPosts);
}

export default postsSaga;
```

In the preceding code, either the successful response or failed response dispatched to the store. This response depends on API call happened through the `call` helper function.

How do you choose between Redux Saga and Redux Thunk?

Both Redux Thunk and Redux Saga middleware are helpful in allowing the Redux store to interact with external API calls (or side effects) asynchronously. But the decision to choose one of them totally depends on your project requirements and personal preference. Redux Thunk is a good choice if you are new to the React or Redux ecosystem and the project is small in size. Moreover, Redux Thunk requires less boilerplate code and is easy to understand.

On the other hand, Redux Saga is suitable for big projects where you need to split the logic into multiple files. However, the main advantage of Redux Saga over Redux Thunk is the ability to write clean and readable tests for asynchronous code.

The plain Redux requires a lot of boilerplate code to fulfill the state management requirements. Developers need to implement common tasks such as store setup, writing reducers and actions, and so on. Also, you may need to import APIs from other packages based on needs. So, this entire process makes it difficult for developers to learn and implement the Redux solution. RTK is going to standardize the process and simplify it with its helpers.

Standardizing Redux logic using RTK

The RTK package provides the necessary tools to ease Redux development. This package not only eases development but also prevents common mistakes, provides suggested best practices, and many more features.

What is RTK?

Redux Toolkit (RTK) is a set of tools that simplifies Redux development and is used as an officially recommended approach to writing Redux logic. It was previously known as Redux Smarter Kit. The node package for this toolkit is available with the name `@reduxjs/toolkit`, which is wrapped around the core `redux` package. In summary, this package provides utilities and common dependencies that are required for building a Redux application.

This tool helps cover common use cases such as setting up the store, creating the reducers and actions, writing immutable update logic, and creating entire slices of state at once.

By default, RTK automatically supports the following officially recommended set of tools or libraries to cover most of the common use cases:

- Redux DevTools
- Immer
- Redux Thunk
- Reselect

RTK supports TypeScript through which APIs provide excellent type safety and reduce the number of types used in the code.

What are the problems solved by RTK?

RTK is helpful to speed up the development process and apply the recommended best practices automatically. It solves the following three major issues found in the Redux library:

- Configuring a Redux store that is too complicated
- This Redux library requires a lot of dependencies for building a large-scale application
- Redux requires too much boilerplate code, which impacts the efficiency and quality of the code

The toolkit provides certain options to configure the global store, creating actions and reducers that make the development simpler by abstracting the Redux API.

What is RTK Query? How do you use it?

RTK Query is a powerful data fetching and client-side caching tool to simplify common use cases in Redux applications. For example, this tool supports use cases such as loading data in the web application, avoiding the need for hand-written data fetching and caching logic, and so on. If you are using the RTK package, this query feature is going to be available as an optional add-on. Also, this feature is built-in on top of the RTK API methods such as `createSlice` and `createAsyncThunk` for its implementation.

Let's explain the usage of RTK Query with a data fetching use case in the web application.

First, you need to import the `createAPI` and `fetchBaseQuery` API methods from the RTK Query package. This `createAPI` method accepts an object that includes the `baseQuery` configuration created by the `fetchBaseQuery` API and a list of API endpoints to interact with the server.

In this example, two endpoints are going to be created – one for creating the user and the other one for listing the users:

```
import { createApi, fetchBaseQuery } from "@reduxjs/toolkit/query/
react";
```

```
export const usersServerApi = createApi({
  reducerPath: "api",
  baseQuery: fetchBaseQuery({
    baseUrl: "https://jsonplaceholder.typicode.com/",
  }),

  endpoints: (builder) => ({
    users: builder.query({
      query: (page = 1) => `users?page=${page}&limit=10`,
    }),

    createUser: builder.mutation({
      query: (name) => ({
        url: "users",
        method: "POST",
        body: { name },
      }),
    }),
  }),
});

export const { useUsersQuery, useCreateUserMutation } =
usersServerApi;
```

As shown in the preceding code, RTK Query auto-generates React Hooks for each endpoint that is available to use in function components through export declaration.

Next, the store needs to be configured by mapping RTK Query's generated slice reducer into root reducer along with a custom middleware that handles data fetching. The setupListeners API is an optional utility to enable refreshOnFocus and refreshOnReconnect behaviors:

```
import { configureStore } from "@reduxjs/toolkit";
import { setupListeners } from "@reduxjs/toolkit/query";
import { usersServerApi } from "./services/usersAPI";

export const store = configureStore({
  reducer: {
    [usersServerApi.reducerPath]: usersServerApi.reducer,
  },

  middleware: (getDefaultMiddleware) =>
    getDefaultMiddleware().concat(usersServerApi.middleware),
});

setupListeners(store.dispatch);
```

After that, you need to wrap our application with the `Provider` component from the `react-redux` package to pass the store as a prop to all the child components, just like any Redux application:

```
const rootElement = document.getElementById("root");

render(
  <Provider store={store}>
    <App />
  </Provider>,
  rootElement
);
```

Once that is done, you can make requests in your component through queries. The list of users on the second page can be retrieved as shown in the following code snippet:

```
const { data, error, isLoading } = useUsersQuery(2)
```

In addition to users `data`, `error` and `isLoading` fields, the preceding query also provides other Boolean utilities such as `isFetching`, `isError`, and `isSuccess`, which might be of use, depending on functional requirements.

Redux is the best state solution for large-scale applications. However, it will be challenging to debug the bugs that arise in these kinds of applications. Redux DevTools makes the development and debugging experience easy by tracing when, where, and how your application's state has been changed.

Debugging applications using Redux DevTools

Just like Chrome DevTools is used to manipulate the content of the web page on the fly, Redux DevTools allows you to directly manipulate Redux operations in the web application. Nowadays, this tool has become a standard development tool for developing any kind of Redux application.

What is Redux DevTools?

Redux DevTools is a development-purpose-only tool for debugging an application's state changes. It is used to perform time-travel debugging and live editing for Redux with hot reloading, actions history, undo, and replay features. If you don't want to install Redux DevTools as a standalone app or integrate it as a React component in the client app, it can be used as a browser extension for Chrome, Firefox, or Edge browsers.

The following is an example DevTools snapshot representing the sequence of fetching todos, completing, and deleting todo operations:

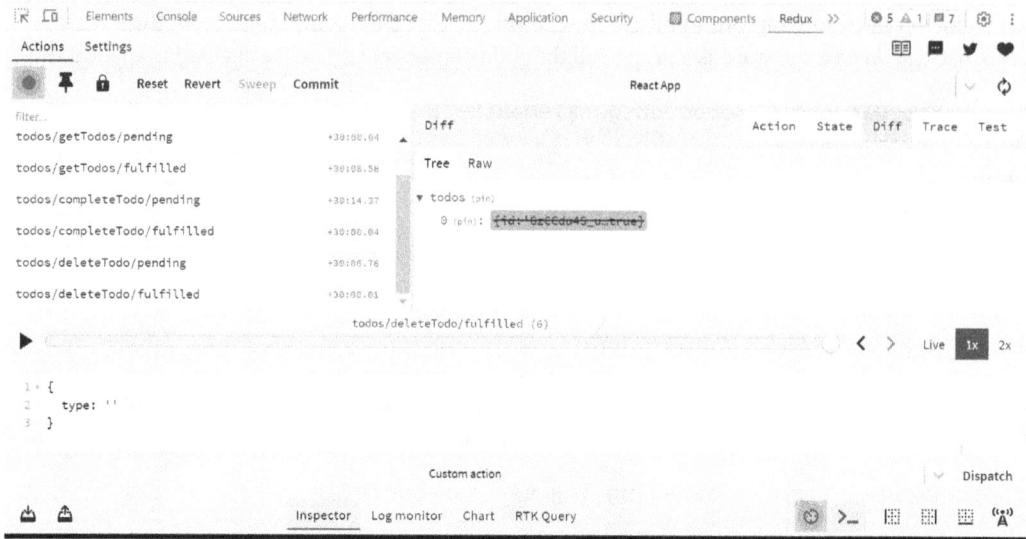

Figure 6.2: Redux DevTools UI

In the preceding screenshot, the left panel represents the list of actions with *Skip* and *Jump* options on selecting the particular action and the right panel describes the current state, differences in state, and other useful features.

> **Note**
>
> RTK's `configureStore` API automatically sets up integration with Redux DevTools.

What are the major features of Redux DevTools?

Some of the major features of Redux DevTools are listed here:

- It provides the ability to inspect every state and action payload

- You can go back in time by canceling the actions

- Once the reducer code changes, each staged action will be re-evaluated

- If there is an error thrown from the reducer, you can trace which action caused the error and what the error is about

- You can persist debug sessions across page reloads using the `persistState()` store enhancer

It is also possible to dispatch actions without writing any code in the application using the **dispatch** option of Redux DevTools.

Summary

This chapter has offered comprehensive knowledge of Redux state management solutions for React applications. We began this chapter with a brief introduction to Flux, its architecture, differences with the MVC pattern, and use cases, followed by Redux fundamentals, differences with Flux, and its advantages as a state management solution. We also covered topics such as the core principles of Redux, their components, various add-ons, and data flows. After that, we went through understanding async tasks, popular middleware libraries in Redux, how to use them in React applications, and their use cases. Finally, we covered the debugging techniques and Redux DevTools to track the state changes.

In the next chapter, we will understand the various approaches to applying CSS in React applications. First, we will start with a regular CSS styling approach in React using inline styles and external styles. Then, we will go through advanced techniques such as locally scoped CSS using CSS Modules and the `styled-components` library based on the CSS-in-JS solution.

7

Different Approaches to Apply CSS in ReactJS

Creating aesthetically beautiful and user-friendly interfaces is critical in modern web development for establishing engaging and effective applications. ReactJS is a popular frontend framework for creating user interfaces and has a number of methods for implementing **Cascading Style Sheets** (**CSS**), the language responsible for styling online content. This chapter attempts to answer many important questions on the topic of CSS that an interviewee might have. By explaining the various approaches for incorporating CSS in ReactJS, we will be able to benefit from an expanded knowledge set that puts us in a much better position when tackling interview questions on this subject.

We will look at five different methods for implementing CSS: **importing external style sheets**, **inline styles**, **CSS Modules**, `styled-components`, and **Atomic CSS** (with the Tailwind CSS framework). Each of these solutions has advantages and disadvantages, depending on the project objectives and preferences. By investigating these options, you will get the knowledge and confidence to navigate these questions in an interview environment, which will be particularly useful when the time comes for you to create a ReactJS application. By learning about the principles of writing and maintaining clean, manageable, and scalable code, you will find it much simpler to come up with good-quality answers in your interviews.

Preprocessors such as Sass and Less will also get an introduction in this chapter, as we aim to cover all of the relevant use cases for implementing CSS into our React projects and have the right answers to any interview questions in these areas.

In this chapter, we will learn about and go into detail on these important CSS-related topics:

- Different ways to apply CSS
- Exploring processors and CSS Modules
- CSS-in-JS approach and `styled-components` and its usage
- How to use styled components in React applications

Technical requirements

Make sure that you have Node and npm installed on your computer and that the JavaScript Node packages for Create React App and Next.js are installed and working. Use your favorite IDE and **command-line interface (CLI)** to work on these projects.

The package for Create React App can be found here: `https://create-react-app.dev/`.

The package for Next.js can be found here: `https://nextjs.org/`.

Different ways to apply CSS

In this section, we will be exploring different ways to apply CSS inside React projects. The knowledge gained will provide us with crucial interview-ready answers to these common questions, and the examples can aid us in explaining in detail the differences and how they work. Let's continue with our learning and take a closer look at these CSS solutions.

While ReactJS is a JavaScript library for creating user interfaces, CSS is a style sheet language used to describe the appearance and formatting of an HTML or XML document. Incorporating CSS with ReactJS helps developers to efficiently style their components, resulting in aesthetically pleasing and consistent interfaces. There are a few ways to use CSS with ReactJS, which we are going to learn about in this chapter.

In the upcoming sections, we will learn about importing CSS, CSS Modules, CSS preprocessors, Atomic CSS, and inline styling. The latter involves adding styles directly to React components using JavaScript objects. While inline styles are useful for small components or dynamic styles, they can cause code duplication and maintainability problems in bigger applications, which we will talk about. First, let us begin with importing style sheets.

How do we import external style sheets?

The standard technique of utilizing CSS in React involves creating separate CSS files and styling components with class names. This solution keeps style and logic concerns separate, making the code more structured and manageable. The official React documentation recommends that developers use production-grade React frameworks when starting new React projects. This includes Next.js, Remix, Gatsby, and Expo (for native apps). This is now considered the most modern way of developing React applications, which you can read about here: `https://react.dev/learn/start-a-new-react-project`.

We will take a look at two code examples, one with Next.js and another with Create React App, to show the contrast between the two (old versus new) processes of building React apps. Next.js is considered to be the most modern recommended way for building ReactJS applications, whereas Create React App is now seen as a legacy tool. This is because Next.js is seen as a more production-grade ready ReactJS framework.

How do we use Create React App to build React apps?

Here's how to implement the traditional method in a React application using Create React App.

Firstly, create a React project and then create a CSS file. Use CSS rules and class names to specify your styles in a separate CSS file called App.css, as follows:

```css
/* App.css */
.container {
  text-align: center;
  margin: 0 auto;
  background-color: #bada55;
  padding: 1rem;
}

.title {
  font-size: 2rem;
  font-weight: bold;
}
```

Now, import the created CSS file into your React component file, which should be App.js:

```js
// App.js
import './App.css';

export default function App() {
  return (

      <div className="container">
        <h1 className="title">Hello, World!</h1>
      </div>

  );
}
```

> **Note**
>
> The className attribute is used in JSX elements to apply the corresponding CSS classes from the imported style sheet. We are using the className attribute instead of class because a class is a reserved word in JavaScript. This is not a problem when writing CSS in CSS files, but it is in JavaScript files. Also, JSX is a nomenclature, which means that it requires element properties such as class names to use the camelCase naming convention.

Initiate the npm run start command in your console, and your application should be up and running.

How do we use Next.js to build React apps?

Next.js is a well-known open source web development framework built on ReactJS. It is intended to make it easier for developers to create server-rendered React apps, allowing them to create high-performance web applications that are optimized for **search engine optimization (SEO)** and give a fantastic user experience.

Next.js has a slightly different project structure, although importing CSS style sheets still works the same way. Fortunately, the process is actually quite similar when using the latest App Router feature in Next.js. This is how we would import a CSS style sheet in Next.js.

Firstly, use Next.js to create a React project and then create a Home.css file inside of the app folder. Use the CSS shown here:

```css
/* Home.css */
.container {
  margin: 0 auto;
  display: flex;
  flex-flow: column nowrap;
  background-color: #0384c8;
  padding: 2rem;
}

.main-content {
  display: flex;
  flex-flow: row nowrap;
  padding: 2rem 0;
}
```

Now, just replace all of the code inside of the page.js file in the app folder with this code here:

```jsx
import './Home.css';
export default function Home() {
  return (
    <div className="container">
      <h1>Heading 1</h1>
      <h2>Heading 2</h2>
      <h3>Heading 3</h3>
      <h4>Heading 4</h4>
      <h5>Heading 5</h5>
      <section className="main-content">
        <p>
          Lorem ipsum dolor sit amet, consectetur
          adipiscing elit. Nullam eu
          mi sit amet velit convallis tincidunt.
```

```
        </p>
        <p>
          Lorem ipsum dolor sit amet, consectetur
          adipiscing elit. Nullam eu mi sit
          amet velit convallis tincidunt.
        </p>
      </section>
    </div>
  );
}
```

Run your application using the npm run dev command, and it should work just as before.

This has been the default method for importing our style sheets since the days of Create React App. It does not, however, enable component-level isolation, and global class names might cause naming conflicts and unwanted style overrides. CSS Modules and CSS-in-JS frameworks, for example, solve these concerns and provide more extensive tools for decorating React components. Some popular CSS frameworks include Tailwind CSS, MUI, Chakra UI, Semantic UI, NextUI, React Bootstrap, Ant Design, and Emotion. Tailwind CSS is actually an option that you can select when configuring your Next.js application for the first time.

It's also worth mentioning that in the CSS web layout model, the two most popular ways to build the structure of a website are by using either Flexbox or CSS Grid. Flexbox is by far more popular, although it is common to use either one or both together depending on the website design and complexity. We can use these web layout models on their own or with a CSS framework. Another area that we might want to look into at some point is animation. Aside from using the usual CSS libraries for creating animations, we can utilize various third-party libraries as well. Some popular libraries are React Spring, Green Sock, Framer Motion, React Move, and many others.

We will now talk about another method of styling our ReactJS apps, called inline styling, which is a common way to do styling in normal HTML and ReactJS applications. It has been one of the default ways of styling HTML for quite some time and is possible in React using JSX, too.

Inline styling provides many advantages too, which makes it a very appealing option for styling our React applications. We are able to use dynamic styling according to component state or props, and there is component isolation, which lowers the possibility of unintended style overrides or incompatibilities with other components. The faster development, ease of use, and the fact that we don't even need CSS class names all increase the benefits of using this method.

How do we use inline styles?

Inline styles in ReactJS applications allow developers to apply styling to specific elements or components directly using JavaScript objects, rather than specifying CSS styles in separate style sheets or classes. They are specified as object literals that include key-value pairs. Basically, they are objects inside JSX curly brackets that look like this {{ backgroundColor: blue }}. Inside the JSX curlies is where we would then use CSS properties and their values. The object's keys are the CSS property names, and the values are the associated property values.

Let's take a look at an example so that we can see what this looks like in real code. Just replace all of the code in the page.js file to convert it to an application that now uses inline styles instead of external style sheets:

```
const container = {
  display: 'flex',
  flexFlow: 'column nowrap',
  backgroundColor: '#7e7dd6',
  padding: '2rem',
};

const mainContent = {
  display: 'flex',
  flexFlow: 'row nowrap',
  padding: '2rem 0',
};

export default function Home() {
  return (
    <>
      <div style={container}>
        <h1>Heading 1</h1>
        <h2>Heading 2</h2>
        <h3>Heading 3</h3>
        <h4>Heading 4</h4>
        <h5>Heading 5</h5>
        <section style={mainContent}>
          <p>
            Lorem ipsum dolor sit amet, consectetur
            adipiscing elit. Nullam eu
            mi sit amet velit convallis tincidunt.
          </p>
          <p>
            Lorem ipsum dolor sit amet, consectetur
            adipiscing elit. Nullam eu
            mi sit amet velit convallis tincidunt.
          </p>
        </section>
      </div>
```

```
    </>
  );
}
```

When we need to apply dynamic styles based on the state or properties of a component, React inline styles might be helpful. For example, based on user interactions or other events, we might declare a style object as a property of the component's state and change it dynamically.

It's possible to use a variable with our inline styles as well by assigning it to state, and this is what it would look like:

```
'use client';
import { useState } from 'react';
export default function Home() {
  const [h1color, setH1Color] = useState('blue');
    return (
  <div>
    <h1 style={{ color: h1color }}>Hello World</h1>
  </div>
);
}
```

Nevertheless, inline styles have certain drawbacks, including the inability to reuse styles across components, the fact that they are less effective than external style sheets for large-scale systems, and the possibility of affecting readability if not utilized carefully.

One way to address these problems is by using CSS Modules. CSS Modules is an approach for writing modular, scoped CSS for your components. It aids in the resolution of typical CSS difficulties such as global scope and name conflicts.

Another good strategy for implementing CSS in React is using `styled-components`. `styled-components` is a well-known CSS-in-JS package used to style React components. It enables you to use tagged template literals to write CSS right in your JavaScript code. `styled-components` produces unique class names and injects styles into the DOM, scoping them to the individual components. This method improves the developer experience and component separation.

Another way we can use CSS in our projects is by using Atomic CSS. Atomic CSS, also known as functional CSS, is a style technique that focuses on developing tiny, single-purpose CSS classes that are combined to create sophisticated user interface components. Each class provides one type of rule or a group of rules that are closely linked, and they are generally labeled in a format that defines their purpose or the attributes that they apply.

The advantage here is that development is fast because by simply mixing existing atomic classes, you can quickly prototype and construct components. A general theme or template is followed so that every developer uses the same documentation and set of classes. This makes for very simple debugging, and the onboarding process is fast because everyone is using the same process.

How do we use Atomic CSS?

Atomic CSS is a strategy for structuring and developing CSS code that emphasizes the usage of brief, specialized classes that could be combined to produce sophisticated styling. The goal is to deconstruct designs into manageable, reusable parts capable of being merged in a variety of ways to produce the desired design.

The Atomic CSS technique is implemented by a number of well-known CSS libraries, including Tailwind CSS, Bootstrap CSS, and Bulma, among many others. These libraries offer pre-defined collections of atomic classes that can be used to quickly generate complicated styling. We will now use the Tailwind CSS library to do some basic styling in our Next.js app because of its popularity in the community and the fact that Tailwind CSS is integrated into Create Next App, which is the official framework for building Next.js applications. It's possible to use any CSS library when you understand the fundamentals.

Installing Tailwind CSS is fairly easy; all you have to do is follow the setup guide here: `https://tailwindcss.com/docs/guides/nextjs`.

With that completed, we can see what the syntax looks like in this example:

```
export default function Home() {
  return (
    <>
      <div class="flex flex-row">
        <div class="basis-1/4 bg-teal-600">01</div>
        <div class="basis-1/4 bg-teal-700">02</div>
        <div class="basis-1/2 bg-teal-800">03</div>
      </div>
    </>
  );
}
```

Next, let us learn about preprocessors and CSS Modules. A CSS preprocessor is a program that allows us to build CSS using the preprocessor's own syntax. In a CSS module, every single class name and animation name is now, by definition, assigned locally. For greater efficiency and security, CSS Modules allow you to create styles in CSS files; however, you need to utilize the styles as JavaScript objects.

Exploring processors and CSS Modules

We can build websites with CSS in two distinct ways—by using CSS processors and CSS Modules. CSS processors have been around for quite a long time and were designed to be an improvement over traditional CSS. They gave us access to nesting our CSS code and the code compiled to regular CSS. CSS Modules, on the other hand, give us scoped CSS code in our files, which is better for avoiding name conflicts. Let's now learn about them both, starting with CSS processors.

What are CSS processors?

CSS processors, commonly referred to as CSS preprocessors, are tools that add extra features to CSS, such as variables, mixins, and nesting rules. They enable you to write in less repetitive and modular ways that are easier to maintain. Sass, also known as SCSS, Less, and Stylus are the three CSS preprocessors that are most widely used. To translate the improved CSS syntax into conventional CSS that web browsers can understand, these preprocessors need a build step. When using build tools such as Webpack, you can incorporate this build phase into your development routine.

How do we use CSS processors?

Sass is supported in Next.js natively, utilizing both the `.scss` and `.sass` extensions. Through CSS Modules and the `.module.scss` or `.module.sass` extension, you can apply component-level Sass. Firstly, install Sass using the `npm install -save-dev sass` command. Then, write your styles in Sass syntax in a new `.scss` file. Import the generated CSS by referencing the `.scss` file in your React component file, as shown here:

```
import './styles.scss';
const MyComponent = () => {
  return <div className="myComponent">Hello, World!</div>;
};
export default MyComponent;
```

Importing a `.scss` file is exactly the same as importing a normal `.css` file.

What are CSS Modules?

A method for locally scoping CSS in a modular approach is CSS Modules. By automatically creating distinct names of classes for each component, it helps prevent conflicts between global styles by making sure that styles don't spread to other areas of your program. Writing your CSS styles in distinct files, often with the `module.css` extension, and importing them into your JavaScript files is how CSS Modules work. The imported styles are handled as an object, having the produced unique class names serving as value pairs and the keys serving as the primary class names.

How do we use CSS Modules?

We can utilize locally scoped CSS in our components by using CSS Modules. Class names are by default locally scoped using CSS Modules, preventing any naming conflicts. This is also the default styling method used in Next.js applications. We can see what this looks like in the following code snippets.

This is the CSS for the Home.module.css file:

```css
/* Home.module.css */
.main {
  display: flex;
  padding: 2rem;
  color: #ffffff;
}

.box {
  background-color: rgb(241, 255, 240);
  color: #000;
  padding: 1rem;
  margin: 1rem;
}
```

And this is the JavaScript for the page.js file:

```javascript
// page.js
import styles from './Home.module.css';

export default function Home() {
  return (
    <>
      <div className={styles.main}>
        <h1>Hello World!</h1>
      </div>
      <div className={styles.box}>
        <p>
          Lorem ipsum dolor sit amet, consectetur
          adipiscing elit. Etiam convallis, nulla non
          laoreet condimentum, turpis felis finibus
          metus,ut molestie risus enim id neque. Integer
          tristique purus non gravida sodales. Maecenas
          ultricies feugiat dolor lobortis commodo. Sed
          maximus vitae neque quis mollis.
        </p>
      </div>
      <div className={styles.box}>
```

```
      <p>
        Lorem ipsum dolor sit amet, consectetur
        adipiscing elit. Etiam convallis, nulla non
        laoreet condimentum, turpis felis finibus
        metus,ut molestie risus enim id neque. Integer
        tristique purus non gravida sodales. Maecenas
        ultricies feugiat dolor lobortis commodo. Sed
        maximus vitae neque quis mollis.
      </p>
    </div>
  </>
  );
}
```

As you can see, it is similar to using inline styles; however, we still have an external style sheet, so it is the best of both worlds. There is another approach to implementing CSS, which is by using styled-components and a CSS-in-JS approach. This gives us another way to set up our project and can offer many advantages when compared with other approaches. Let's learn more about this implementation now.

CSS-in-JS approach and styled-components and its usage

This is a fundamental learning area for us as the CSS-in-JS methodology applies throughout the React framework. We will learn about the approach and how it's possible for us to use a third-party library such as styled-components as an alternative to the other CSS techniques we learned earlier.

What is CSS-in-JS?

CSS-in-JS is an innovative web development style solution that incorporates CSS into JavaScript code. Instead of having separate CSS files, this method allows developers to define and oversee styles for their components right inside their JavaScript or TypeScript scripts. CSS-in-JS allows for improved component encapsulation, scoped styles, and simpler dynamic styling. It also enables you to use the entirety of JavaScript in your styles, which includes dynamically applying styles according to the state of the component or computing style values using JavaScript variables.

What are styled-components and how are they used in React projects?

With the help of a popular third-party tool for React, called styled-components, programmers can specify component styles in JavaScript rather than external CSS files. It offers a method for crafting CSS code that is focused on a particular component, simplifying the management and reusing styles throughout an application.

Styled components adopt a CSS-in-JS methodology, which implies that JavaScript functions and variables are used to define CSS styles for component styles. This enables programmers to create dynamic styles by utilizing all of JavaScript's capabilities, such as functions, variables, and other language constructs. When using `styled-components`, we have **server-side rendering (SSR)**, which guarantees that our styles are rendered appropriately on the server. In comparison to other CSS such as inline styles, it has an advantage because it does not need extra effort to ensure good SSR support. The developer experience is additionally improved since styled components include syntax highlighting, linting, and auto-completion support in most code editors.

This results in a more positive development experience and increased productivity because they also enable you to segregate styles from the JSX of the component, resulting in cleaner and more maintainable code. We can also use styled components to produce unique class names for each component, ensuring that styles are scoped to the appropriate components and avoiding inadvertent style leaks or conflicts.

Another bonus we get access to is built-in theming support via React's context API when we use `styled-components`. This makes it simple to build and manage uniform themes across our application, which is not possible with other CSS techniques. It's a great plus to have support for all CSS features, such as pseudo-selectors, media queries, and keyframes.

How to use styled components in React applications

To reinforce this learning, let us go through an example to see what the syntax looks like. We will take a quick look at a simple, easy-to-understand, basic setup that should make this very clear.

How do we use styled components?

Basically, a styled component can be created in four easy steps. Firstly, we have to install the package for the `styled-components` library, which can be found here: `https://styled-components.com/`. Next, we import the package into the top of our file. Following that, we create a JavaScript-type object for our HTML, which has CSS styling. We use the `styled` method followed by the HTML element we want to use, such as a `div`, `section`, or `p` tag, and so on.

And lastly, we render the object on the screen by returning it in our code. The following code snippet shows a working example:

```
import styled from 'styled-components';

const ContainerDiv = styled.div`
  color: blue;
  font-size: 30px;
`;

export default function Home() {
  return <ContainerDiv>Hello World!</ContainerDiv>;
}
```

We successfully concluded this section and learned about many different CSS-related interview questions, which is going to put us in a great position to do well in interviews when it comes to this subject area.

Summary

We looked at several ways to utilize CSS in ReactJS apps, emphasizing the significance of design and styling in creating aesthetically appealing user interfaces. Importing external style sheets, inline CSS styles, CSS Modules, `styled-components`, and Atomic CSS frameworks such as Tailwind CSS were the five primary options explored.

We discussed how to connect and import external CSS files into a React component, allowing for centralized administration and separation of stylistic and component logic concerns. This method is perfect for using classic CSS in React apps.

We also looked into Atomic CSS and its utility-first approach, focusing specifically on the popular Tailwind CSS framework. By offering a broad collection of utility classes that can be used to build bespoke designs, this technique reduces the requirement for custom CSS.

On the subject of CSS Modules, we looked at how CSS Modules can help handle component-specific styles in a modular fashion. CSS Modules eliminate global style conflicts and encourage component reusability by utilizing locally scoped class names. We also discussed the popular `styled-components` package, which allows you to create styled components using tagged template literals. This method encourages component encapsulation, theming support, and a prop-based dynamic style.

You will easily design and style your application components while keeping clean, manageable, and scalable code bases by knowing and utilizing these various CSS methods in your ReactJS applications.

In the next chapter, we will learn how to test and debug our ReactJS applications.

8

Testing and Debugging the React Application

React has become the most popular frontend library in the field of web development, enabling programmers to build effective, scalable, and maintainable apps. To ensure the stability and dependability of your application, comprehensive testing and efficient debugging have become increasingly crucial as projects become larger and more complicated. This chapter provides a thorough examination of the tools and methods required to master testing and debugging React apps, laying the groundwork for you to build on as you hone your abilities.

We'll start by talking about React testing helpers, which facilitate testing and boost productivity. Then, we will review the most well-liked and adaptable testing tools accessible right now for the JavaScript and React ecosystem, including Enzyme, Jest, and **React Testing Library**. By doing this, you will be able to choose the appropriate tools for your unique needs and requirements. The setup and takedown phases of the testing life cycle will then be covered in detail.

We have devoted a section to discussing the best practices for addressing data fetching and mocking issues inside our tests because they are essential components for applications. We will dive into the details of testing user events, controlling timers, and modeling real-world interactions, giving you the necessary tools to confirm the responsiveness and performance of your application.

Finally, we'll present React DevTools, a vital tool for troubleshooting and evaluating your React apps.

By the end of this chapter, you will be equipped with the knowledge, abilities, and self-assurance necessary to successfully test and debug your React apps. You will be well equipped to build applications that are both dependable and robust in the face of constantly changing circumstances if you have a firm grasp of the tools and approaches at your disposal. So, let's start on the path to becoming experts in testing and debugging React apps so that your projects can withstand the test of time.

In this chapter, we are going to take a deep dive into the subject of testing and debugging from a software point of view as we learn the fundamentals, ideology, and concepts for testing our React applications. The following topics will be covered:

- Introducing React testing helpers
- Testing our software
- Managing data in our applications
- Code execution using events and timers
- Using React DevTools for debugging and analysis

Technical requirements

You can find the projects and code of this chapter, here: `https://github.com/PacktPublishing/React-Interview-Guide/tree/main/Chapter08`

Introducing React testing helpers

In this section, we are going to learn about the fundamentals of RTL. But first, let's try to understand what testing means when it comes to programming so that we can learn about the core concepts and methodology.

What is testing in software development?

Reviewing a software program or system to verify it satisfies its functional and non-functional criteria and certifying its overall quality, performance, and dependability is known as testing in software development. It comprises running the program under controlled settings to find mistakes, flaws, or possible problems before the product is delivered to end customers. Testing is usually done at many levels, from the individual component level to the completely integrated system, and it is a critical part of the software development life cycle.

Depending on the project, there could be any number of testing phases. Let's see what some of these testing-level phases could look like:

Testing phase	Description
Unit tests	Testing isolated code or its parts is known as unit testing. It guarantees that every unit operates according to its specifications and acts as intended.
Integration tests	Testing the integration and relationships among various software units, modules, or components is known as integration testing. It guarantees that the components talk effectively with one another and that the combined system functions as a whole.

Testing phase	Description
Regression tests	Regression testing is done to make sure that new code modifications or improvements don't negatively impact already-existing functionality. It entails re-running earlier tests following software modifications.
Security tests	The product's security features and weaknesses are evaluated during security testing. It pinpoints possible security concerns such as data leaks, unauthorized access, and coding flaws.
Functional tests	Software functioning is compared to the stated requirements through functional testing. It comprises testing numerous features, use cases, and situations to evaluate the program from the viewpoint of the end user.
Alpha and beta tests	Before distributing the program to a select group of external users, internal testers do alpha testing in a restricted environment. Beta testing involves making the program available to a wider number of outside users to obtain input from actual users and spot any possible problems.
Performance tests	The software's adaptability, rapidity, ability to scale, and stability under various load levels are assessed during performance testing. This involves testing variables such as the speed of response, resource use, and constraints in the system.

Table 8.1: Software development testing phases

As you can see, there are many different types of testing that we can perform during a project's life cycle. Next, let's learn how we can do testing in React applications.

How do we do testing in React applications?

In React, testing is the method of confirming and validating each component and the entire application to make sure they work as intended and adhere to the set criteria. This often involves testing each individual React component, user interactions, and any potential changes to the application state. There are a few ways that we can do testing in React applications and these are typically unit testing, integration testing, and **end-to-end** (**E2E**) testing.

How do you set up a test environment for a React application?

For your React application to be reliable, maintainable, and of the highest quality possible, you must set up a testing environment. You can perform tests in a controlled, isolated setting that closely mirrors the production environment if your test environment is set up correctly. This aids in locating and resolving possible problems before they impact end customers. All test environments require us developers to write tests for them, which is known as **test-driven development** (**TDD**).

The following figure describes the TDD cycle in a software development workflow. Coding, testing, and design are closely knitted together in this programming approach. There are many variations of this; however, the fundamental principle remains the same:

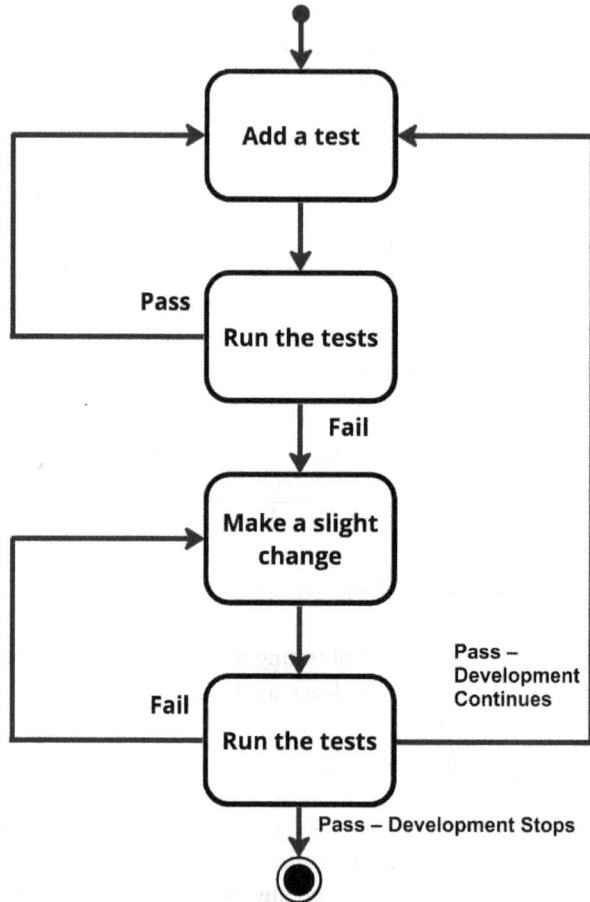

Figure 8.1: The TDD cycle in software development

Now that we have learned about the TDD cycle in software development, let's move on to testing frameworks/libraries to see how we can best use them in our apps.

How do you choose a testing framework or library?

When building a React application, it's a good idea to consider a good testing library. Having a good testing structure means that our software should operate as expected and live up to the user's expectations. So, let's take a look at some of the popular testing libraries available right now:

- **React Testing Library (RTL):** The lightweight RTL focuses on testing the functionality of your components. Compared to other testing frameworks, it offers a more straightforward API.

- **Jest:** The popular testing framework Jest is already set up to operate with React. It has built-in capabilities for testing React apps, such as mocking and snapshot testing.

- **Enzyme:** Shallow rendering, complete DOM rendering, and snapshot testing are just a few of the testing tools offered for React by the potent testing framework Enzyme.

- **Vite:** The frontend build tool Vite has a unit testing framework called **Vitest**. It is a good unit test framework with numerous contemporary features, including support for TypeScript, JSX, and component testing for React.

- **Cypress:** Cypress is an E2E solution for advanced web test automation that is JavaScript-based. Frontend developers and QA engineers can build automated web tests with the help of this tool, which is designed for developers and runs directly in the browser

When it comes to testing, there are multiple ways that we can get it set up inside our React projects. Every developer has their personal preference. Some choose to have a dedicated folder where all of their test files go that is separate from their main components. Others prefer to have their test files in the same folder as their component and in both cases, the test files follow the same naming conventions as their components – so, for example, `index.js` and `index.test.js`.

The following figure shows an example of both use cases. It is a Next.js project that has the default setup for a Jest and RTL project. There is a folder named `__tests__` that contains a test called `index.test.tsx`. There is another `index.test.tsx` file inside of the `pages` folder next to the `index.tsx` component. Both tests can be run using the `npm test` command:

```
EXPLORER                        ...

∨ OPEN EDITORS

∨ REACT-APP
  ∨ 🗀 with-jest-app
    ∨ 🗀 __tests__
      > 🗀 __snapshots__
        ⚗ index.test.tsx
        ⚛ snapshot.tsx
    > 📁 .swc
    > 🧶 .yarn
    > 📁 node_modules
    ∨ 🗁 pages
        ⚛ _app.tsx
        🗐 index.module.css
        ⚗ index.test.tsx
        ⚛ index.tsx
    > 📁 public
    > 📁 styles
      ◎ .eslintrc.json
      🔶 .gitignore
      🗐 .pnp.cjs
      🗐 .pnp.loader.mjs
      🗐 jest.config.js
      🗐 jest.setup.js
      ⊤ₛ next-env.d.ts
      🗐 package-lock.json
      🗐 package.json
      📕 README.md
      🗐 tsconfig.json
      ⊤ₛ types.d.ts
      🧶 yarn.lock
```

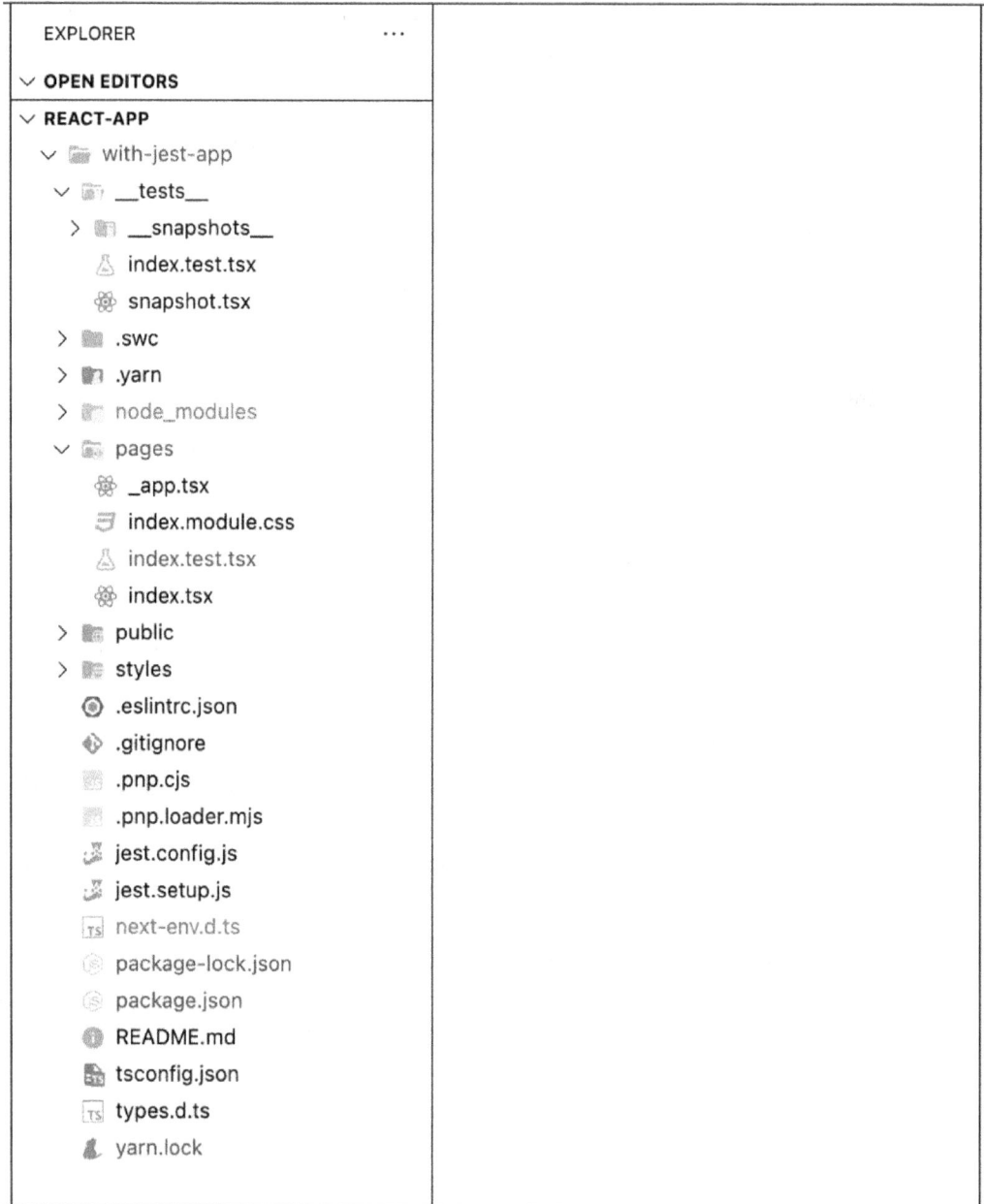

Figure 8.2: React project testing file structure

Now that we have learned a bit about testing conventions in general, the next topic we'll cover will be the fundamentals of RTL.

What are the fundamentals of React Testing Library?

With the help of the well-liked testing tool RTL, developers are urged to test their components in an approach that closely matches how consumers will interact with the application. RTL encourages testing components according to what individuals observe and perform instead of on implementation specifics, ensuring that the program stays accessible, manageable, and user-friendly. RTL is a family of packages, and it can be used on both React and React Native projects. So, it's good to know that we can use the same package to test our web and mobile apps.

RTL has many different core principles that we should become familiar with:

- **Events**: RTL provides the `fireEvent` method, which lets you start a variety of DOM events, such as click, change, or submit, to imitate user interactions. This enables you to verify that the anticipated behavior is displayed by testing how your components respond to user interactions.

- **Queries**: We can use query options to help locate certain items inside the displayed component. The searches are focused on what the user can see or do, such as text, labels, or responsibilities. `GetByText`, `GetByRole`, and `GetByTestId` are a few often-used queries.

- **Custom render**: There is a default render function that you can use to render your components, but you can also design your own render function to wrap your components in a particular context or with a particular provider. When your components depend on unique context settings, such as theme or localization, this is very helpful.

- **Screen**: You can use `screen` to output an object that gives you easy access to the displayed parts and query methods without you having to manually break them down. You may streamline your exams and make them easier to read by using `screen`.

- **Asynchronous utilities**: It is possible to use utilities such as `waitFor`, `waitForElementToBeRemoved`, and `find*` searches when working with components that download data or depend on asynchronous activities. By guaranteeing that your tests wait for the necessary components or actions before continuing, these methods assist in managing the asynchronous operation of your components.

- **UserEvent**: For a more accurate simulation of user interactions, is advisable to use the `@testing-library/user-event` package in addition to `fireEvent`. The advanced event simulation functions in this package more closely resemble user behavior than the fundamental `fireEvent` method.

So, now that we have grasped the idea of using React testing helpers to set up a robust testing environment, let's take what we've learned and see how we can best set up our test environments when using these tools. This is also going to be a chance to see some example test cases.

Testing our software

Now, let's focus on learning how we can set up and clean up our project and code base to isolate the effects of tests – that is, setup and teardown. Setup and teardown are the actions that are taken before and following each test or collection of tests in the context of programming, particularly in software testing. Doing this ensures that we have good test coverage and that our tests are reliable. It's crucial to adhere to a methodical approach while setting up and deconstructing tests to isolate their impacts. This guarantees that tests are independent of one another and do not affect one another, producing precise and trustworthy findings.

In automated testing, the setup and teardown steps are critical for separating the effects of specific tests. Before each test, the setup process helps establish a consistent state. This stage may include tasks such as generating required objects, connecting to a database, or initializing particular settings. By conducting these procedures before each test, we guarantee that each test begins from the same starting point, regardless of the outcomes during previous tests. This implies that a test's behavior is not impacted by the side effects of a preceding test, which is critical for accurate, trustworthy testing.

Any modifications that are made during the test can be undone during the teardown phase. This could require actions such as cutting off database access, removing test data, or erasing objects made during the test. We don't have to worry about changes made during one test affecting subsequent tests if we clean up after each test. Without a breakdown step, a test could ultimately leave behind certain modifications that might affect the behavior of subsequent tests.

Each test runs in the same starting environment and has no impact on the environment for any other tests thanks to the setup and teardown stages, which work together to make sure each test is isolated and reproducible. One of the guiding principles of automated testing is to make sure that the tests are trustworthy and that any flaws that are discovered are attributable to the code being tested and not to the test configuration or cross-test interaction.

There are some rules that we can follow that will help us generate an effective test plan. Let's walk through them and see how following them can give us a good strategy:

- **Set up the test environment**: Ensure that the testing environment is the same for all tests. This covers any prerequisites that are required for the test to perform as well as the software, devices, and network setups.

- **Version control**: Use version control tools such as Git and GitHub to keep track of changes to your code and tests so that you can see any problems that fresh code or tests could cause.

- **Create good tests**: Choose the exact tests you wish to run, and then list the variables and testing conditions for each.

- **Utilize test isolation**: Create your tests so that they have no dependence on other tests. This implies that each test must have its own setup and teardown and cannot rely on the results or state of any other test.

- **Use monitoring**: To gather test results and spot any anomalies or trends in the test data, use logging and monitoring.

- **Make continuous improvements**: Always enhance your tests and testing environment based on the findings and suggestions from each cycle of testing.

- **Use methods**: Implement the setup and takedown procedures that are carried out before and following each test. These techniques may be used to build and remove resources that the tests require, such as temporary files or database connections.

- **Parallel or sequential testing**: Run the tests sequentially to ensure there is no conflict between them or run them in parallel based on the kind of test to expedite the process.

- **Mock external functions**: An approach to testing that isolates the unit of code being evaluated from its dependencies, such as external libraries, services, or functions, is mocking external functions. Usually, this is done to provide predictable and controlled test conditions. For a variety of testing scenarios, mocking enables you to imitate the behavior of external dependencies before actually calling them.

Now that we have learned some of the basics of setting up our projects for testing it's time to take it a step further and move on to learning all about writing tests for our React.js projects.

How do we write tests for components, props, and events?

Once you've selected a testing framework and libraries, you can start developing tests for your React application. You will create a variety of tests, with each one having a different purpose and scope. There are several types of tests we can write, including component tests, unit tests, integration tests, event tests, and E2E tests. The aim is to get as much test coverage across all of the tests to set a benchmark and give you credibility and confidence that your application has thorough testing in place.

What are component tests?

A React component test is a form of unit test that specializes in individually testing React components. React components are the building blocks of a React application and define the UI, encapsulate functionality, and manage the application's state. Testing React components ensures that they behave properly and meet the desired functionality and criteria.

In this code example, we can see what a component test looks like for a component called `Counter.tsx`. We have an accompanying `Counter.test.tsx` file that tests for increments and decrements on the buttons.

Here's the code for the `Counter.tsx` file:

```
import { useState } from 'react';
const Counter = () => {
  const [count, setCount] = useState(0);
```

```
    const increment = () => setCount(count + 1);
    const decrement = () => setCount(count - 1);

    return (
      <div>
        <h1>Counter: {count}</h1>
        <button onClick={increment}>Increment</button>
        <button onClick={decrement}>Decrement</button>
      </div>
    );
};

export default Counter;
```

This is the code for our test file, `Counter.test.tsx`:

```
import { render, screen, fireEvent } from '@testing-library/react';

import '@testing-library/jest-dom/extend-expect';

import Counter from './Counter';

describe('Counter component', () => {
  test('renders Counter component', () => {
    render(<Counter />);

    expect(screen.getByText(/Counter:/i)).toBeInTheDocument();
  });

  test('increases the count when the Increment button is clicked', ()
=> {
    render(<Counter />);

    fireEvent.click(screen.getByText(/Increment/i));

    expect(screen.getByText(/Counter: 1/i)).toBeInTheDocument();
  });

  test('decreases the count when the Decrement button is clicked', ()
=> {
    render(<Counter />);

    fireEvent.click(screen.getByText(/Increment/i));
```

```
    fireEvent.click(screen.getByText(/Decrement/i));

    expect(screen.getByText(/Counter: 0/i)).toBeInTheDocument();
  });
});
```

We have now learned the basics of component and component test files.

What are unit tests?

React unit tests are a method of testing that focuses on individual React components. Their purpose is to guarantee that each component behaves appropriately, follows the intended functionality and requirements, and tests the logic and output of the component. Unit tests are an essential aspect of the testing process since they assist developers in identifying and resolving issues at the most granular level, ensuring that each component of the application performs properly.

We saw what a unit test looks like in our component test example.

What is an integration test?

A React integration test is a type of test that verifies the right interaction and behavior of many React components or between a React component and other system components such as APIs or external services. Integration tests, as opposed to unit tests, analyze how well components interact together inside the program, ensuring that general functionality is proper and data flows easily between different areas of the system.

Integration tests are multiple tests that run inside of a `describe()` function block scope, as shown in our earlier component test example.

What are event tests?

React event tests are a form of testing that focuses on confirming the behavior and functioning of React component event handlers. User interactions or system occurrences that trigger specified actions inside a React application are referred to as events. Button clicks, form submissions, mouse movements, and keyboard inputs are all examples of events. By testing event handlers, you guarantee that your application responds to user interactions appropriately and that the necessary actions are taken when events are triggered.

What is snapshot regress testing?

In React, we can use snapshot tests as a way to confirm that our UI has not changed and remains the same as it was prior. This helps us check that there were no unexpected changes that can affect the way that our design is rendered on screen. With snapshot testing, it is common for a snapshot of our code base to be taken that can then be compared to a reference snapshot file that is combined with a test. The test fails if the snapshots are not the same, and this is how we can ensure that there have been no changes to the UI. We can always update the snapshot to the latest version to match any changes we have made to the UI.

What are end-to-end tests?

E2E tests are a form of testing that tries to validate the functionality of a whole program, from the UI through to the backend services and databases. E2E tests are used to model real-world user situations and guarantee that the overall structure works as planned, giving seamless user experience and accurate functionality.

Cypress is a popular E2E testing library that does not come bundled with React projects but can be installed as a separate package. You can learn more from the documentation: `https://www.cypress.io/`.

We can use our earlier Counter project example to see what the code looks like when doing an E2E test with Cypress. It is quite similar to Jest and RTL and all three packages can work together seamlessly.

Let's take a look at our modified Counter file:

```
import { useState } from 'react';
import './App.css';

function App() {
  const [count, setCount] = useState(0);

  return (
    <div className="App">
      <h1>Counter App</h1>
      <h2 data-testid="counter-display">Count: {count}</h2>
      <button onClick={() => setCount(count + 1)}
        data-testid="increment-button">
        Increment
      </button>
      <button onClick={() => setCount(count - 1)}
        data-testid="decrement-button">
        Decrement
      </button>
    </div>
  );
}

export default App;
```

Here's our Counter test file:

```
describe('Counter App', () => {
  beforeEach(() => {
    cy.visit('/');
  });

  it('increases the counter', () => {
    cy.get('[data-testid="increment-button"]').click();
    cy.get('[data-testid="counter-display"]').
      contains('Count: 1');
  });

  it('decreases the counter', () => {
    cy.get('[data-testid="decrement-button"]').click();
    cy.get('[data-testid="counter-display"]').
      contains('Count: -1');
  });

  it('increases and decreases the counter', () => {
    cy.get('[data-testid="increment-button"]').
      click().click();
    cy.get('[data-testid="decrement-button"]').click();
    cy.get('[data-testid="counter-display"]').
      contains('Count: 1');
  });
});
```

These examples have provided us with a comparison between E2E tests and component tests; the similarities are quite clear.

Managing data in our applications

We are now going to learn how to manage the data in our applications. This is also known as data fetching and mocking, which are two important concepts to grasp. When doing testing in this area, it is necessary to have a working knowledge of how data-fetching APIs operate and how to mimic their data. This knowledge is necessary for several reasons, including development efficiency, independent testing, integration and interaction with external systems, and cost and rate limiting.

In the case of developer efficiency, developers can separate portions of the application for testing and development by mocking API replies. This means that even if the backend portion of a feature is not yet completed, a frontend developer can still work on it by simulating an API response. As for independent testing, programmers can confirm that their tests are not impacted by the status or behavior of other systems by mimicking the data given by APIs, producing more dependable and consistent outcomes for tests.

When we use external systems such as APIs, we can communicate and exchange data between various software systems. To get data from databases, communicate with other apps, or offer services to users, many current applications are built on top of APIs. That's why creating, maintaining, and enhancing these apps requires a functional understanding of how these APIs function.

When we think about cost and rate limiting, many APIs contain use restrictions or extra fees. To prevent reaching these restrictions or spending needless money, we can mock API answers during development and testing.

To use data in an application or system, data must be fetched from a data source, such as a database, API, or filesystem. In online applications and other software systems, data fetching is frequently used to display, analyze, or change data. It often entails sending queries to a local storage location or distant server, processing the answer, and then using the data in the application.

While testing, developing, or designing processes, mocking data refers to creating fictitious or mock data to replicate the behavior of actual data. When building features for a system, testing code, or designing UIs, mock data can be used as a stand-in for real data. It enables programmers to test their programs and apps without relying on potentially private, erratic, or unreachable external data sources or live data.

How do we mock data for tests?

Mock data will most likely be required while testing your React application to imitate real-world circumstances. This is especially helpful for testing components that rely on APIs or third-party services. Numerous libraries are available for mimicking data:

- **Axios Mock Adapter**: The Axios Mock Adapter library intercepts Axios requests and returns mocked data
- **Nock**: Nock is an HTTP request interceptor that returns faked data
- **JSON Server**: JSON Server is a package that uses JSON data to imitate a REST API

Why should we use mock data in tests?

There are many reasons why it's a good idea to use mock as opposed to real data in our tests. We can separate sections of our system using mock data, which makes it simpler to find problems and test particular components without being impacted by other dependencies. Controlled mock data ensures that tests are reproducible and produce consistent findings, which is another advantage. Developers can also verify their code and apps without having to wait for access to actual data thanks to the speedy generation of mock data. Also, during development and testing, sensitive or private data might be exposed, which can be a major worry for organizations. Using dummy data helps prevent this.

In the next section, we will learn about events and timers, which is crucial learning as it relates to asynchronous or time-dependent actions in programming. Asynchronous programming is a technique that allows your program to begin a potentially long-running operation while being responsive to other events, rather than needing to wait until that work is completed.

When that task is completed, the outcome is shown in your program. An extremely flexible asynchronous and concurrent programming language such as JavaScript is very powerful because, like sync, it is single-threaded, but unlike async, it also does not block code execution, which is great for our React applications.

Code execution using events and timers

Now, let's move on to learning about the subject of events and timers. In software development, events and timers are implemented to keep track of the precise moment in time when something outside the program takes place. Events and timers are critical concepts in programming, especially when dealing with asynchronous or time-dependent actions. They also play a crucial part in testing such systems. Let's go through each subject in further depth to drill these concepts in.

What are events?

Events are activities or occurrences that arise during program execution and are frequently prompted by input from users, system changes, or other sources. In event-driven programming, system components respond to these occurrences by executing specified routines known as event handlers or callbacks.

Simulating events is critical in testing to guarantee that the application responds as intended when the events happen. You might wish to test how your web application reacts to user activities such as button clicks, form submissions, or navigation events. By simulating these events in your tests, you can ensure that your application's event handlers are functioning properly and handling various circumstances as planned.

What are timers?

Timers serve a purpose in programming as they plan the execution of certain functions or code snippets after a certain amount of time has passed or at regular intervals. In JavaScript, common timer functions are `setTimeout` and `setInterval`, which allow you to run a function immediately following a delay or periodically at predefined intervals.

Timers can complicate testing since they require asynchronous activities, which can result in unexpected behavior or race situations. A race situation, also known as a race hazard, is a circumstance in which the substantive behavior of software or other systems is reliant on the sequence or timing of other uncontrolled occurrences. When one or more of the alternative behaviors is undesired, it constitutes a bug.

It is critical to handle timers appropriately when testing code that depends on them to produce accurate and trustworthy test results. Now that we have learned about timers, the next section will take what we've learned further as we look into debugging and making the best use of our knowledge of timers, which can be used in conjunction.

Using React DevTools for debugging and analysis

React DevTools is a browser plugin that offers a variety of tools for testing your React application. It allows you to investigate the component hierarchy, view the React component tree, and verify the props and state of your components. We will dive into the various debugging techniques available to us and how using them will give us more confidence in the code that we write.

React DevTools can be seen in the following figure. It is available in the Chrome web store:

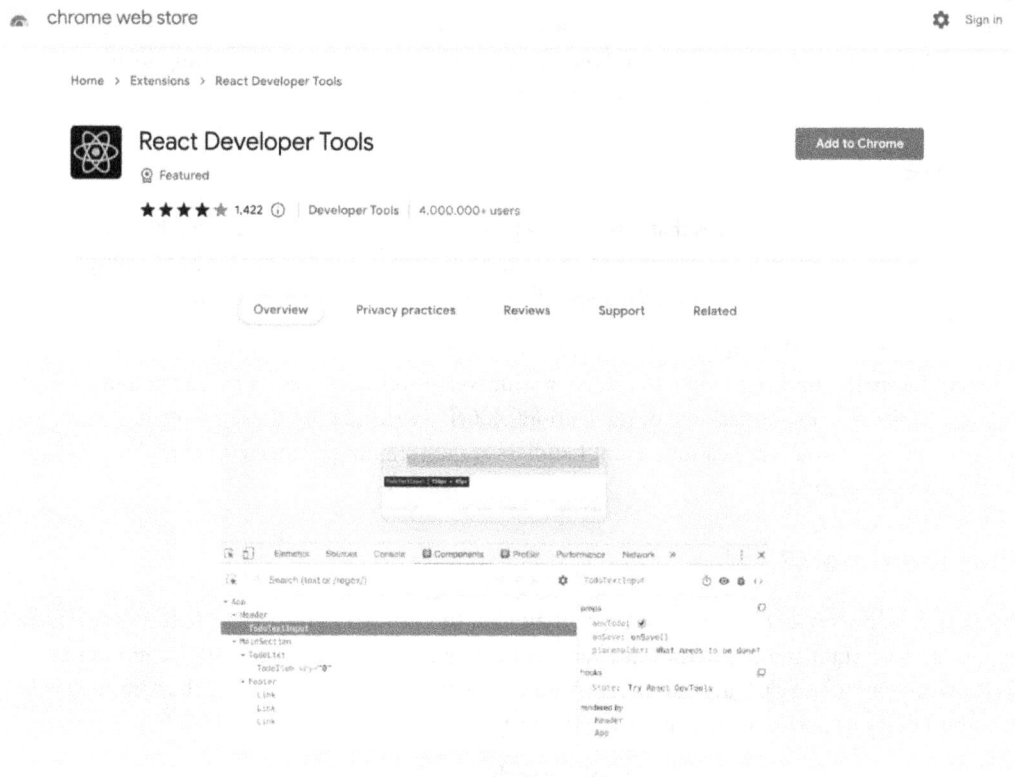

Figure 8.3: React DevTools

With that, we have learned about React DevTools. Next, we'll learn how to configure CI/CD pipelines for our automated tests, another useful tool in our debugging toolkit.

How do we configure a CI/CD pipeline to automate tests?

To ensure that our tests run every time we make code changes, we can configure a **continuous integration/continuous deployment (CI/CD)** pipeline that runs tests automatically. This allows us to catch issues early and ensure that our code meets the expected standard. Using a CI/CD pipeline to automate tests in a React application has several advantages, including higher code quality, faster feedback, greater collaboration, and more efficient deployment procedures. These advantages enable teams to create high-quality software more quickly and consistently, making CI/CD pipelines a vital tool for modern software development.

It is common practice to use a code hosting platform such as GitHub, GitLab, or Bitbucket combined with a CI/CD testing platform such as GitHub Actions, Jenkins, Docker, Kubernetes, or CircleCI to name a few.

How do we debug a React application?

Debugging a React application might be difficult, but it is a necessary skill for any React developer. In this subsection, we'll go over some fundamental strategies and tricks for properly debugging a React application.

How do we utilize the debugging tools inside our IDE/code editor?

Popular code editors such as Visual Studio Code include debugging capabilities for JavaScript and React apps. You can debug your React application immediately within the editor by configuring a launch configuration, which allows you to create breakpoints, walk through code, and inspect variables.

How do we set up breakpoints with DevTools?

Debugging a React application begins with the use of breakpoints, which interrupt the execution of your code at a certain moment in time. You can set breakpoints, analyze variables, and go through your code line by line using the browser's built-in developer tools. Use DevTools and browse the **Sources** tab to establish a breakpoint in your program. Locate the necessary file, scroll to the line where you wish to establish a breakpoint, and then click on the line number to do so.

If you reload the page once you've set a breakpoint, your code will halt at the breakpoint.

How do we use logging to track application behavior?

Another key tool for troubleshooting a React application is logging. You can use `console.log()` commands to output variable values, trace the flow of your code, and troubleshoot problems.

Just put `console.log()` followed by the value you wish to log into your code to add a `console.log()` statement.

How do we create error boundaries?

Error boundaries are React components that can detect JavaScript problems anywhere in your component hierarchy, report them, and replace the crashed component with a fallback UI. You can prevent your application from crashing if an unhandled error in a single component is wrapped in an error border component.

How do we understand JavaScript error codes?

React apps can experience a variety of issues, ranging from syntax mistakes to runtime faults. Knowing these issues and the error codes associated with them is critical for effective troubleshooting. For example, a typical problem that's seen by React developers is `TypeError: Cannot read property 'propName' of undefined`. When you try to access a property of an undefined object, this error occurs.

You can pinpoint the problem and repair it faster if you understand the error code and its associated problems.

How do we install a debugger extension?

Browser debugger plugins can also assist you in debugging your React application. The React DevTools extension, for example, contains various tools that have been developed expressly for debugging React applications, such as the ability to explore the component hierarchy, check properties and states, and highlight the selected component in the browser. Similarly, we can use the Redux DevTools extension to debug our application's state changes. Using Redux is more applicable when we are working with a more complex application that requires a global state.

How do we use the ESLint plugin for React?

ESLint is a popular JavaScript linting tool that can help you find and correct syntax problems, possible bugs, and code quality concerns. The ESLint plugin for React adds extra linting rules tailored to React applications, assisting you in detecting frequent mistakes and best practice violations.

What are error monitoring tools?

Tools for tracking, identifying, and reporting mistakes and anomalies that arise in applications throughout development, testing, or deployment are known as error monitoring tools. These tools assist programmers in locating problems, determining their root causes, and promptly resolving them. For developers to achieve better software, error monitoring systems frequently include capabilities such as real-time error tracking, alerts, and thorough error reporting.

There are quite a lot of error monitoring tools available, and some stand-out ones include LogRocket, Sentry, and Rollbar.

We have reached the end of this section and also this chapter. Our knowledge of testing and debugging will be crucial at interviews because this is an area that many companies expect developers to be good in.

Summary

This chapter has offered a thorough understanding of the critical parts of testing and debugging React applications. We began by discussing the significance of testing in software development and the necessity for a strong testing environment geared toward React apps. Next, we looked at various testing frameworks and libraries, highlighting their unique characteristics as well as the criteria to consider when choosing the best tools. Learning about the importance of setups and teardowns was also covered.

We covered building tests for components, props, and events throughout this chapter, highlighting the need to create extensive test suites to ensure the dependability and maintainability of our React applications. To take the testing process even further, we talked about mocking data for tests, which allows us to simulate real-world scenarios without relying on external dependencies. Understanding events and times when doing testing was another hot topic we talked about.

We also introduced React DevTools, which assists developers in evaluating and understanding the internal structure and behavior of their apps throughout the testing phase, as well as CI/CD pipelines. Another important topic we discussed in this chapter was debugging React apps and using error monitoring tools. Understanding the art of testing and debugging is critical for React developers looking to build high-quality, long-lasting applications because these skills will make us better developers. Being capable of solving problems is a quality that is highly sought after in the world of programming.

In the next chapter, we will get the chance to learn about some of the most modern React.js build tools available. Next.js, Gatsby and Remix are three popular choices for React.js development so let's expand our knowledge further and get a grasp on these amazing libraries

Rapid Development with Next.js, Gatsby, and Remix Frameworks

Developers are continuously searching for tools and frameworks that can speed up the development process without compromising the flexibility and resilience of their apps in the rapid digital environment of today. Full stack React frameworks such as **Next.js**, **Gatsby**, and **Remix** have become crucial participants in the contemporary web development environment as the need for seamless user experiences and dynamic, data-driven apps keeps rising. This chapter thoroughly examines these three formidable frameworks, focusing on their distinctive features, advantages, and application use cases.

We'll look at how each framework approaches different technologies such as **server-side rendering** (**SSR**), SEO, and creating static sites. These frameworks can be used to create blazing-fast, scalable, and highly performant apps, so we will see how they do it. Knowing the difference between popular React build tools will help us justify our choices for using them when asked at an interview. So, let's continue our learning and see how Next.js, Gatsby, and Remix can revolutionize our approach to web development and help us realize our digital goals. By the end of the chapter, we should have much better knowledge in this area to help us give great answers to interview questions.

These are the topics that we will be going through in this chapter:

- Using React as a full stack framework
- Static site generation
- Server-side rendering
- Adding page metadata
- SEO best practices

Using React as a full stack framework

Let's begin our journey by learning about Next.js, Gatsby, and Remix. If you are a modern developer then you should be using one of these three build tools to develop your React applications. They are recommended in the official React documentation, and understanding how they work and when to choose one over the other is paramount to putting together excellent interview answers. First, we will see what Next.js has to offer us.

What is Next.js?

Next.js is an open source framework for creating contemporary, scalable, and high-performance online apps with the help of React. Next.js, developed and maintained by **Vercel**, provides a complete collection of capabilities and optimizations that make it an excellent choice for both **static site generation (SSG)** and SSR.

Developers who choose to use Next.js for their React projects are blessed with a diverse tool that is rich in features. This has made Next.js the best framework for building React projects and replaces **Create React App** as the default choice. Some of its standout features are shown in the following table:

Features	Explanation
Code splitting	It can automatically break the JavaScript code into smaller bits, ensuring that users only load the code required for a given page. This enhances the web application's overall speed and loading times.
Dynamic importing	Next.js enables developers to leverage dynamic imports to load JavaScript modules and components as needed, reducing the initial bundle size and improving speed.
API routing	Support for building serverless API endpoints is included, so it's simple to build **RESTful** or **GraphQL** APIs within your online application.
File routing	It uses a file-based routing method that makes it simple to add new routes and pages by just adding new files to the `pages` folder.
Built-in TypeScript	There is TypeScript support, allowing developers to create type-safe code while also benefiting from improved tools and refactoring.
Hybrid renders	With Next.js, we can enable static site creation as well as SSR, permitting developers to select the optimal solution for their particular situation or even combine both ways inside a single application.

Features	Explanation
Hot reload	Hot reloading adds dynamic capabilities to a React application's frontend UI. This implies that any changes we make to the application's code are immediately reflected on the web application frontend that the user sees in real time.
Built-in support for CSS	Next.js works out of the box with many CSS libraries and has the option to configure it with **Tailwind CSS** on setup.

Table 9.1: Next.js features

As a whole, Next.js is a strong and adaptable framework that can handle a variety of web development requirements, from SSG to the construction of static websites, making it an attractive choice for programmers creating efficient online applications.

Now, let's have a look at Gatsby, which is another popular choice.

What is Gatsby?

Gatsby is a free and open source static site generator based on React for creating contemporary, high-performance web apps and static websites. Gatsby uses GraphQL, an API query language, to retrieve data from many sources and integrate it with your React components throughout the build process to produce static HTML, CSS, and JavaScript files. The end result is a website that is lightning-fast, SEO-friendly, and well optimized.

It shares a few similarities with Next.js. However, it does differ in a few key areas. For starters, it is powered by GraphQL and it can also be used as a headless **content management system** (**CMS**). A CMS with a headless CMS separates the presentation layer, where the content is displayed, from the backend, where content is maintained. It distinguishes between knowledge and display. This allows for the reusing and rearranging of material across different digital media platforms. Basically, it is the equivalent of developing a WordPress website, but in this case, it is built for JavaScript developers, so we get access to the full suite of features.

We can have a look at some of the unique features that make Gatsby a great React build tool:

Features	Explanation
GraphQL integration	Gatsby leverages GraphQL to build a uniform and flexible data layer, allowing developers to retrieve data from a variety of sources, including Markdown files, CMSs, APIs, and databases, and utilize it through their React components.
Plugin library	It features an extensive library of plugins that let programmers customize its capabilities, integrate it with multiple services, and tailor the development process to their own requirements.
Progressive web app (PWA)	PWAs can be simply created by Gatsby-generated websites, enabling capabilities such as offline access, quick launching, and app-like performance on phones and tablets.
Performance enhancements	To guarantee rapid loading times and an effortless user experience, Gatsby automatically performs several speed optimizations such as code splitting, inlining crucial CSS, and lazy-loading of pictures.
Versatile hosting choices	The framework works nicely with a variety of hosting systems and provides continuous deployment, ensuring that it's simple to set up and maintain your website.

Table 9.2: Gatsby features

Gatsby is a strong and adaptable framework for creating rapid, SEO-friendly, and thoroughly optimized React and GraphQL web apps and static web pages. Because of its emphasis on speed, developer satisfaction, and flexibility, it is a favored option for programmers and enterprises.

Finally, let's see what our final option, the Remix framework, is capable of doing and how its capabilities and features match up with the previous two options.

What is Remix?

Remix is a cutting-edge web framework that uses React. Remix, which was built by the creators of **React Router**, seeks to deliver a fantastic user experience for developers while emphasizing the significance of web basics and best practices. Just like Next.js and Gatsby, the Remix framework also has a wide array of qualities that make it a great option when considering a starting point for your React projects. Remix has quite a lot of features, including the ones highlighted in the following table:

Features	Explanation
Flexibility	Remix is built to interact with a variety of backend technologies, server systems, and data sources of information, which makes it an ideal choice for programmers who work on a variety of applications.
Nested routes	It is an easy-to-use and robust nested routing framework that allows you to design complicated and multilevel structures while maintaining the state and scroll location throughout browsing.
Rendering outputs	The framework features SSR, SSG, and **client-side rendering (CSR)**, allowing programmers to select the best rendering technique for a particular use case or even blend multiple ways inside one application.
Web standards	Because of its reliance on internet standards and its emphasis on the significance of exploiting browser-native technologies, it has enhanced speed and ease of use when using features such as the **Fetch** API, other HTML methods, and browser navigation.
Data-fetching improvements	Users can access the Remix "loader" methods, which provide a distinctive information-fetching strategy, enabling programmers to retrieve information from the server or client side, ensuring fast processing of data and rapid page transitions.

Table 9.3: Remix features

In a nutshell, Remix is a strong and adaptable web framework for creating high-performance, feature-rich React apps. It distinguishes itself from other frameworks by focusing on web principles, best practices, and developer experience, making it an enticing alternative for developers wanting to build modern online apps. These features make it developer friendly, and the documentation is easy to understand.

Now, moving on to the next section, we will learn about SSG, which is a popular tool for web developers to swiftly and effectively design websites. All of the frameworks we are discussing use it for builds.

Static site generation

It's now time for us to learn about SSG and why it's so important. We will present an overview of static site creation, the way it works, and the reason why it has become so popular among millions of developers worldwide. With this technology, you will be able to rapidly develop stunning sites without having to be concerned about installing complicated server settings or handling obtrusive backend operations. Let's do it.

Why should you care about SSG?

It's a popular approach to developing websites, and for good reason. Instead of depending on a server to produce site content on the fly each time a user demands a page, static site creation pre-builds all required files and sends them through a user's computer as soon as a page is requested. This leads to speedier load times and overall better performance. Static sites are also easier and less expensive to host because there is no dynamic material to handle. So, whether you're a developer trying to streamline your workflow or a company owner looking to increase the performance and accessibility of your site, static site creation is absolutely something to think about.

What are the advantages of using a static site generator?

For developers aiming to simplify and improve their processes, static site generators are game changers. Static site generators, which do not rely on a database or server-side scripting, tend to be dependable even under tremendous traffic, making them an excellent choice for both corporations and individuals. Additionally, with the flexibility of a large choice of themes, developers can keep total control over the aesthetic of their website while benefiting from the performance of a static site. With advantages such as performance, security, and personalization, it's no surprise that static site generators are gaining favor.

Using a static site generator leads to further advantages and better maintenance. Let's now understand how these can make our applications safer and more robust.

Why are speed and performance so good in static websites?

Static site generators are tools that assist with the creation of static websites through the transformation of source files (such as Markdown or templates) into static HTML, CSS, and JavaScript files. They are well known for outperforming dynamic websites in terms of speed and performance for many different reasons that we are going to learn about now:

- **On-demand page content**: In contrast to dynamic websites, which construct pages on the spot according to every request, static site generators pre-build all pages throughout the build process. When a user requests a page, the website's server can just send the already created HTML file, making it quicker.

- **Caches static files**: **Content delivery networks** (**CDNs**) and websites can readily cache static files. CDNs can keep replicas of static files on hosts all around the globe, enabling users to view material from a location near them. This decreases latency and speeds up loading times.

- **Data compression**: Static site generators frequently contain tools for minimizing and compressing assets such as HTML, CSS, and JavaScript. This decreases file sizes, resulting in quicker transmission and loading times.

- **Decreased web page loading times**: Because the web pages are pre-built, the computer running them does not have to spend time performing server-side code or searching databases. This minimizes system strain and enables the computer to process additional requests at the same time.

- **Robust security settings**: Given that static internet pages do not have databases or server-side programming, they are less susceptible to attacks such as **SQL injection** and **cross-site scripting (XSS)**. This can boost performance immediately by lowering the chances of the website being hacked and dragged down by criminal activity.

So, basically, static site generators provide various advantages to website developers, including faster performance, improved security, and simpler maintenance and upgrading. It is critical to be aware of the most common static site generators on the market, as well as the step-by-step instructions for installing a static site generator.

Knowing the best practices for configuring a static site generator is also useful in ensuring that your brand's website functions properly from the start. Finally, as with all computer users, it is critical to track your static website on a regular basis to maintain constant peak performance and to detect any possible dangers. Using a static site generator is a good option for people who want to take their website-building skills to the next level.

With our knowledge in this area boosted, let's move on to SSR so that we are also able to talk about this topic in depth when asked about it.

Server-side rendering

In this section, we'll look at one of the most efficient and successful methods for creating fast-loading web pages: SSR. Using SSR techniques ensures that the website loads swiftly and looks good on all devices. We will discuss what it implies, how it works, why it is essential, and the benefits of employing this strategy over other ones.

Then, with the aforementioned information, we will learn how it becomes much easier to improve our site's user experience and have greater control over loading times so our users can access material more quickly and without interruption. When we are done with this chapter, we will have all the knowledge we need to explain what SSR is. Now, let's answer some of the biggest questions about SSR.

What is SSR and why is it important?

Websites must load as quickly as possible. This is where SSR enters the picture. The process of producing a web page on the server side before delivering it to the client's browser is known as SSR. This significantly speeds up the process because the server could provide a pre-populated HTML file to the browser, instead of waiting for the browser to request the necessary assets and construct the HTML file itself.

This not only enhances the user experience but also provides major SEO benefits, because search engines can crawl server-side-rendered material more readily than client-side-generated content. In brief, SSR is an important strategy for assuring faster load times and improved search engine exposure.

How does SSR work? The fundamentals of SSR page loading

SSR is a method that can significantly enhance a website's speed and user experience. SSR is a means of rendering a web page on the server before transmitting it to the client (browser). When a user requests a page, the server creates the HTML, populates it with basic data, and returns it to the client as a pre-rendered page. This strategy greatly decreases the amount of time it requires to load a website and enables quicker CSR. SSR, in basic terms, gives a quicker, more efficient, and more intuitive experience by generating a page with preliminary material on the server.

What are the advantages of SSR?

One of the most crucial elements for websites right now is their loading speed. Nobody likes waiting for a website to load, which is where SSR comes in. SSR enables the server to build a website's HTML code before it is transmitted to the browser, resulting in quicker loading times, enhanced SEO, and greater user accessibility. Additionally, SSR can aid in the prevention of frequent difficulties, such as content loading before it's ready (which may lead to broken designs) and content moving around the screen. This results in a smoother user experience. Overall, the benefits of SSR make it an essential component in the development of successful and efficient websites.

When utilized in web applications, SSR offers various benefits. Among these many advantages, we can find many reasons why it is seeing such high usage these days. Let's learn more:

- **Strong SEO**: Because the final programming files are created on the server before being transmitted to the client's web browser, search engines can simply scan and index server-rendered content. This helps search engines comprehend and rate your website, increasing its prominence in the search results.

- **Dynamic data**: SSR is appropriate for apps that demand regular updates or that require clients to see personalized content. Because the content is created on the server, it is able to be readily changed or customized depending on input from users, cookies, or additional factors without requiring the whole website to be rebuilt.

- **Fast loading times**: When compared to CSR, SSR can give quicker initial page load times because the browser obtains completely rendered HTML content from the server, removing the requirement to wait on JavaScript to load and run before showing the content on the screen. This can lead to improved user perception of website performance.

- **Web browser legacy support**: With SSR, we can improve support for outdated browsers and devices with restricted JavaScript capabilities. As the data is displayed on the server, regardless of whether certain JavaScript capabilities are available or not, these browsers can view them.

With SSR, we gain a lot of advantages, but we also need to take into account how SSR can have a detrimental effect on our applications. Next, we will see what the disadvantages are and learn whether they are dealbreakers.

What are the disadvantages of SSR?

Although SSR has advantages such as increased SEO and faster beginning load times, it also has some drawbacks. Let's take a look at some of these drawbacks:

- **Application server requirements**: To display and transmit the content, SSR depends on the server. If the server is experiencing latency or is down, this can lead to problems because the whole website could become unreachable or load slowly.

- **More complex architecture**: The application architecture becomes more complicated when SSR is implemented because server-side programming and administration are needed. Debugging and upkeep could become more difficult as a result, while development time might go up.

- **Caching issues**: Compared to static files, dynamic material produced by SSR is frequently harder to adequately cache. As a result, caching's performance advantages might be diminished, and the workload of servers can escalate.

- **Decreased server efficiency**: SSR will raise server load and CPU use, particularly on sites with heavy traffic, because it necessitates the server rendering the pages for each request. As a result, there may be a demand for more robust and pricey infrastructure for servers and longer turnaround times.

Regardless of these drawbacks, SSR can still be a useful option in some circumstances, such as if SEO is a necessity or if dynamic material has to be displayed rapidly. Before selecting a rendering strategy, it is crucial to analyze the benefits and drawbacks and consider the specific needs of your project.

Remaining on topic, let's now segue into the subject of SEO, which is related to page metadata. This will give us answers to the interview question on how we can improve the SEO for our applications and websites.

Adding page metadata

Adding page information to enhance SEO does not have to be challenging. Once we have gone through this section, we should be able to grasp and talk about the fundamentals of increasing a website's visibility via the use of SSG and other techniques. As soon as we grasp the principles, it becomes so much easier to develop pages, giving us the real-world experience needed for coming up with answers to questions on creating better SEO.

What is page metadata and why is it important for SEO?

In order to increase traffic to your website, SEO is essential. Page metadata is possibly one of the most crucial components of a good SEO strategy, but there are many more. Title tags, meta descriptions, and keywords are examples of metadata, which is information that characterizes the content of a web page. The material on your website might be better understood by search engines and made more interesting to potential visitors by optimizing your metadata. In simple terms, page metadata functions as a roadmap for both visitors and search engines, making it a crucial part of any SEO plan.

What types of page metadata can be used for SSG?

Understanding the significance of page information is essential for creating static sites. In principle, metadata is information about information, and it aids search engines in understanding the purpose of your website. Title tags, meta descriptions, and alt text are just a few examples of the several kinds of information that are regularly used on a website. The words that show in your web browser's tab are called title tags, and meta descriptions give a one-sentence overview of the contents of the page. Images are frequently accurately classified by search engines when they include descriptive alt text. You can boost the search engine ranking of your website and make a guarantee that what you publish is correctly indexed by including these various sorts of metadata.

To make it clear how much of an impact metadata can have, we are going to learn about some popular types. We will now learn about meta titles, meta descriptions, meta viewports, meta robots, meta authors, meta language, and open graph tags.

What is a meta title?

Any website's SEO plan has to include title tags. Make sure they appropriately represent the content on each page, because they are the first thing that search engines such as Google notice when they crawl your website. In addition to essential keywords, title tags should be clear, comprehensible, and interesting. Your search engine rankings can be enhanced, and the number of clicks can be increased with a well-written title tag. So, whether you're developing a new website or optimizing an existing one, pay special attention to your title tags and make sure they're successful in drawing attention to your website.

We can see what that looks like in an example:

```
<title>Home page - Programming content</title>
```

The title tag basically describes a website page.

What are meta descriptions?

Meta descriptions are now a crucial component of website optimization in the ever-changing world of SEO. These text excerpts offer an ideal chance to persuade potential customers to visit your website. Standing out from the crowd is accomplished by creating an engaging meta description that uses your chosen keywords. Meta descriptions can help your website's overall search engine rankings, so it's not only about gaining clicks. Spend some time creating a clear, direct meta description that appropriately summarizes your content and draws visitors who are looking for the things you are able to provide.

Here's an example of it in action:

```
<meta name="description" content="This is a website about
programming">
```

The content of this tag gives a summary of the web page's content.

What is a meta viewport?

A meta viewport is a form of metadata element that is used in a web page's HTML code to manage the layout and scaling of the website's content on multiple devices, particularly mobile devices with various screen sizes and resolutions. The meta viewport tag is critical to rendering a website responsive and easy to use on phones, tablets, and other mobile devices.

Here is an example of a meta viewport:

```
<meta name="viewport" content="width=device-width, initial-scale=1">
```

This code tells the browser how to control the width of the page and to give it a scale of 1, which is useful when viewed on mobile devices. It helps the page to display better on mobile and these options enable a website to adjust and be responsive.

What are meta robots?

Meta robots are a form of metadata element that is used in a web page's HTML code to guide search engine crawlers (also known as robots, spiders, or bots) on how to index or follow links on a website. Website administrators can regulate the behavior of search engine crawlers when they view their website's pages with the use of meta robot tags, which helps to optimize indexing and avoid potential SEO concerns.

Let's see an example of it:

```
<meta name="robots" content="noindex, nofollow">
```

In this example, the `noindex` value instructs the crawler not to index this page, meaning it won't show up in search results, while the `nofollow` value instructs the crawler not to follow any links from this page.

What are meta authors?

The meta author tag is a form of metadata element that is used in a web page's HTML code to denote the writer or creator of the material on the website. This tag is not directly connected to SEO, but it can give useful details about the individual or organization that manages the written material on a website's page to users or search engines.

Let's see an example of what this looks like:

```
<meta name="author" content="Sarah Thomas">
```

This tells everyone looking at the HTML that Sarah Thomas created the web page.

What is a meta language?

The meta language tag, commonly referred to as the *Content-Language* meta tag, is a form of metadata element that specifies the principal language of a home page's information in the HTML code. This tag assists search engines, web browsers, and other online services in understanding the content's language, which might be important for searching, interpreting, and accessibility.

We can see what that looks like in this code example:

```
<meta http-equiv="Content-Language" content="en-us">
```

The HTML element in this example uses the `lang="en"` property to specify that the entire HTML page is written in English. The `<meta http-equiv="Content-Language" content="en-us">` tag further states that the content is written in American English.

What are open graph tags?

Open graph tags are responsible for making links on social media platforms look more visually appealing than others. You can decide how links to your website appear on social networking sites such as Facebook, Twitter/X, and LinkedIn, among others, by using open graph tags, which are HTML code snippets. You can customize the picture, title, and description that appears when someone shares the link by using open graph tags on your website. As a result, you have the ability to provide your audience with a more interesting and aesthetically appealing link preview, which can eventually result in increased interaction and clickthrough rates. So, think about using it if you want your website to stand out on social networking sites.

We can see an open graph tag example in the code here:

```
<!-- Twitter Example -->
<meta property="twitter:card" content=
  "summary_large_image" />
<meta property="twitter:url" content=
  "https://www.yoursite.com/page" />
<meta property="twitter:title" content=
  "Your Website Title" />
<meta
  property="twitter:description"
  content="A description of your website."
/>
<meta
```

```
      property="twitter:image"
      content="https://www.yoursite.com/image.jpg"
  />

  <!-- Facebook Example -->
  <meta property="og:type" content="website" />
  <meta property="og:url" content=
      "https://www.yoursite.com/page" />
  <meta property="og:title" content=
      "Your Website Title" />
  <meta property="og:description" content=
      "A description of your website." />
  <meta property="og:image" content="https://www.yoursite.com/image.
jpg" />
```

This code demonstrates the use of open graph tags using examples from Twitter/X and Facebook.

Now that we have a better understanding of the usage of these tags, another important area that we should be aware of is website auditing. This is where we essentially run tests on our web page to test its SEO capability with those meta tags that we learned about, which are going to give us a much higher website score. The **Lighthouse** Chrome extension is a very popular choice for website auditing. Let's learn about it now.

How can we use the Lighthouse extension to audit our website?

Lighthouse is an open source, automated tool for enhancing web app performance, quality, and accuracy. Lighthouse audits a page by running a series of tests against it and then generating a report on how effectively the page performed. Based on the results, you can take advantage of the failed tests to determine what you need to do to enhance your app.

In the next section, we will be learning about SEO best practices, where we will get even more valuable knowledge that will be useful when it comes to deploying a real-world application online.

SEO best practices

SEO is the process of improving a website's ranking in search engine results by optimizing its content, structure, and other aspects. So, we should be implementing SEO best practices that can assist our website in ranking better in search engine results. By doing this, it increases our chances of being able to attract more organic visitors and improve its overall online visibility. There are many ways we can accomplish this and some of them are listed as follows:

Strategy	Description
Meta tags	Create distinct and captivating meta titles and descriptions for each page. Because these are the snippets that appear in search engine results, they should be accurate representations of the material.
Page load speed	Optimize the loading speed of your website to create a better user experience and improve search engine results. Compress pictures, reduce code, and make use of browser caching.
URL structure	Use descriptive, easy-to-read URLs that indicate the theme of the item. Avoid using long, complicated URLs with extraneous arguments.
Good content	Create relevant, insightful, and entertaining content that speaks to your target audience's requirements. The writing should be correctly written, understandable, and related to the subject or keywords.
Mobile optimization	Websites tend to get high traffic from mobile users, even higher than that from desktop users. As mobile compatibility is a ranking criterion for search engines, make sure that the site is responsive and mobile-friendly. An excellent mobile experience increases user interest and their subsequent return.
Great UI and UX	Focus on giving an enjoyable user experience by making navigation simple, calls to action obvious, and material organized properly.
Security certificate	Install an SSL certificate on your website to ensure data encryption and to improve your search engine ranking. HTTPS is a ranking indication for Google.

Table 9.4: SEO best practices

We have successfully reached the end of this chapter and learned a great deal about the differences between the different metadata types. We will now be able to apply what we have learned when working on our React projects and when under interview conditions, as this knowledge will always be useful.

Summary

This chapter has offered a thorough examination of Next.js, Gatsby, and Remix, three potent, full stack React frameworks. We have gotten a greater grasp of how these technologies can be used to expedite the web development process and easily construct dynamic, data-driven apps by exploring their special features and use cases. We have covered key topics in contemporary web development along the way, including the creation of static sites, SSR, and the addition of page information for SEO. We have paved the way for wise decision-making when picking the best tool for a certain project by analyzing the benefits and drawbacks of each framework.

Next.js, Gatsby, and Remix provide us with different choices for developing React applications. We have looked at the differences between all three of them, which gives us good interview answers because we can compare these differences and give a valid reason for why we would choose one over the other in our projects.

Throughout this chapter, we have covered useful information that has encouraged us to learn more about these frameworks and their strengths to ace interviews and stand out in an increasingly crowded market. The road to mastering Next.js, Gatsby, and Remix is only getting started, and there are countless opportunities for development and creativity. The ultimate potential of these technologies resides in your imagination, inventiveness, and resolve to push the limits of what is feasible in the field of web development as you continue to study and explore.

In the next chapter, we will learn how to crack real-world programming tasks.

Part 4:
Hands-On with
Programming Tasks

In this part, you will learn about how to crack the coding tasks given in the interview process at a high level in a stipulated time. We will also get useful tips and recommendations before deep-diving into the projects. Then, we will build two React applications to showcase your programming skills – one app is based on Redux and styled-components along with the Firebase backend, and another app is based on the Next.js toolkit, GraphQL, and SWR using the REST API.

This part has the following chapters:

- *Chapter 10, Cracking Any Real-World Programming Task*
- *Chapter 11, Building an App Based on React, Redux, Styled Components, and the Firebase Backend*
- *Chapter 12, Building an App Based on the Next.js Toolkit, Authentication, SWR, GraphQL, and Deployment*

10
Cracking Any Real-World Programming Task

To effectively perform a real-world programming assignment in today's quickly expanding tech landscape, programmers must manage an ever-increasing number of hurdles and complexity levels. In this chapter, we will look at the basic stages, tools, and best practices that will allow you to approach any programming project with confidence and generate high-quality, maintainable software. Our interview preparation becomes so much better when we can confidently talk about this subject and give real-world examples. Over time, we will be able to provide more of our own personal experiences, which, as a result, makes us a far better candidate for hiring when going through an interview process.

This chapter will give you the knowledge and confidence you need to overcome every programming assignment that comes your way, from setting up your development environment to organizing your code base and sharing your work. We'll go through how to pick the correct scaffolding tools and templates to help you construct an excellent foundation for your application while saving you time and effort. We will also look into the optimal application architecture for your project's needs, striking a balance between versatility and ease of use.

As we go along, you'll realize how important it is to test your code to assure its dependability, scalability, and security. We will provide you with practical guidance on how to include a testing strategy in your workflow and show you how to use **test-driven development** (**TDD**) to generate higher-quality code from the start. Finally, we'll lead you through the steps of setting up and managing your Git repository, writing a clear and informative README, and sharing your work with the rest of the world. Not only will this increase the exposure and effect of your work, but it will also stimulate cooperation and continual development.

By the end of this chapter, you will have gained the necessary abilities and methods to conquer any real-world programming work, and you will be well on your way to being an invaluable asset in the field of software development.

In this chapter, we will go through subjects related to solving programming assignments, giving you the confidence required in this programming area. These fundamental skills are key to performing well on the job as well as during interviews because your ability to problem-solve determines how good a programmer you are. As developers, we often get asked about our development environment and tech stacks, and if we are to work effectively within another team at a company, then we have to know about the tools that we will have to use. So, having the right answers to these questions when at an interview can show that we know what we are talking about and can integrate into any team.

These are the topics we will discuss in this chapter:

- Preparing your development environment
- Choosing the right scaffolding tools or templates
- Deciding on the application architecture
- Testing your code
- Creating a Git repository with a README and sharing it

Technical requirements

On your machine, please ensure that you have downloaded and installed the latest version of Node.js and npm, which you can find here: `https://nodejs.org/en`. Also, ensure that you have a code editor installed, such as Visual Studio Code, which you can download from here: `https://code.visualstudio.com/`.

Preparing your development environment

Let's now learn how to make excellent React applications. The most diffiicult step is setting up your development environment, but it doesn't have to be. You'll be one step closer to your dream job as a React developer with the assistance of workflow background knowledge and these basic guidelines for setting up a successful JavaScript development environment. This section will walk you through every stage of the process, from selecting the best scaffolding tools for your project to debugging and fixing any difficulties that arise. Every developer should know the basics of setting up a development environment and getting a framework working. In an interview setting, we might be expected to work on a technical test, so being able to find the right tools, install them, and get your code base working is all required knowledge for us as developers. It is absolutely paramount to be able to do so when at an interview. So, let's get going.

Why do you need a good development environment?

A development environment is an essential part of the software development process for a developer. A development environment provides an isolated environment in which you can generate and test your code without fear of interfering with a live production environment. This decreases the danger of end user or customer disruptions and allows you to play around with and test different ways of coding. A development environment also allows you to test your source code against many platforms, browsers, and devices to verify that your application works flawlessly for all users. You can write code more effectively, identify mistakes and defects earlier, and ultimately offer a high-quality product to your consumers if you utilize a development environment.

A development environment requires us to have either an **integrated development environment** (**IDE**) or a text editor/code editor. But what is the difference between them? Let us have a look.

What is the difference between an IDE and a text editor/code editor?

There are many ways for us to set up our development environments. Developers, particularly those using JavaScript and React, have a variety of tools to pick from according to their personal needs. An IDE is a popular choice since it includes a full array of tools for developing, debugging, and testing. A text editor, which is a basic tool that enables effective and simplified coding, is another choice. An online code editor, on the other hand, might be the greatest option for those who like to work directly in the browser. These environments enable quick and easy testing and deployment without the need for any software to be installed on your desktop or laptop.

Now that we have an understanding of these tools, it's time to move on to learning about the basic steps for setting up a modern React development environment.

How do you set up a React development environment?

It might look difficult to set up a React development environment, but with the appropriate steps, anyone can accomplish it. First and foremost, you must be familiar with JavaScript and the command line. Then, download and install Node.js and npm here: `https://nodejs.org/en`, both of which are required for React development. Choose a coding editor, such as Visual Studio Code, which you can download from here: `https://code.visualstudio.com/`. Following that, it is recommended to use Next.js, Remix, or Gatsby commands to build a new React project.

You can learn about the setup process here:

`https://react.dev/learn/start-a-new-react-project`

Installing software requires us to use a package manager, which is basically a collection of tools bundled together that automate a process. This enables us to install, upgrade, configure, and delete software from our computers. npm is the most popular package manager for the JavaScript ecosystem. Alternatives include `yarn` and `pnpm`, and they all have their pros and cons. There is also `npx`, which is an abbreviation for **Node Package eXecute**. It's just an npm package runner that enables developers to run any JavaScript package accessible on the npm registry without the need to install it.

Developers usually use npm or npx depending on the documentation for the tool that they are using. Anyway, we will be using npm and npx in these upcoming examples. The commands for setting up a React project are quite simple. Let's take a look at the syntax for each React framework, as follows:

- *Next.js*

    Running this code will scaffold a Next.js starter project:

    ```
    npx create-next-app
    ```

    It's straightforward, and when you have completed the setup, you will be ready to go.

- *Remix*

    The code here is for Remix and will create a new project for us:

    ```
    npx create-remix
    ```

    Once again, the setup is easy to follow, so creating a Remix project does not take long.

- *Gatsby*

    Using this code sets up a Gatsby project for us:

    ```
    npx create-gatsby
    ```

- *Vite.js*

    With this command, we can set up a Vite.js project:

    ```
    npm create vite@latest
    ```

Gatsby has a similar setup to Next.js and Remix, so it's pretty easy to alternate between the three of them.

Finally, start the development server and see your project come to life. While the setup procedure could appear time-consuming and tedious, the end product is definitely worth it. You'll be able to start developing dynamic and interesting web applications when you have a fully working development environment.

A development environment is only as good as the tools that we use to create it. Let's learn more about React scaffolding tools to see how they can make our job much easier.

Which tools can we use for scaffolding a React project?

We're certain to come across some new and intriguing tools and frameworks as we explore the world of web development. There are a few scaffolding tools that stand out from the rest. webpack is an open source bundle runner that simplifies the process of bundling code for deployment. Next.js, Remix, and Gatsby all use webpack. Then, there's Babel, a tool that allows us to write in the most recent version of JavaScript and have it compiled into a format that most browsers support. These technologies work together to provide a seamless and fast scaffolding experience, freeing up our time to focus on providing the greatest possible user experience.

Scaffolding tools are essential for having a project that is easy to maintain, and we are going to discover why this is the case.

Why are scaffolding tools so important to our project's success?

It is critical to have the correct tools for any profession, and project management is no exception. Having the right tools, from kanban boards to collaborative software, can make or ruin a project. These tools improve communication, boost productivity, and simplify operations. Without them, projects can become disorganized and difficult to manage. The correct tools can help teams stay on track, meet deadlines, and ultimately succeed. Investing in the correct project management tools may appear to be an unnecessary cost, but it may save time, money, and your sanity in the long run. Similarly, it's just as important to check that you have the latest version of Node.js installed or a compatible version that works with your software. This can help you avoid breaking changes, which can affect the software you are using because there can be compatibility issues.

Setting up an environment can be both exhilarating and intimidating. It might be aggravating to experience technical issues throughout this process, so we are going to learn how we can overcome some of these problems.

How do you troubleshoot common issues that can arise in the process of setting up the environment?

To make the process less unpleasant, you can tackle typical difficulties. First, double-check that you have all of the required gear and software. Then, make sure your internet connection is reliable and stable. Try refreshing your browser or clearing your cache if you are experiencing issues or missing files. Follow any instructions carefully and, if necessary, seek assistance. Remember that a little patience and effort will go a long way toward resolving any problems that might emerge throughout the setup process.

To summarize, having an effective React development environment is incredibly beneficial for any web developer. It not only allows you to develop and test your projects successfully but also allows you to jump right into coding chores rather than battling with integration concerns. The tools and frameworks discussed previously have proven to be essential in creating the required environment and providing excellent scaffolding. A thorough grasp of these components will enable us to deploy our application without bugs or technical concerns. When developing React applications, the correct environment and structure are critical to success.

Let's now dive deeper into scaffolding tools and learn how to choose a good architecture for our programming tasks.

Choosing the right scaffolding tools or templates

Scaffolding tools, templates, programs, and other resources are all accessible to assist you in realizing your idea. However, in order to get the most out of your project, you must take the time to properly assess those options. In this section, we will look at the many components of choosing a feasible architecture for React-based applications and how to use them effectively.

What is scaffolding in programming?

Scaffolding is the process of creating a structured framework, layout, or template for an application in order to offer a stable basis for subsequent development. Scaffolding saves time and effort for developers by automating repetitive operations and establishing an effective structure for the project. For a variety of programming languages and technologies, scaffolding tools and frameworks exist to assist developers in launching their projects with the least amount of manual setup. These tools frequently include best practices and suggested patterns, which can result in code bases that are easier to maintain and scale.

Scaffolding tends to include the following:

- **A file structure**: Establishing a consistent, sustainable system for organizing files and folders that makes it simple to navigate and understand how the project is set up

- **Configuration and setup file**: Creating configuration files for tools and libraries such as linters, bundlers, and transpilers that support maintaining a standardized development environment and streamlining the build procedure

- **Code examples**: Giving simple examples of how to utilize the framework, libraries, or project components can aid users in getting up and running fast and grasping recommended practices

- **Boilerplate starter kit**: Producing reusable code snippets or components that are able to be quickly customized for certain use cases, including establishing a build system, setting up a web server, or developing standard **user interface** (**UI**) elements

Aside from scaffolding, we also need to consider the project size, complexity, and technologies required to complete our React programming tasks. Moving on to the next section, we are going to talk about and learn more about the project aspects.

How do you determine which project factors to take into account when creating a project?

There are various ways to analyze which project factors we should be taking into account as we create projects. This can include the following:

- Each project's size
- Complexity
- Required technologies

You can develop great frontend designs that are responsive to the organization's demands by properly taking these variables into account. While simpler code and testing might be needed for smaller projects, more complicated frameworks for implementing React components may be needed for bigger projects. Knowing which technologies could be necessary to complete the work at hand is crucial. You can make sure that you're producing high-quality work, meeting client needs, and offering smooth user experiences by having a thorough awareness of all these factors.

We will now learn about evaluating the functionalities of tools and templates because this is required for the project setup and specification.

How do you evaluate the functionalities of each tool or template and determine which one best suits your needs?

Carefully compare the features of each tool or template before choosing one that best suits your requirements. You can be sure that you select the tool that is the greatest fit for your particular requirements by taking the time to thoroughly analyze the features and capabilities of each one. There are many solutions available to fit any demand, whether you're searching for a tool with a wide range of customization possibilities or a template that's simple to use right out of the box. In the end, the decision you make will be influenced by a number of variables, such as your financial situation, your degree of expertise, and the precise objectives you want to accomplish with the tool or template you select.

Analyzing the attributes of a project is something that we take into account when working on our own projects and those for clients as well. Let's find out why it's so significant to do so.

How do you analyze these adaptability, compatibility, scalability, and security features?

Businesses require software that can keep up with their changing needs in today's fast-paced environment. Analyzing the software's adaptability, compatibility, scalability, and security aspects is essential when choosing a program. Software needs to be able to adapt as a business develops and evolves, therefore adaptability is essential. Scalability enables the software to expand in line with changing company requirements, while compatibility guarantees that it integrates seamlessly with other important internal systems. On the topic of scalability, there are many ways that we can make our applications scalable. If we choose to use a modern framework such as Next.js, for example, then we guarantee that we are getting access to the latest tools and features. This can be further enhanced when we have the mindset to use some popular coding standards and methodologies to keep our projects robust.

A few ways this can be accomplished are set out here:

- **Using engine locking**: With this, we confirm which version of Node.js and the package manager we are using to ensure that everyone working on the project uses the same versions. Typically, we would have a `.nvmrc` and `.npmrc` file for this.
- **ESLint setup**: For JavaScript code analysis and spotting problematic patterns.

- **Prettier configuration**: So that every developer's code follows the same formatting.

- **Commit linting**: A way to lint our commit messages and ensure they adhere to a set of standards.

- **Framework customizations and plugins**: A framework can be further extended by enabling features and customizations that are outlined in the documentation or by installing third-party packages and tools.

Last but not least, security is the backbone of any software, safeguarding private information and making sure the program is resilient enough to fend off attackers. Businesses can make sure they have the software they need to succeed in today's competitive environment by examining these essential qualities.

Choosing the right tool from the start of the project can save you a lot of time and give you more confidence in the code base. Let's now read about how this can affect us in the long run.

How do you choose the right tool or template that meets all your requirements to ensure a successful outcome?

You must use the appropriate tool or template that satisfies all of your needs if you want to obtain a good conclusion. It might be difficult to choose the right tool or template, especially with so many possibilities available. However, you will be setting yourself up for success if you take the time to do your research and select the one that is most suited to your needs. Finding the ideal match for your project can ultimately save you time and effort, whether it's a software program, a project management template, or an app. Avoid opting for a tool that is only *good enough*; instead, look harder to locate the one that will enable you to reach your goal.

For React applications, it's crucial to pick the appropriate scaffolding tool or template. Prior to anything else, be sure to comprehend what scaffolding is and its significance. The size, complexity, and technology needed to complete your work should then be taken into account. Research all accessible tools or templates for the duties after that. Determine which tool or template best meets your needs by comparing its functionality to others. To achieve a good end result, consider each option's adaptability, compatibility, scalability, and security characteristics before choosing one that best suits your needs. By following these steps, you'll be able to pick a solid framework for your project and eventually simplify your work.

Staying on topic, we will now segue into the theme of application architecture, which is connected to scaffolding.

Deciding on the application architecture

A number of aspects and considerations must be taken into account when choosing an application architecture for a React project. Maintainability, scalability, and reuse are encouraged by a well-designed architecture. The architecture ought to be adaptive and change with the needs of the project. As you get more expertise and familiarity with React, you'll find yourself better able to make educated architectural design decisions. When the project expands and fresh demands arise, be willing to refactor and reconsider your decisions.

What do we need to think about when choosing an application architecture?

Every project is different and, as a result, requires a different configuration. We have to take into account many different factors, which is something we have to do right at the start before we start to work on our project. There is no right or wrong answer because ultimately, it can come down to our personal preferences, team tech stack familiarity, or even client requirements.

For example, if we were building a website that was taking payments, then many factors would need to be considered, such as a secure way to manage and take payments, and a way for users to sign up and create accounts. So, figuring out why we would choose one state management solution over another one or why we would choose a payment gateway such as Stripe instead of a different one are all options that we should be able to talk through.

Again, there is no right or wrong answer here; the main thing is that we can explain and justify our choices.

To choose the best application architecture for our React project, we should consider the following characteristics:

- **State management**: Thinking about the component-to-component level of interaction and the level of detail of your application's state, determine whether you require a state management tool such as Redux.

- **Routing**: If your application has to switch between various views or pages, configure your framework for routing or use an external routing framework such as React Router.

- **Recognizing project specifications**: Start by comprehending the project's needs, scale, and scope. Decide on the main characteristics, the performance standards, and the different deployment platforms.

- **Future-proofing**: To provide for future expansion and modification, modularity and adaptability should be considered while designing your components, state management, and API design.

- **The folder structure**: Ensure that your file and folder structures are logical, scalable, and well maintained. Group by category, such as components, media, and testing, or group by feature set.

- **Application programming interface (API)**: Determine any external libraries or APIs required for your task, such as those for data analysis, authorization, or other specialized functionality.

- **Static site generation (SSG) versus server-side rendering (SSR)**: To enhance performance and **search engine optimization (SEO)**, use an SSR or SSG solution such as Next.js, Gatsby, or Remix, which can be chosen based on the requirements of your project.

- **Apply programming best practices and criteria**: Use linters such as ESLint, code formatters such as Prettier, and documented rules such as the popular Airbnb JavaScript style guide to enforce code standards and best practices throughout the project so that every developer's code and project setup is consistent.

- **UI libraries**: For determining how we are going to design the structure for our applications. We have many options at our disposal, such as the Tailwind CSS framework, `styled-components`, Sass, or just plain CSS.

Now, we are going to learn about the aspects of testing our code in projects.

Testing your code

All programmers must be able to take advantage of **version control systems** (**VCSs**) and conduct adequate tests on their code. Through testing your code, you can make sure that it performs as intended and that there are no mistakes when various potential inputs are used. Smooth team cooperation will be made possible by having efficient version control, and future job deployments will be able to manage source files more effectively. We will go into these crucial subjects in this section so that you're equipped with the knowledge required for success.

Testing is significantly better when combined with version control. Let's find out how it can help us in this next section.

Why should you use version control while testing your code?

There have been occasions when I forgot what I changed in my code or accidentally rewrote a piece of work and forgot what it was before. Version control solves these problems. It's a mechanism that keeps track of modifications you've implemented in your code over time and lets you go back to earlier iterations if necessary. When testing your code, having a VCS set up is essential. It not only enables you to keep track of changes, but it also makes organized and secure teamwork possible. Version control can speed up the testing process, minimize mistakes, and overall make the whole process more effective.

We have learned some use cases for version control in this section. Now, we are going to find out about ways to track changes in our code base in the next section.

Which testing and change-tracking tools you should utilize for your code base?

It might be difficult to test and keep track of changes in your code base, but the correct tools can really help. With so many alternatives available, it's critical to select tools that are most effective for your particular need. Cypress and Selenium are two well-liked testing solutions that enable automated testing across several browsers. Version management tools such as Git and **Subversion** (**SVN**) can also make it simpler to track changes. In the case of mistakes, these technologies facilitate cooperation and simple rollbacks. Finding tools that will optimize your workflow and assist you in achieving your goals requires time-consuming study and testing out a variety of solutions.

Finally, let's tie up this chapter by learning about the importance of creating a code repository with well-written documentation as we learn how to create a Git repository.

Creating a Git repository with a README and sharing it

For many different kinds of reasons, building a code repository with excellent documentation is crucial. Let's continue to read on so that we can understand why.

Why is creating a code repository with good documentation crucial?

Developers can more easily comprehend the functionality, purpose, and design of a code base with the aid of clear documentation. They can utilize, contribute to, or alter the code more successfully as a result. A well-documented code repository makes it easier for team members to work together since everyone is aware of the code's structure and intended use. This makes it simpler to talk about adjustments, work out problems, and monitor advancement.

In essence, onboarding refers to the process of integrating new team members into a project. They rapidly become comfortable with the code base thanks to clear documentation, which lowers the learning curve and cuts down on the effort required to ask queries or look for solutions. There is another benefit of quality control. Test cases, anticipated results, and instructions for assisting with the project are frequently included in the documentation. This guarantees that updates comply with the project's objectives and maintain the quality of the code.

We explain our code as it is produced, which generally results in time savings over the long term. Developers do not need to sift through the code or seek assistance from other developers; they can just turn to the docs for direction and clarification. The ability to maintain docs becomes considerably simpler when all of the aforementioned suggestions are integrated. Whenever the documentation is clear, it is simpler to preserve the code base as time goes on since it gives developers a complete guide to use when adding updates or addressing errors. This lessens the possibility of creating new problems or compromising current functionality.

These enhancements could indicate a developer's expertise and self-assurance. The repository reflects favorably on the developers and organizations participating with well-documented code. It exhibits a dedication to best practices, meticulousness, and consideration for the requirements of other developers. A well-documented code base increases the likelihood that others will find it valuable and expand upon it. This could result in more widespread developer community acceptance, cooperation, and innovation. To ensure comprehension, maintainability, and cooperation, it is essential to have a code repository with clear documentation. It enhances a project's longevity and viability and favorably portrays the project's developers.

How do you create a Git repository?

Creating a new Git repository is a very easy process. Details of how to do so can be found here: `https://github.com/new`.

Essentially, all you have to do is create a new repository and then run the setup code inside your local project folder. An example of the code can be seen here:

```
echo "# myapp" >> README.md
git init
git add README.md
git commit -m "first commit"
git branch -M main
git remote add origin https://github.com/yourusername/myapp.git
git push -u origin main
```

The code is autogenerated every single time we create a new repository, and it is configured for our project, so all we have to do is copy and paste the code into our command line to get our project set up and version controlled on Git.

Summary

As we get to the end of this chapter on solving any real-world programming problem, it is clear that a solid foundation and a systematic approach will substantially speed up the software development process. We have created a basis for a successful project by carefully configuring our development environment, selecting suitable scaffolding tools and templates, and selecting an acceptable application architecture.

With everything that we have learned, we now have knowledge we can use when we get asked about setting up our development environment and some good reasons for choosing the right project architecture. These tend to be common interview questions or, at the very least, talking topics where we can show our experience and way of thinking when it comes to creating React projects.

The importance of testing also cannot be understated, and we are capable of talking about the reasons why it is an area that React developers should be taking seriously and using during the development process.

We have emphasized the significance of implementing a rigorous testing plan to ensure the stability, scalability, and security of our code throughout this chapter. You can find and solve issues early in the development process by embracing TDD and adding a rigorous testing framework, thereby enhancing the overall quality of your product.

On top of that, we have emphasized the need to build a well-structured Git repository with a clear and informative README. This not only acts as a great reference for yourself and other developers in the future, but it also develops a working atmosphere that promotes ongoing growth.

Ultimately, mastering the art of real-world programming necessitates a blend of technical knowledge, strategic planning, and good communication. You are now better prepared to handle any programming challenge with confidence and sophistication after polishing these abilities and adopting the best practices mentioned in this chapter. Remember that a software developer's career is an ongoing learning experience, and as you continue to mature and evolve, you will find yourself more capable of overcoming even the most complicated obstacles in the field of software development.

In the next chapter, we will be building an app based on React Hooks/Redux, `styled-components`, and Firebase. This will allow us to build on the knowledge we have gained up until now, further progressing our React and interview skills.

11

Building an App Based on React, Redux, Styled Components, and the Firebase Backend

As we progress through this book, we will cover many concepts and skills related to the React ecosystem, popular libraries, and the best practices to build robust React applications in the modern era of web apps. This chapter is dedicated to creating a full stack React application with the help of knowledge gained in the previous chapters. As part of the interview process, the interviewer might ask you to build a full-fledged React project based on certain functional and technical requirements, or assign a quick coding challenge to assess your abilities in a particular domain. This chapter will guide you on how to tackle the coding rounds, by creating a React project from scratch following standard guidelines and asking interview questions on the implemented project. In this chapter, we will build an e-commerce application by implementing various UI components, applying styles, verifying the identity of the registered users through an authentication mechanism, integrating with the Firebase backend, and deploying the application to make it available for public usage.

First, we will start with the process of scaffolding the project using an official **Redux Toolkit** template. This will help you to quickly create a runnable project and avoid confusion over the project folder structure and minimum required dependencies for the project, using one simple command. In the same section, we will also add dependencies such as styled-components, which is helpful to encapsulate CSS styling inside the component, React Router to navigate pages, the `react-intl` library to support internationalization, and the Firebase package to implement the backend. Then, we will quickly introduce the Firebase backend and its services, integrating Firebase inside our React project and authentication features.

Thereafter, we will build business logic following Redux standards to work with various actions triggered from a UI. To increase the user base from various regions, we will enhance the application with the support of an internationalization process. Then, we will write a couple of unit tests to make our code flawless and work as per business requirements. At the end of the chapter, we will host our Git repository on GitHub and make it available online to showcase our skills.

In this chapter, we will cover the following main topics:

- Scaffolding and configuring a project
- Introducing Firebase services and configuring an application
- Implementing Firebase Authentication and its backend
- Building the Redux components for state management
- Building the presentation layer
- Supporting internationalization
- Implementing testing using the Vitest framework
- Creating a Git repository with README documentation
- Deploying the application for public access

Technical requirements

Before starting our project's journey, your workstation should have the latest Node.js and npm (https://nodejs.org/en) packages installed on it. You will also need to have a Netlify account (https://www.netlify.com/) for the deployment section while building this project and a GitHub (https://github.com/) account to host the Git repository. The code base of this project can be found online in the git Repository: https://github.com/PacktPublishing/React-Interview-Guide/tree/main/Chapter11/one-stop-electronics.

Let's first talk about the scaffolding and project configuration to build a React application.

Scaffolding and configuring the project

In *Chapter 6*, we covered various topics about Redux and its workflow to build React web applications, based on a Redux state management solution. To reduce the boilerplate code involved with Redux logic, the Redux team recommends using **RTK** to simplify many common use cases, apply best practices, and prevent common mistakes.

If you create a project from scratch, doing so using the **Redux and TypeScript template for Vite** is one of the suggested approaches from the Redux team. So, we will use the same approach to build the project in this section. In this project, we will build an e-commerce application, named *One Stop Electronics*, where one can buy electronic devices.

The following `degit` project scaffolding command is helpful for creating a project structure based on RTK:

```
npx degit reduxjs/redux-templates/packages/vite-template-redux
onestop-electronics
```

This template creates a project based on TypeScript (`.tsx` or `.ts` files), with the required type definition dependencies for the `react`, `react-dom`, and `jest` packages.

The project will use React Router to navigate the pages in the application and `FormatJS`, which is a modular collection of JavaScript libraries to support internationalization, using the `React Intl` library. The commands to install these packages are listed here:

```
npm install --save react-router-dom
npm install --save react-intl
```

There are various approaches to styling React components. We will use styled-components for this project to write component-based styling. This package will be installed along with its type definition dependency, as shown here:

```
npm install --save styled-components
npm install --save-dev @types/styled-components
```

styled-components was discussed in *Chapter 7*. You can also find more details and features on the official website: `https://styled-components.com`.

The Firebase cloud-based development platform will be used for this application to implement an authentication mechanism and backend data storage. So, let's install the latest Firebase version with the following command:

```
npm install --save firebase
```

Once the application folder structure is created and the aforementioned dependencies are installed, let's create a few more folders to customize the project as per the tech stack. The important folders are listed as follows:

- `app/store`: The `store` folder is used to create various components of RTK, such as actions or action creators, reducers, and selectors
- `assets`: This folder holds all the image and icon files
- `backend`: This contains the Firebase-related API and e-commerce application data
- `features`: The folder is dedicated to the main pages for the web application
- `i18n`: This contains all the internationalization-specific files

Visual Studio (VS) Code is widely used and quite popular for React development. So, we will use it for this project and the folder structure, after adding all the aforementioned folders, as shown in the following figure:

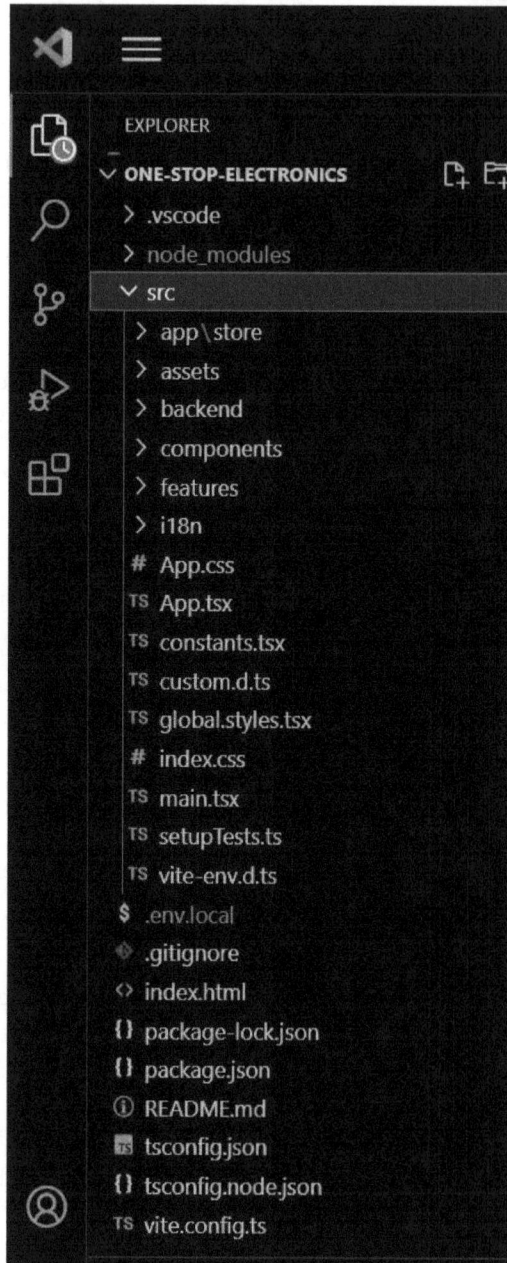

Figure 11.1: The application folder structure

VS Code provides a big list of extensions in its marketplace. In this project, the `vscode-styled-components` extension will be used to highlight the syntax of styled-components, and the `Prettier` code formatter extension will be used to format code.

> **Note**
>
> There is no restriction to use a specific IDE. You can use any popular IDE based on your preference and required features.

In the following section, we will be introduced to Firebase's services and required configuration and learn about Firebase Authentication and the backend, before proceeding with its implementation.

Introducing Firebase services and configuring the application

Firebase is a comprehensive **backend as a service** (**BaaS**) provider offered by Google that provides database, authentication, cloud storage, analytics, and many other services on the fly. These backend services help developers to build apps faster and more securely without requiring much programming code.

What are the main features of Firebase?

To get a clearer idea of Firebase, we will look at some of its main features. They are listed as follows:

- **Realtime Database**: The Firebase Realtime Database is a cloud-hosted NoSQL database. The data is stored in the JSON format and synchronized in real time for every connected client. The database supports all types of platforms such as Android, iOS, and web platforms.

  Here, *Realtime* means that any changes to data are reflected immediately across the platforms and devices within a few milliseconds. Moreover, the Realtime Database provides great offline support by caching all the data you have queried and retrieving it from the cache whenever there's no internet connection. Once a device is connected back to the internet, the database synchronizes the local data changes to the original remote data to avoid any conflicts occurring with the internet outage. As a result, the apps remain responsive.

- **Authentication**: Firebase Authentication is a backend service used to provide user authentication, using email, password, phone number, and popular federated identity providers, such as Google, Facebook, Twitter/X, GitHub, and Apple.

  Once you upgrade from a basic Authentication product to Firebase Authentication with Identity Platform (`https://firebase.google.com/docs/auth#identity-platform`), you will get additional features such as **Multi-Factor Authentication** (**MFA**), enhanced logging, user activity, blocking functions, **Security Assertion Markup Language** (**SAML**) support for web and OpenID Connect providers, multi-tenancy, and enterprise-grade support. Even though this Identity Platform product is a paid service, you will be able to use the service without being charged if you keep within the daily limits.

You will get the flexibility to use either the Firebase Authentication SDK to manually integrate sign-in methods or the `FirebaseUI` library as a complete ready-made UI authentication solution.

- **Cloud Storage**: Cloud Storage is a simple cost-effective storage service for application developers who need to store and process user-generated large-content files, such as images, audio, videos, and any other object type. You can use either the Firebase SDKs or Google Cloud Storage APIs to access those content files. The Firebase SDKs enable secure uploads and downloads from clients directly.

- **Google Analytics and Crashlytics**: Google Analytics for Firebase is a free app measurement solution that helps you get insights into app usage and user engagement. This service provides unlimited reporting of up to 500 distinct events, defined using the Firebase SDK. This analytics information can be used for business growth by retaining more users and making wise decisions for marketing and performance optimizations.

  Crashlytics is a real-time crash reporting tool that collects details about errors and crashes that occurred in your application. This is helpful to troubleshoot an issue by logging the error details, such as the line number where the error happened, the device name, the OS version, and when the issue happened.

How do you set up and configure Firebase for authentication and data storage?

If the project that you build is based on the Firebase backend, you need to take the following steps to create a Firebase app:

1. Go to the official Firebase console at `https://console.firebase.google.com/` and log in with your Google account.

2. Click on the **Add Project** link and give your project a name – for instance, let's name it `onestop-electronics`. After that, click on the **Continue** button to proceed with the configuration wizard.

3. You will get the option to enable Google Analytics for your project. This is optional and not required for this project.

4. Then, click on **Create project**. You need to wait for a while to provision the resources and finish the setup of the project.

5. Click on the web icon on the home page of your project to create your web app. This opens a form to enter the web app name. Then click on the **Register App** button to integrate the web app with Firebase.

6. Then, copy the web app's Firebase-generated configuration, and save it for later usage in the project.

7. After that, add Firebase products named `Authentication` to build a secure authentication system and `Cloud Firestore` for the cloud-hosted NoSQL database used in the project.

> **Note**
>
> The `Authentication` product is used to store the authenticated user on sign-up, and update the user on every sign-in operation, whereas the Firestore database will store the application data.

8. By default, Firestore doesn't provide read or write permissions. This permission flag can be enabled inside the **Rules** tab. The updated security rule looks like this:

```
rules_version = '2';

service cloud.firestore {
  match /databases/{database}/documents {
    match /{document=**} {
      allow read, write: if true;
    }
  }
}
```

9. In the `Authentication` product, you can choose sign-in methods such as *email/password* and *Google* providers. You can also find several other third-party providers under the sign-in provider section.

You can create multiple projects under a single account, but there is a limit for the free plan.

Where do you put Firebase configuration securely in the project?

It is not recommended to store the Firebase configuration in a repository that will be available on a public development platform, such as GitHub. You can keep the configuration in the following `.env.local` file in the key-value format, and add it to the `.gitignore` file of the project:

```
VITE_FIREBASE_API_KEY = "yourfirebaseapikey"
VITE_FIREBASE_AUTH_DOMAIN = "yourfirebaseauthdomain"
VITE_FIREBASE_PROJECT_ID = "yourfirebaseprojectid"
VITE_FIREBASE_STORAGE_BUCKET = "yourfirebasestoragebucket"
VITE_FIREBASE_MESSAGING_SENDER_ID =
  "yourfirebasemessagingsenderid"
VITE_FIREBASE_APP_ID = "yourfirebaseappid"
```

The keys should start with the VITE keyword in a Vite-based project, as shown in the preceding code. The same keys are accessible in the project through import.meta.env.VITE. For instance, this configuration is useful to instantiate the Firebase app in the config.ts file:

```
import { initializeApp } from "firebase/app"

const firebaseConfig = {
  apiKey: import.meta.env.VITE_FIREBASE_API_KEY,
  authDomain: import.meta.env.VITE_FIREBASE_AUTH_DOMAIN,
  projectId: import.meta.env.VITE_FIREBASE_PROJECT_ID,
  storageBucket: import.meta.env.
    VITE_FIREBASE_STORAGE_BUCKET,
  messagingSenderId: import.meta.env.
    VITE_FIREBASE_SENDER_ID,
  appId: import.meta.env.VITE_FIREBASE_APP_ID,
}

export const firebaseApp = initializeApp(firebaseConfig)
```

The exported firebaseApp from the preceding code can be used anywhere in the project when it is required.

> **Note**
>
> If you create a React project based on the **create-react-app** tool, the keys should start with REACT_APP and be accessible through the process.env variables.

Once the Firebase project is configured, we need to implement the Firebase authentication methods that will be invoked upon sign-up and sign-in form submission. Simultaneously, Cloud Firestore data operations should be implemented in the form of methods to store and retrieve product information. The following section will focus on this Firebase API implementation.

Implementing Firebase Authentication and its backend

Once the Firebase app is configured in the Firebase console, you can implement authentication for the One Stop Electronics application using the Firebase Authentication API. These API methods are helpful to authenticate legitimate users when they sign up and sign in to purchase products in this e-commerce application. Usually, we create all the API handlers inside a separate folder (in our case, backend->firebase->api) to keep it separate from the frontend code.

How do you implement Firebase authentication for sign-in, sign-up, and sign-out scenarios?

We need to import several Firebase functions and utilities from the `Firebase/auth` package to work with the authentication mechanism. The Firebase package provides separate methods for sign-in, sign-up, and sign-out scenarios. Let's start by importing all these API methods along with a Firebase instance inside the following `api/auth.ts` file:

```
import { firebaseApp } from "@/backend/firebase/config"
import {
  signInWithEmailAndPassword,
  signInWithPopup,
  signInWithRedirect,
  GoogleAuthProvider,
  createUserWithEmailAndPassword,
  updateProfile,
  signOut,
  getAuth,
  onAuthStateChanged,
  NextOrObserver,
  User,
} from "firebase/auth"

const auth = getAuth(firebaseApp)

const googleProvider = new GoogleAuthProvider()

googleProvider.setCustomParameters({
  prompt: "select_account",
})
```

In the preceding code, the `auth` instance has been created based on the Firebase app instance. Also, the Google provider has been configured to prompt for Google account details to perform Google sign-in authentication.

Using the preceding API utilities, write down the two sign-in methods in the same file mentioned above – one with an email address and a password, and another one using Google sign-in authentication. Similarly, the sign-up method can be created based on an email address and a password, along with a username. The sign-out method will be used to end the current user session. The following `auth.ts` file is updated with these authentication methods:

```
export const signInEmailAndPassword = async (
  email: string,
```

```
  password: string,
) => {
  if (!email || !password) return
  return await signInWithEmailAndPassword(auth,
    email, password)
}

export const signInGooglePopup = () => signInWithPopup
  (auth, googleProvider)
export const signInGoogleRedirect = () =>
  signInWithRedirect(auth, googleProvider)

export const signUpEmailAndPassword = async (
  displayName: string,
  email: string,
  password: string,
): Promise<User> => {
  Const userInfo = await createUserWithEmailAndPassword
    (auth, email, password)
  await updateProfile(userInfo.user, { displayName })
  return userInfo.user
}

export const signOutUser = async () => await signOut(auth)
```

The preceding exported methods will be integrated with UI screens, especially for sign-in or sign-up forms, in the upcoming section where we will build the presentation layer.

Lastly, it is also possible to listen to the authenticate state changes using the following method. This method is helpful to update the current user details in the application:

```
export const onAuthStateChangedListener =
  (callback: NextOrObserver<User>) =>
  onAuthStateChanged(auth, callback)
```

Now, we are ready with all the backend authentication methods, which are helpful to create an active user session in the e-commerce application. Once the user is authenticated, they can usually perform **create, read, update, and delete (CRUD)** operations on the application data, based on business needs.

How do you implement cloud store data operations? Can you explain data operations with any collection?

Unlike a SQL database, there are no tables and rows within a cloud store database. Here, you store data as key-value pairs in the form of documents, which are organized into collections. The stored product information is displayed as a part of a landing page, which is crucial in this e-commerce application. So, let's explain data operations with a product collection.

First, we need to create a product collection to store the electronic device data in Firebase's *Cloud Firestore* database. If the collection does not exist in the database, it will be created automatically and insert the product data. In this application, the product records (or documents, using Firebase's terminology) are uploaded to the database through a JSON file, available at `firebase/data/ products-data.json`.

Let's start by importing all the required functions from the `firebase/firestore` package, along with the product type, inside the following `firebase/data/db-utils.ts` file:

```
import {
  getFirestore,
  doc,
  collection,
  writeBatch,
  query,
  getDocs,
  QueryDocumentSnapshot,
} from "firebase/firestore"
import { Product } from "@/app/store/product/product.types"

export const db = getFirestore()
```

In the preceding code snippet, the database instance is created through the `getFirestore()` function to perform database operations on the application collections.

Using the previously imported functions, you can create read and write operations for the product collection in the same file:

```
export const insertProductsData = async <T extends Product>(
  collectionKey: string,
  productItems: T[],
) => {
  const collectionRef = collection(db, collectionKey)
  const batch = writeBatch(db)

  productItems.forEach((product) => {
```

```
    const docRef = doc(collectionRef)
    batch.set(docRef, product)
  })

  await batch.commit()
}

export const fetchProductsData = async () => {
  const collectionRef = collection(db, "products")
  const queryRef = query(collectionRef)
  const querySnapshot = await getDocs(queryRef)

  return querySnapshot.docs.map((docSnapshot) =>
    docSnapshot.data())
}
```

In the preceding code, the product data is inserted with the help of the following four steps:

1. First, create a collection reference, which is based on the database instance and unique key.

2. Then, create a batch reference based on the database instance to insert multiple products at a time.

3. Iterate each product, and create a document reference to update the batch.

4. Finally, commit the batch to insert multiple records simultaneously.

Similarly, the product data is retrieved in four steps:

1. First, create a collection reference for products.

2. Then, create a query reference based on the collection reference created in the previous step.

3. Fetch all the documents of the product collection using the getDocs method, and store them as a snapshot.

4. Finally, iterate through the query snapshot and return the results.

All the preceding cloud store data functions are imported from the firebase/firestore package.

It is also possible to create a user collection based on each sign-up action, triggered through the new user. You can find this specific API handler within the code and extend the functionality of this project as per the requirements. However, this is out of the scope of this specific section and is the code snippet is only commented on for reference.

Now, we have completed the backend code. In the following section, let's create all the Redux components to implement a state management solution for this application.

Building the Redux components for state management

The Redux store-related components cover most of the application actions, such as calculating the business logic, creating or updating the data inside the store, and fetching the latest data to display on the UI. In this project, the store components are categorized into product, cart, and user folders. Each folder contains files such as the entity type (`*.type.ts`), a slice that contains actions or a reducer (`*.slice.ts`), and a selector to retrieve the data (`*.selector.ts`).

In our e-commerce application, the `Product` entity is required to display details such as product name, brand, price, and quantity to showcase all the available products. So, let's create the store components for the product entity first. The following `product.type.ts` file creates the product and its relevant types, with all possible properties:

```
export type Product = {
  id: number
  productImageUrl: string
  name: string
  brand: string
  price: number
  category: string
}


//Holds the list of products,product category and boolean flag to
indicate loading state
export type ProductsState = {
  products: Product[]
  category: string
  isLoading: boolean
}

export type ProductMap = {
  [key: string]: Product[]
}
```

Once the product types are created, the product slice should be created to update the product list and product category in the store. RTK simplifies things by keeping these actions inside a reducer as a product slice. The following is a product slice with the name `product.slice.ts`:

```
import { createSlice } from "@reduxjs/toolkit"
import { ProductsState } from "./product.types"

const INITIAL_STATE: ProductsState = {
  products: [],
  category: "all",
  isLoading: true,
```

```
}

export const productsSlice = createSlice({
  name: "products",
  initialState: INITIAL_STATE,
  reducers: {
    setProducts(state, action) {
      state.products = action.payload
      state.isLoading = false
    },
    setCategory(state, action) {
      state.category = action.payload
    },
  },
})

export const { setProducts, setCategory } =
  productsSlice.actions
export const productsReducer = productsSlice.reducer
```

The preceding actions are exported in order to use them on the respective product UI page, in response to user actions, whereas the exported reducer is used to fetch the store state, such as the products, the category, and the product map, based on a category name using the reselect library.

The following code is for the product.selector.tsx file. The code for this file is quite long, so let's break it down into smaller code blocks. The first code block contains selectors to fetch products, the loading state of the products, and the product category:

```
import { createSelector } from "reselect"
import { RootState } from "@/app/store/store"
import { Product, ProductMap, ProductsState }
  from "./product.types"

const selectProductReducer = (state: RootState):
  ProductsState => state.products

export const selectProducts = createSelector(
  [selectProductReducer],
  (productsSlice) => productsSlice.products,
)

export const selectCategory = createSelector(
  [selectProductReducer],
  (productsSlice) => productsSlice.category,
```

```
)

export const selectProductsIsLoading = createSelector(
  [selectProductReducer],
  (productsSlice) => productsSlice.isLoading,
)
```

The following code block contains a product map with respect to each category:

```
export const selectProductsMap = createSelector(
  [selectProducts],
  (products): ProductMap =>
    products.reduce(
      (acc, product) => {
        const { category } = product
        acc[category]
          ? acc[category].push(product)
          : (acc[category] = [product])
        acc["all"].push(product)
        return acc
      },
      { all: [] } as ProductMap,
    ),
)
```

The One Stop Electronics application uses the preceding `selectProductsMap` to filter the products based on a category. Our application has various categories such as all types of laptops, tabs, and mobiles.

Similarly, we can create store components for the `User` and `Cart` entities.

How do you work with multiple reducers in a Redux application?

Once you complete all the Redux entities for the project, all the reducers need to be combined in a single root reducer named the `root-reducer.ts` file. Here, we will use the `combineReducers` method from Redux, which accepts all the reducers as an object in a single argument:

```
import { combineReducers } from "redux"
import { userReducer } from "./user/user.slice"
import { productsReducer } from "./product/product.slice"
import { cartReducer } from "./cart/cart.slice"

export const rootReducer = combineReducers({
  user: userReducer,
  products: productsReducer,
```

```
   cart: cartReducer,
})
```

Thereafter, the store can be configured using the aforementioned root reducer inside the `store.ts` file:

```
import { configureStore } from "@reduxjs/toolkit"

export const store = configureStore({
  reducer: rootReducer,
})
```

RTK automatically calls the `combineReducers` method, so you don't need to invoke it directly.

Now, the store is ready to be used for any `read` or `update` operations on the application data.

The Redux development is now completed for the entire application using RTK. The next section is dedicated to building the presentation layer using UI components and web pages based on these reusable components.

Building the presentation layer

It is a common practice to keep reusable components under the `components` folder. In this project, we will create customized form components such as button, input, select, and spinner, layout components such as header and footer, and reusable functional components such as products and categories inside the `components` folder.

How do you implement a custom button using styled-components?

The HTML button element doesn't come with different variations in terms of styling, but it is possible to create multiple button variations using React and styled-components. Let's look at a button component and how it can be customized for the purposes of this project.

The project requires basic buttons that are bigger in size (mainly used for sign-up and sign-in pages), inverted buttons with constrasting colors for Google sign-in, and small buttons in scenarios where there is not a lot of space on screen (which are often used to add products to a cart). As a first step, the styled-component should be created with these different styles inside the `button.styles.tsx` file.

Let's break down the code into small code blocks because of the large content in the file. The first code block contains the `BasicButton` styled-component:

```
import styled from "styled-components"

export const BasicButton = styled.button`
  min-width: 10rem;
```

```
    width: auto;
    height: 2.5rem;
    line-height: 2.5rem;
    letter-spacing: 0.5px;
    padding: 0 2rem;
    background-color: rgb(112, 76, 182);
    color: white;
    font-size: 0.7rem;
    font-family: "Barlow Condensed";
    font-weight: bolder;
    text-transform: uppercase;
    border: none;
    border-radius: 0.2rem;
    cursor: pointer;
    display: flex;
    justify-content: center;

    &:hover {
      background-color: white;
      color: black;
      border: 1px solid black;
    }
`
```

The following code block contains two more styled button components that extend the basic button. The inverted button inverts the background and text colors of the basic button, and while the small button appears to be similar to the basic button, it will actually be smaller in size:

```
export const InvertedButton = styled(BasicButton)`
  background-color: white;
  color: rgb(112, 76, 182);
  border: 1px solid black;
  &:hover {
    background-color: rgb(112, 76, 182);
    border: none;
    border: 1px solid white;
    color: white;
  }
`

export const SmallBasicButton = styled(BasicButton)`
  width: 4rem;
  height: 1.5rem;
  min-width: 0rem;
  padding: 0rem;
```

```
letter-spacing: 0.1rem;
line-height: 2rem;
font-size: 0.4rem;
align-items: center;
letter-spacing: 0rem;
`
```

In the preceding styled-components, we have used the rem relative unit instead of an absolute unit such as px to have dynamic sizing or spacing, depending on screen size.

Then, we import these button styles into the following button.tsx file and dynamically render the respective button component, based on the button's type prop value. The component also accepts children and other button props:

```
import { FC, ButtonHTMLAttributes } from "react"
import { BasicButton, InvertedButton, SmallBasicButton }
  from "./button.styles"

export enum BUTTON_TYPE_CLASSES {
  basic = "basic",
  inverted = "inverted",
  small = "small",
}

const getButton = (buttonType = BUTTON_TYPE_CLASSES.basic) =>
  ({
    [BUTTON_TYPE_CLASSES.basic]: BasicButton,
    [BUTTON_TYPE_CLASSES.inverted]: InvertedButton,
    [BUTTON_TYPE_CLASSES.small]: SmallBasicButton,
  }[buttonType])

export type ButtonProps = {
  buttonType?: BUTTON_TYPE_CLASSES
} & ButtonHTMLAttributes<HTMLButtonElement>

const MyButton: FC<ButtonProps> = ({ children, buttonType,
  ...otherProps }) => {
  const CustomButton = getButton(buttonType)
  return <CustomButton {...otherProps}>
  {children}</CustomButton>
}
export default MyButton
```

The preceding `MyButton` component is typed in such a way that it accepts only the `button` type and other built-in HTML button attributes as props. If you pass any other button prop that doesn't belong to the button element, there will be a compile-time error due to `TypeScript` usage. The usage of the previously customized button appears on several pages of our application.

Implementing business-specific UI components

Similar to a button component, you can create a product box component. The product component should display the product image, name, brand, and price details in a particular style layout. Let's apply all the required styles for each field inside the `product.styles.tsx` file.

The first code block contains the styled-components import and the type declaration for the image background prop:

```
import styled from "styled-components"

type ImageBackgroundProps = {
  $hasWhiteBackgroundImage: boolean
}
```

The following code block has a `ProductContainer` styled component, which is used to wrap the product image and other product details:

```
export const ProductContainer = styled.div<ImageBackgroundProps>`
  display: flex;
  flex-direction: column;
  background-color: #f1f1f1;
  padding: 1rem;
  border-radius: 0.125rem;

  img {
    width: 7rem;
    height: 5rem;
    object-fit: fill;
    background-color: #f1f1f1;
    transition: 0.5s all ease-in-out;
    mix-blend-mode: ${(props) =>
      props.$hasWhiteBackgroundImage ? "multiply" :
        "normal"};

    &:hover {
      transform: scale(1.1);
    }
```

```
  }

  &:hover {
    img {
      opacity: 0.8;
    }

    button {
      opacity: 0.85;
      display: flex;
    }
  }
}
`
```

The following code block contains a `Footer` styled-component, which is used to style and wrap around the product fields:

```
export const Footer = styled.div`
  width: 100%;
  display: flex;
  flex-direction: column;
  justify-content: space-between;
  font-size: 1rem;
  padding-left: 1rem;
`
```

Finally, we have the styled-component for each product field declared in order to give them a unique look:

```
export const Name = styled.h2`
  font-size: 0.8rem;
  line-height: 1rem;
  font-weight: 600;
  text-transform: capitalize;
  margin-bottom: 1rem;
`

export const Brand = styled.div`
  font-size: 0.6rem;
  line-height: 1rem;
  color: rgb(75 85 99);
  margin-bottom: 0.5rem;
  span {
    font-weight: 600;
    text-transform: capitalize;
  }
```

```
export const Price = styled.span`
  font-size: 0.6rem;
  line-height: 1rem;
  color: rgb(75 85 99);
  margin-bottom: 1rem;
  span {
    font-weight: 600;
    text-transform: capitalize;
    color: rgb(85, 118, 209);
  }
`
```

In the preceding styled-component, each product field has its own style. For example, the name of the product should be in a bigger font size, and the price should be in a different font color to highlight the important data while showcasing the products.

The styled-components of the previously completed `product.styles.tsx` file will be used in the markup, as shown in the following `product.tsx` file. The component code is quite long, so let's break it down into smaller code chunks.

First, define the imports of our page, the product's prop type, and the utility function to verify the non-white background images:

```
import { FC } from "react"
import { useDispatch } from "react-redux"
import { useAppSelector } from "@/app/store/hooks"
import { selectCurrentUser } from
  "@/app/store/user/user.selector"
import MyButton, { BUTTON_TYPE_CLASSES } from
  "@/components/button/button"
import { Product } from "@/app/store/product/product.types"
import { addProductToCart } from
  "@/app/store/cart/cart.slice"
import { BRAND_NAMES } from "@/constants"
import { ProductContainer, Footer, Name, Brand, Price }
  from "./product.styles"

type ProductProps = {
  product: Product
}

const hasWhiteBackground = (brand: string) =>
  BRAND_NAMES.includes(brand)
```

Now, let's add the `ProductItem` component, which accepts `product` as a prop without having any markup code. The component declares `currentUser` and `addCartProduct` to dispatch the product to the cart:

```
const ProductItem: FC<ProductProps> = ({ product }) => {
  const currentUser = useAppSelector(selectCurrentUser)
  const { name, price, productImageUrl, brand } = product
  const dispatch = useDispatch()
  const addCartProduct = () => dispatch
    (addProductToCart(product))

  return (
   //Markup goes here
     )
 }
export default ProductItem
```

Finally, the rendered product markup is added, as follows:

```
<ProductContainer $hasWhiteBackgroundImage=
  {hasWhiteBackground(brand)}>
  <img src={productImageUrl} alt={`${name}`} />
  <Footer>
    <Name>{name}</Name>
    <Brand>
      Brand: <span>{brand}</span>
    </Brand>
    <Price>
      Price:{" "}
      <span>
        ${price}
      </span>
    </Price>
    {currentUser && (
      <MyButton
        buttonType={BUTTON_TYPE_CLASSES.small}
        onClick={addCartProduct} >
        Add to cart
      </MyButton>
    )}
  </Footer>
</ProductContainer>
```

The preceding `ProductItem` component hides the button to add a product to the cart if the application is not authenticated by the user.

Similarly, you can create other UI components to reuse them in the required pages. Now, let's build the application pages based on all these reusable UI components.

Implementing application pages using UI components

Each web page in a React application is composed of UI components. Our application requires product landing, add product to cart, sign-up, and sign-in pages. These pages should be created under the `features` folder as per the scaffolding structure. The product's landing page is created by iterating the `Product` component with a list of products. The following code is for the `products.tsx` file.

This file code is quite long, so let's break it down into smaller code blocks. This first code block has imports related to React Hooks, components, selectors, and styled-components, as follows:

```
import { useState, useEffect, Fragment } from "react"
import { useParams } from "react-router-dom"
import { useAppSelector } from "@/app/store/hooks"
import ProductItem from "@/components/product/product"
import MySpinner from "@/components/spinner/spinner"
import { insertProductsData } from
  "@/backend/firebase/api/db-utils"
import { Product } from "@/app/store/product/product.types"
import {
  selectProductsMap,
  selectCategory,
  selectProductsIsLoading,
} from "@/app/store/product/product.selector"
import { Categories } from "@/components/
  categories/categories"
import {
  ProductsContainer,
  Title,
  LayoutContainer,
  LoaderContainer,
} from "./products.styles"

const Products = () => {
    // The component code goes here
}
export default Products
```

The following code block is updated with the components code, which has product information (i.e., `productsMap` and `category`) retrieved from the store using selectors. It also includes the `useEffect` Hook to set the latest products when there is a change in the category and product data:

```
const Products = () => {
  const productsMap = useAppSelector(selectProductsMap)
  const category = useAppSelector(selectCategory)
  const isLoading = useAppSelector(selectProductsIsLoading)
  const [products, setProducts] = useState
    (productsMap[category])

  useEffect(() => {
    setProducts(productsMap[category])
  }, [category, productsMap])

  return (
    // Markup goes here
  )
}


export default Products
```

Finally, the rendered markup for our products page looks like this:

```
<Fragment>
  <LayoutContainer>
    <Categories></Categories>
    <ProductsContainer>
      {isLoading ? (
        <LoaderContainer>
          <MySpinner />
        </LoaderContainer>
      ) : (
        products &&
        products.map((product: Product) => (
          <ProductItem key={product.id} product=
            {product} />
        ))
      )}
    </ProductsContainer>
  </LayoutContainer>
</Fragment>
```

In the preceding code, the `Products` screen displays a page loader until the data is retrieved. Once the data is ready, a list of products appears in the grid format.

Conversely, the sign-in page can be created using input and button UI components to authenticate the Firebase backend. It follows the sign-in process through either regular email or the Google sign-in mechanism. The sign-in page to authenticate the user appears as follows:

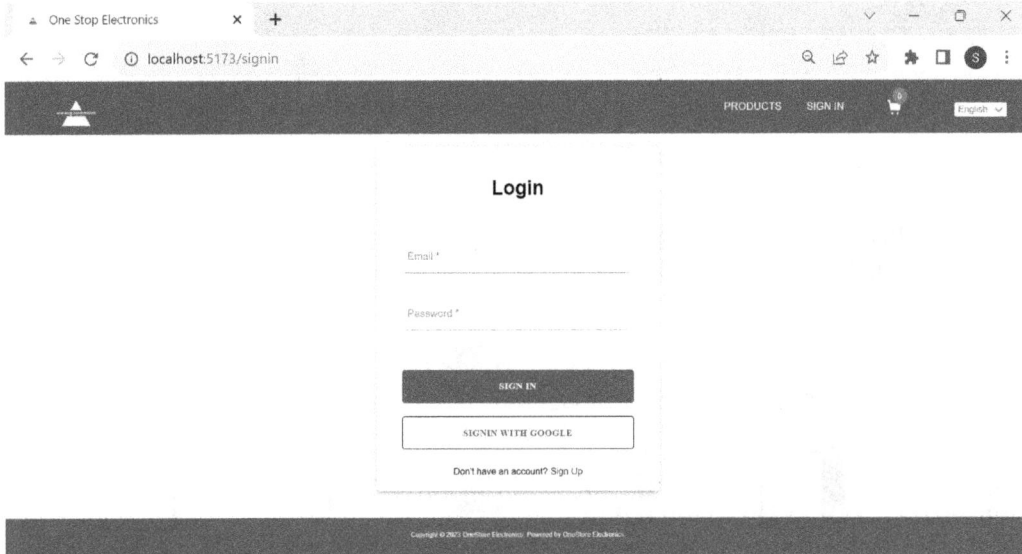

Figure 11.2: The sign-in page

Authentication through the sign-in page is helpful for adding products to the cart. It also provides a link at the bottom for sign-up if there are new users. In a similar fashion, you can implement sign-up and cart pages.

> **Note**
>
> It is still possible to see the available products irrespective of whether a user signs in to the application.

Now, we have reached a position with all the required UI components and pages ready to use. As a last step, the application layout can be designed with the `Header` and `Footer` UI components, along with the previously implemented pages mapped for each route, inside the following `App.tsx` file:

```
function App() {
    return(
      <Fragment>
        <Header></Header>
        <div className="app-content">
```

```
        <Routes>
          <Route path="/" element={<Products></Products>} />
          <Route path="/signin" element={<SignIn />} />
          <Route path="/signup" element={<SignUp />} />
          <Route path="/cart" element={<CartProducts />} />
        </Routes>
      </div>
    <Footer></Footer>
    </Fragment>
  )
}
```

In the preceding code, the routes are configured for each page. The products page is configured as a default route. That means that this page will be displayed immediately after running the npm run dev command in the project root folder.

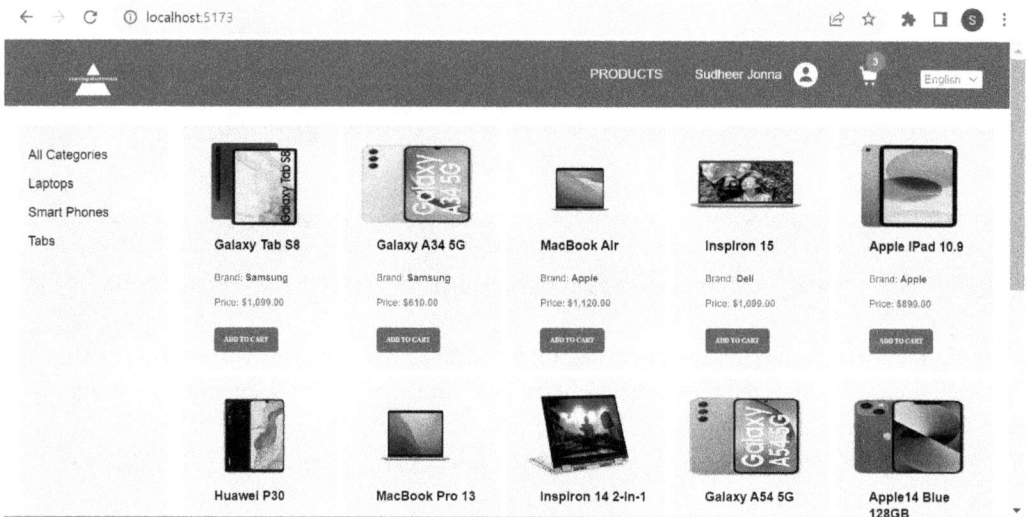

Figure 11.3: The product showcase

Upon adding each product to the cart, the count of cart products will appear on the cart icon. If a user doesn't log in to the application, the add to cart button will be hidden. Moreover, you can filter the product list based on the selected category, as an additional feature.

Even though we have completed all the pages, the text messages are hardcoded in the English language. This means that it will be difficult for non-English readers to read the messages. In the following section, the application will be enhanced with internationalization support to increase our user base across the globe.

Supporting internationalization

If you want to launch your current services in the international market, your web application should support internationalization to meet the needs of global users. In *Chapter 4*, we covered internationalization through the `FormatJS` library.

This project mainly uses the same `FormatJS` library to translate the text messages and support the formatted currency amounts. The entire process of extending the application with internationalization involves just a few instructions.

First, create all the translations inside the `i18n->translations` folder in the form of JSON files. These translations will be loaded based on the respective locales defined inside the `i18n->locale. ts` file:

```
import ENGLISH from "./translations/en-US.json"
import FRENCH from "./translations/fr-FR.json"
import GERMAN from "./translations/de-DE.json"

export const LOCALES = {
  "en-US": ENGLISH,
  "fr-FR": FRENCH,
  "de-DE": GERMAN
}
```

Then, you need to configure `IntlProvider` at the root of the application. This provider loads specific locale messages, as mapped in the previous step, using the `locale` value:

```
import { IntlProvider } from "react-intl"
import { LOCALES } from "@/i18n/locale"
import { DEFAULT_LOCALE } from "@/constants"
import { useAppSelector } from "./app/store/hooks"
import { selectCurrentLocale } from
  "@/app/store/user/user.selector"

function App() {
  const userLanguage = useAppSelector(selectCurrentLocale)
  return (
    <IntlProvider
      messages={LOCALES[userLanguage]}
```

```
       locale={userLanguage}
       defaultLocale={DEFAULT_LOCALE}
  >
     // Main layout goes here
   </IntlProvider>
 )
}
```

In the preceding code, the current locale value is dynamic, and its value gets updated based on the locale dropdown that appears in the header section of the UI.

Now, you can start localizing the text messages and formatting the currency number using the FormattedMessage and FormattedNumber components, respectively, from react-intl, as shown here:

```
import { FormattedMessage, FormattedNumber } from
  "react-intl"

const CartProducts = () => {
   return(
     <CartContainer>
      // UI markup goes here
         <FormattedMessage id="cart.total" />:
           <FormattedNumber
             value={cartProductsTotalCost}
             style="currency"
             currency="USD"
           ></FormattedNumber>
      // UI markup goes here
     </CartContainer>
   )
}
```

The preceding translation related to currency amounts not only includes the currency symbols but also adds comma separators. For instance, the following add to cart screen displays a list of added products with the page text in the German language and formatted currency amounts.

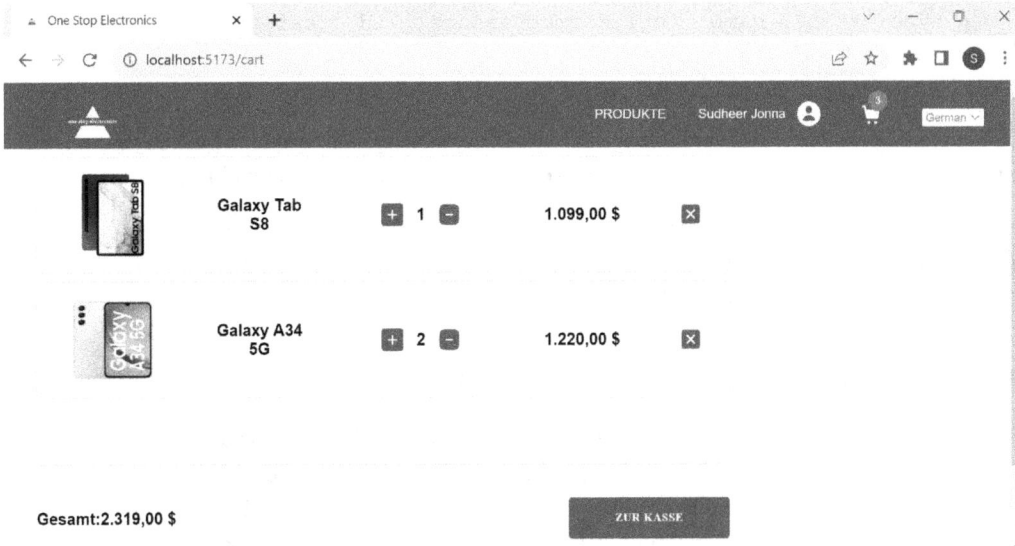

Figure 11.4: Products added to the cart

As you can see, the comma and decimal separators and the currency symbol position are modified based on the selected language. The product quantity and the amount values and their formats will be updated upon clicking the increment, decrement, and clear buttons on the page.

How do you achieve internationalization through an imperative API?

It is not always possible to use `react-intl` components such as `FormattedMessage`, `FormattedNumber`, or `FormattedDate` to format text messages, numbers, or dates – that is, you cannot use built-in components to format text messages inside text attributes such as `title` and `aria-label`, outside the markup area of React components and non-React ecosystems such as Node.js, a Redux store, and the testing section.

After you declare `IntlProvider`, you can get access to the `intl` object (with a type of `IntlShape`) by calling the `useIntl()` hook inside the React function component. For example, this Hook is used to support internationalization to prepare a category list outside the markup section:

```
import { useIntl } from "react-intl"

const categories: Category[] = [
  { type: "all", name: intl.formatMessage({ id: "categories.all" }) },
  { type: "laptop", name: intl.formatMessage({ id: "categories.
    laptops" }) },
  { type: "phone", name: intl.formatMessage({ id: "categories.phones"
    }) },
```

```
          { type: "tab", name: intl.formatMessage({ id: "categories.tabs" })
     },
     ];
```

If you want to support internationalization outside a React component, you need to use the `createIntl` API method by passing `locale` and `messages` properties in the form of an object.

Currently, we have reached a stage with the completion of a full-fledged backend and frontend implementation. In the following section, we will see how to write unit tests to ensure that functionality works as per the business requirements.

Implementing testing using the Vitest framework

Jest is quite a popular testing framework, with a full pack of testing features and an easy-to-use API, which makes it a standard testing framework in the web ecosystem. This project is based on Vite frontend tooling, and it is also possible to integrate Jest in Vite setups. However, this leads to a workspace where you have to configure and maintain two different pipelines, which is hard for developers. So, we will use **Vitest** for this project, which is a blazing-fast unit testing framework based on Jest and Vite tooling. This framework provides similar functionality and syntax to the Jest framework, using the existing configuration or plugins of Vite tooling.

In this project, we will write unit tests for all the actions that exist under `cart.slice.ts`. First, let's create the test suite with an initial cart state:

```
describe("Cart Reducer", () => {
  let initialState: CartState = {
    cartProducts: [
      {
        id: 1,
        productImageUrl: "someurl.com",
        name: "Inspiron 15",
        price: 1200,
        quantity: 2,
      },
    ],
  }
});
```

In the preceding code, the initial state is available, with one cart product having a quantity of 2.

Then, we will write a test case to verify the functionality of increasing quantity within the cart, as follows:

```
it("Should handle adding or incrementing products
   quantity inside cart", () => {
```

```
      const productToAdd: Cart = {
        id: 1,
        productImageUrl: "someurl.com",
        name: "Inspiron 15",
        price: 1200,
        quantity: 1,
      }
      const { cartProducts } = cartReducer(
        initialState,
        addProductToCart(productToAdd),
      )
      expect(cartProducts.length).toEqual(1)
      expect(cartProducts[0].quantity).toEqual(3)
})
```

The preceding test case verifies that the quantity of products increased to 3 and the number of distinct products in the cart remains the same.

Similarly, the test case to decrease the product quantity in the cart is as follows:

```
it("Should handle removing or decreasing products
   quantity inside cart", () => {
      const productToRemove: Cart = {
        id: 1,
        productImageUrl: "someurl.com",
        name: "Inspiron 15",
        price: 1200,
        quantity: 1,
      }
      const state = cartReducer(
        initialState,
        removeProductFromCart(productToRemove),
      )
      expect(state.cartProducts.length).toEqual(1)
      expect(state.cartProducts[0].quantity).toEqual(1)
})
```

The preceding test case checks the quantity of products after decreasing the quantity in the cart. The quantity of products becomes 1 after decreasing or removing one item from the cart, which has an initial state quantity value of 2.

Similarly, we have test cases to clear and reset the cart actions. Once you run the npm run test command, you can see a summary of all the passed tests and failed tests for any incorrect code.

Now, our application is ready with full-fledged development code and covered with unit test cases to detect early flaws in the code. Let's publish this code on GitHub as a Git repository to support version control and to make our app work smoothly online.

Creating a Git repository with README documentation

Currently, the project is ready and able to run the application in a local system successfully. To enhance the project further, a hosting platform such as GitHub is required, as it provides storage and version control, deploys the project, and offers collaboration between various team members seamlessly. Let's apply the following Git commands to push our local code to the GitHub platform:

```
git init
git add .
git commit -m "Add one stop electronics"
git branch -M main
git remote add origin https://github.com/yourname/one-stop-
electronics.git
git push -u origin main
```

Now, our project is on GitHub, which enables us to easily deploy the application on Netlify.

The final version of the One Stop Electronics GitHub project with README.md instructions is available in the Git repository for quick reference: https://github.com/PacktPublishing/React-Interview-Guide/tree/main/Chapter11/one-stop-electronics.

The following section will discuss the deployment process to make the project accessible for the public.

Deploying the application for public access

There are several options to deploy an app, such as Netlify, Vercel, GitHub Pages, and Firebase Hosting. We will use Netlify for the deployment by signing in through a GitHub account on the Netlify website. On the dashboard, you will have the option to select the repository and configure the site through settings. It is also possible to change a random site name to a new name. Since an environment variable file (e.g., .env.local) is not available in the root of the GitHub repository, you need to import the environment variable file into the dashboard before clicking the **Deploy site** button.

By following all these steps, the application is now available online for everyone to access around the world. You can quickly go through all the screens, which are available at the Netlify domain for your reference: https://onestop-electronics.netlify.app/.

Through continuous deployment, Netlify automatically updates your site when the code is updated on the GitHub repository.

Summary

We have reached the end of the chapter and applied all the programming concepts learned in the previous chapters to build a robust full stack React application. At the beginning of the chapter, we had a quick introduction to scaffolding a React project using the standard templates of the Redux library. Later, we briefly covered Firebase services and provided step-by-step instructions to set up and configure authentication mechanisms, using the Firebase console. Then, we provided a detailed implementation of Firebase authentication and Cloud Firestore database operations for our One Stop Electronics application.

After the backend was ready to use, we moved on to building the UI layer by writing a few React UI components, building the application layout and pages for sign-in, sign-up, the product showcase, and cart items. This section was followed by implementing a business layer as per the RTK guidelines. Then, the project was further enhanced through internationalization support and writing unit tests. As the application reached the completion stage, the final step was creating a Git repository and making the application accessible online, with a deployment process.

After learning all these major milestones of application development, you should now be confident enough to showcase your skills in coding challenges and answer interview questions, especially armed with your practical working experience. In the following chapter, we will build another React app based on different skill sets, such as Next.js, GraphQL, SWR, and Vercel, for deployment. This will help you to enhance your knowledge of building various types of projects, with a different set of techniques and concepts that were not covered in this chapter.

12

Building an App Based on the Next.js Toolkit, Authentication, SWR, GraphQL, and Deployment

Throughout our journey in this book, we have learned new skills, methodologies, and better ways of thinking. This chapter is the culmination of our efforts, so let's move forward, as it is now time for us to put everything we have learned together as we seek to develop an exciting application that features an up-to-date modern tech stack. This chapter will allow us to progress from concept to the deployment of a Next.js application that has implementations for authentication, **stale-while-revalidate (SWR)**, GraphQL, and deployment.

We will start with a quick introduction to REST APIs, which will be a fantastic refresher if you are already familiar with them, or a great introduction if it's your first time learning about this essential methodology. Then, we shall move on to figuring out how best to plan the architecture for an application, where we will go into how authentication works. This will be followed up by how effective SWR is and why it's worth using, as it's a very useful aspect that can enhance the performance of our applications. Next, we will learn about GraphQL and how it compares with traditional REST APIs. Then, we will end with deployment, which is where we finally publish our local development build online so that the whole world can use it.

In the sections that follow, we will talk about the ideas behind business logic and how the code we write has significant importance not just for the way our application runs but also for how it can reflect positively or negatively on our team and company depending on how well it is written. Moving on, we will go through creating the presentation layer, which is essential to the user interface and user experience. Testing is going to be the next major feature that we touch on, as it's highly recommended that production-ready applications have a robust testing suite set up to guarantee that it is stable and in a state that is ready to be published as a **minimum viable product (MVP)**.

With those features completed, we will finish off by learning how to deploy our application so that the public can access it. In the last sections, we will create a Git repository with a README file.

In terms of topics, the following will be the themes that we will be focusing on in the upcoming sections:

- Quick introduction to REST APIs

- Planning the application architecture including authentication, SWR, GraphQL, and deployment

- Building the business logic

- Building the presentation layer

- Implementing testing

- Creating a Git repository with README documentation

- Deploying the application for public access

Technical requirements

On your machine, confirm that `https://nodejs.org/en` is up to date and that the JavaScript Node package for Next.js is set up and operational. You can use whatever package manager you want, be it `npm`, `yarn`, or `pnpm`. Just make sure that you use the appropriate commands when doing the installation. For simplicity's sake, we will be using `npm`. Work on your project with your preferred **integrated development environment (IDE)** and **command-line interface (CLI)** tool. You will also need to have an account on `https://vercel.com/` for the deployment section when we build our app. For the authentication section, we will use GitHub and Google, so in the unlikely event that you don't have accounts for both of these services already, create one now. GitHub is also required for the version control section, so it's essential for you to have an account.

The package for Next.js can be found at `https://nextjs.org/`.

The project and code base can be found online at `https://github.com/PacktPublishing/React-Interview-Guide/tree/main/Chapter12/coffee-restaurant`.

To begin, let's first talk about REST APIs to understand their core concepts.

Quick introduction to REST APIs

A **Representational State Transfer Application Programming Interface** (**REST API**) is a particular technology that has established itself as the cornerstone of contemporary web development. By using REST APIs within JavaScript and React applications, developers can develop robust and dynamic web apps that can communicate with other platforms and information sources. Developers can transfer data between the server and client using the REST API without worrying about the architecture of the underlying apps. In simple terms, the REST API standardizes communication protocols, which simplifies development. With the correct tools and skills, REST APIs can totally alter the way web developers work.

We can easily understand the core methodology and concept of a REST API by using a restaurant as an example. This is considered to be a popular way to describe how the process works. For example, let's say that a user has a restaurant application. Basically, the user requests some data for their menu page, which is equivalent to a user in a restaurant asking a waiter for some food. In this case, the waiter who is taking the food request is the same as the API taking the request to display the menu. The waiter then goes to the kitchen to get the food, which is equivalent to the API getting the application.

So, let's imagine that the application has a list of food on the menu. A customer takes a look at the menu and then gives their order to a waiter. The waiter goes to the kitchen with the customer's order and waits for the meal to be completed. When the food is ready, the kitchen staff give the food to the waiter, who then responds by returning to the customer with the food they requested. In a real-world situation, the customer now has a meal to eat. If we imagine this as a website, then a page has now loaded with a table that shows food from the menu inside it. This information was fetched via the API to the backend server application, which returned it.

This example is perfectly illustrated in *Figure 12.1*.

USER   **API**   **APPLICATION**

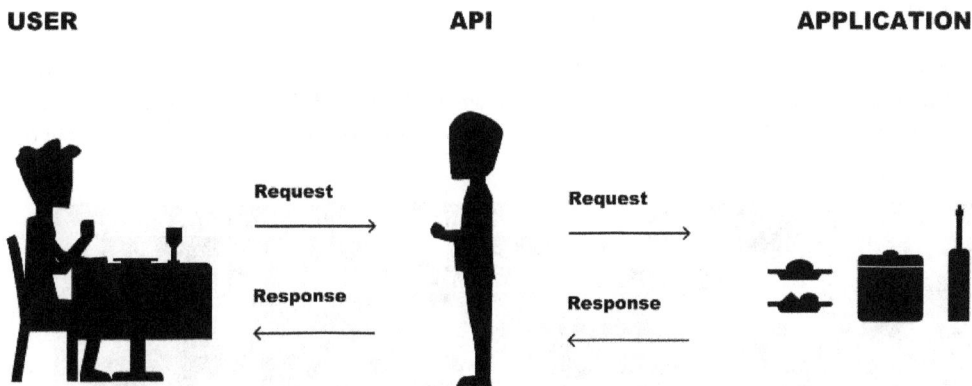

Figure 12.1: Describing a REST API

Let's now learn how we can manage our APIs using various tools. This is another important skill for developers to have.

What tools can we use for testing our APIs?

When doing API development, it is normal for a developer to use an API tool for managing, testing, and interacting with the API. Some of the most popular API development tools for JavaScript development can be seen in *Table 12.1*:

API tool	Website address
Postman	`https://www.postman.com/`
Insomnia	`https://insomnia.rest/`
Swagger	`https://swagger.io/`
Thunder Client	`https://www.thunderclient.com/`

Table 12.1: Popular JavaScript REST API tools

With these tools, we can thoroughly test our REST APIs and it is even possible to use this as a basis for creating the documentation. There is something that we need to be aware of though when building APIs, and that is **cross-origin resource sharing** (**CORS**). CORS is basically an application integration method. CORS specifies a method for client web applications loaded in a single domain to communicate with assets located in another domain. So, essentially, if we do not specify or allow CORS access in our APIs, then we will be blocked from accessing them unless they are on the same server.

For example, we could have an API hosted online on a website, and let's say that we have a React application that is online on a different server somewhere. If our API is not set up for CORS, then our React application can't connect to it to retrieve any data, and we will just get a CORS error in our browser console, as shown in the following figure:

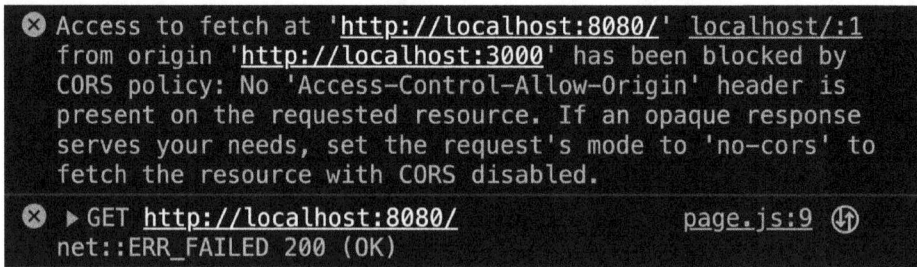

```
⊗ Access to fetch at 'http://localhost:8080/' localhost/:1
  from origin 'http://localhost:3000' has been blocked by
  CORS policy: No 'Access-Control-Allow-Origin' header is
  present on the requested resource. If an opaque response
  serves your needs, set the request's mode to 'no-cors' to
  fetch the resource with CORS disabled.
⊗ ▶ GET http://localhost:8080/                    page.js:9 ⊕
  net::ERR_FAILED 200 (OK)
```

Figure 12.2: A CORS error web browser console message

It's time to move on to learning about REST APIs in more detail now that we have a better understanding of how they are set up. So, let's see what features are on offer.

Which features are available in a REST API?

A REST API is a strong tool that gives developers access to a wide range of functions. The REST API's excellent security system is one of its most important characteristics. It guarantees that any malicious attacks won't be made on the data given over the API. Additionally, the REST API's capacity to scale is another crucial aspect, which implies that it is a great option for apps with heavy traffic because it can manage a lot of queries. Another remarkable quality of REST APIs is their flexibility, which lets developers use any architecture or technology of their choosing. REST APIs are an excellent tool for developers who wish to create dependable and durable apps thanks to all these features taken together.

A REST API is capable of requesting and responding to requests, but what does that mean? Let's find out.

What is the difference between requests and responses when making requests to a REST API?

Understanding how HTTP requests and responses operate is essential if you want to create a web application that connects to a REST API. Data is sent from a client to a server using HTTP requests, and it is sent back from the server to the client using HTTP responses. REST APIs interact between clients and servers using **GET**, **POST**, **PUT**, and **DELETE** standard HTTP protocols. We can build web apps that easily interface with REST APIs by designing them with greater effectiveness and efficiency by knowing how these requests and responses operate. There are other HTTP protocols available, but the standard ones are the most common. Now, let's understand the difference between these HTTP protocols.

What is a GET request?

A GET request is a method that is used to obtain data from the server. It is a read-only procedure so there is no negative impact on the server. GET requests do not cause the data or the server to change its state.

What is a POST request?

A POST request is used to transmit information to the server in order to establish new data. It is not immutable, which means that submitting the same POST request many times might get different results. POST requests generally return the URL or an instance of the newly created resource.

What is a PUT request?

A PUT request can be utilized to add new information to preexisting server data. It is capable of change, so you can send the same PUT request to get different results. Based on the way it's done, if the data does not exist, the server could create it.

What is a DELETE request?

The DELETE request is used to remove data from the server. It is also immutable, which means that sending the same DELETE request multiple times has the same outcome. Following the deletion of data, the server normally provides a status indicating whether the action was successful or unsuccessful.

We can see an example REST API application in this code example here:

```
const express = require('express');
const cors = require('cors');
const path = require('path');
require('dotenv').config();
const app = express();
app.use(cors());
app.use(express.urlencoded({ extended: false }));
app.use(express.json());
app.use('/static', express.static(path.join
   (__dirname + '/public')));
app.get('/api', (req, res) => {
res.json({ msg: 'API Route' });
});
app.post('/post/:data', (req, res) => {
const data = req.params.data;
console.log(data);
res.json({ msg: `Data logged ${data}` });
});
const port = process.env.PORT || 8080;
app.listen(port, () =>
console.log(`Server running on port ${port},
   http://localhost:${port}`)
);
```

In this example, we have a `static` route, which is used for serving files such as images, CSS, and JavaScript, for example, so long as they are in a public folder in our app. We have a `GET` route for the API, which just returns a JSON object. Lastly, we have a `POST` route, which logs to the console and returns a JSON object of whatever text a user sends as a `POST` request, as in this example: `http://localhost:8080/post/helloworld`.

HTTP protocols are just one aspect of a REST API. It is also important to have good authentication set up. Continue reading to see why this is the case.

Why is authentication important when using a REST API?

Using a REST API requires authentication to ensure that private data is kept secure. Authentication requires confirming the user's identity before giving access to API capabilities. This helps to avoid unauthorized data access or usage, which might endanger users. When communicating with an API, you'll probably utilize a variety of authentication mechanisms, including token-based authentication and OAuth. These methods guarantee that only authorized users have access to the API and are allowed to send requests or get data. Understanding authentication while interacting with a REST API can potentially assist us in building a more secure and efficient solution. It is possible to understand authentication flow if we see it in a diagram such as this one:

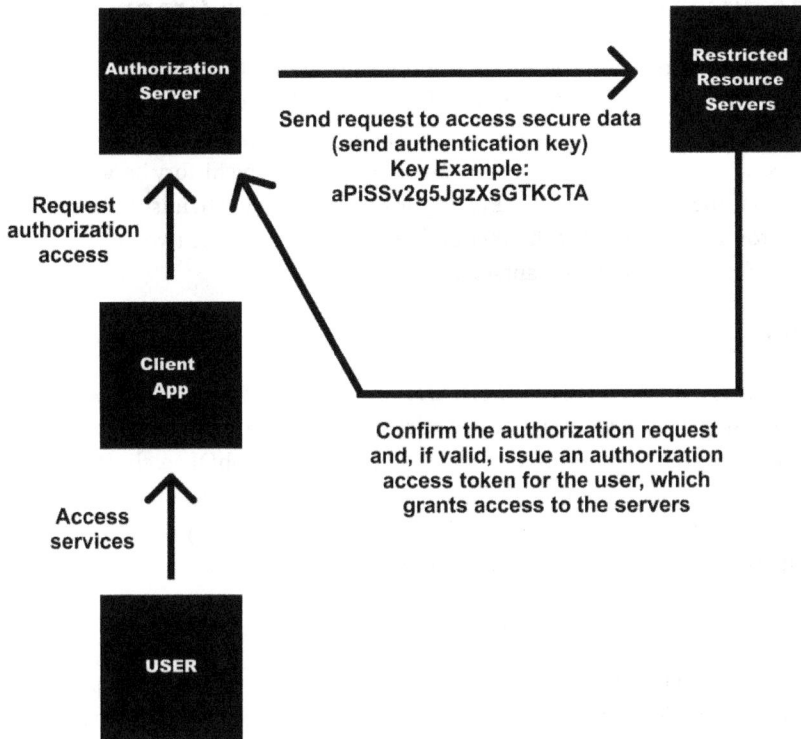

Figure 12.3: The REST API authentication flow

Another aspect worth discussing is error handling because it's crucial that we check for mistakes, which is very important when authentication and user details are involved. Let's discover how having effective error handling can make our application more trustworthy.

How can we use error handling when integrating with a REST API?

Connecting with a REST API is occasionally difficult, especially when confronted with errors. However, having a robust error-handling plan in place could spare us time and hassle in the long term. One useful strategy is to specify error codes and messages that our application can recognize and respond to. Furthermore, installing automatic retries and monitoring systems can assist in identifying and addressing issues more rapidly. Another important topic is dealing with data validation mistakes, as API inputs must be thoroughly scrutinized before being utilized in our application. We can ensure easy integration with a REST API and deliver an improved user experience for our clients by being proactive and comprehensive in our approach to error management.

The last topic we'll cover in this section is GraphQL. So, let's now see how GraphQL compares with a traditional REST API.

What is the difference between a REST API and GraphQL?

REST and GraphQL are two techniques for the creation and operation of web service APIs; however, they differ in numerous ways. GraphQL tends to be more flexible because you can request only the data you need and not all at once as with REST APIs. This is great because it means fewer data transfer requests on the network. Another area GraphQL excels in is versioning history because it is not reliant on versions, which is the case with REST APIs, requiring more manual hands-on work. Despite this, they both have pros and cons over each other and, when comparing the two, we can see how they offer us different advantages and disadvantages.

Fetching data

The end user often uses a REST API to access resources through preset endpoints, where each endpoint is associated with a single resource or a group of related resources. The client makes HTTP requests to these endpoints in order to get or modify data. When using GraphQL, a client sends queries or mutations to a single endpoint, indicating the data it requires or the modifications it wants to make. In comparison to REST API, this allows the client to only retrieve the data they actually need, eliminating the need for requesting more data than required or too little data.

Caching data

To improve efficiency and lessen server load, REST APIs can make use of ETags and cache-control headers, two common HTTP caching methods. In contrast, because of GraphQL's flexible query form, caching is more difficult. The usage of unique caching techniques offered by GraphQL client-side libraries such as Apollo Client or application-level caching is frequently required by clients.

Documentation

Within REST APIs, documentation is frequently given separately, and it is the responsibility of the programmers to keep it up to date. If not kept up with, this can result in contradictions and inaccurate data. On the other hand, since GraphQL includes built-in introspection, users can dynamically learn about the different kinds and features of the API. Engineers can explore and comprehend the API more easily, frequently using tools such as GraphiQL.

To end this section, we are going to take a look at some code examples of fetching some data using REST and GraphQL so it becomes clear how the two methods differ from each other.

How do we fetch data using REST APIs and GraphQL?

We will take a look at code examples for fetching data using REST and GraphQL, starting with REST APIs. In these examples, we will use authors and posts.

How do we fetch data using REST APIs?

The first step is to get a post that has an ID of 1:

```
GET /posts/1
```

This is what a potential sample response might look like:

```
{
  "id": 1,
  "title": "Hello World",
  "content": "Welcome to my first blog.",
  "authorId": 64
}
```

When using a REST API for data retrieval, requests return all of the information in the data object. It is not possible to request, let's say, only the id and title information. We would have to write business logic in JavaScript to filter the object so that we only get the data we want to use in our application.

So, if we wanted to get details for the author, then we would have to send a second GET request:

```
GET /authors/64
```

Now, we'll have the author's info:

```
{
  "id": 64,
  "name": "Jack Thomas",
  "email": "jackthomas@gmail.com"
}
```

So, now that we have understood the basic concept of fetching data using REST APIs, let's see how we can do the same but this time using GraphQL.

How do we fetch data using GraphQL?

When we use GraphQL, we first need to create a schema for our API, as shown in the following example:

```
type Post {
  id: ID!
  title: String!
  content: String!
  author: Author!
}
type Author {
  id: ID!
```

```
    name: String!
    email: String!
}
type Query {
  post(id: ID!): Post
}
```

Then, we need to write a GraphQL query to get the author and a post:

```
query {
  post(id: 1) {
    id
    title
    content
    author {
      id
      name
      email
    }
  }
}
```

The response will look something like this:

```
{
  "data": {
    "post": {
      "id": "1",
      "title": "Hello World",
      "content": " Welcome to my first blog.",
      "author": {
        "id": "64",
        "name": " Jack Thomas",
        "email": " jackthomas@gmail.com"
      }
    }
  }
}
```

GraphQL allows us to retrieve the necessary data with a single request by defining the fields we desire.

Ultimately, deciding between a REST API and GraphQL boils down to our specific use cases and requirements. Both have distinct characteristics and abilities that can help us optimize the development process while creating web or mobile apps. However, as with many technological issues, it is critical for us to consider all of our alternatives before settling on the best method. We can safely use a REST API or GraphQL within our React applications to obtain the desired outcome if we can grasp their common qualities and special benefits. Whatever technology we employ, the objective should always be to provide safe, scalable, and effective solutions for those who use the app.

Now that we have completed this introductory refresher section, let's take the next step and create the foundation for building our app as we learn about the planning required for the architecture.

Planning the application architecture including authentication, SWR, GraphQL, and deployment

In today's fiercely competitive marketplace, it is imperative to possess the know-how of designing, developing, and deploying an application architecture that is efficient, secure, and meets user needs. However, with the advent of evolving technologies such as Next.js, authentication methods transitioning from traditional OAuth 2.0 to SWR, and GraphQL gaining popularity, planning our application architecture might seem like a daunting task.

In this section, we will get valuable insights to assist us in organizing our application for success, from selecting the appropriate technologies to incorporating user experience design elements. By the end of this section, we will have a roadmap to guide us through building our next project, with clear steps to follow through to completion.

Our next topic focuses on serverless frameworks. So, let's read on and see why they are a brilliant choice for building modern apps.

Why are serverless frameworks such as Next.js a brilliant choice for building modern applications?

New frameworks and architectures are developed as digital technology advances to better the effectiveness of building web applications. Next.js is one of these architectures because of its speed and flexibility. Next.js apps have a distinct design that separates server-side code from client-side logic, resulting in faster processing times and better performance. This architecture employs **server-side rendering (SSR)** to generate HTML pages on the server, significantly reducing client-side load. Next.js apps also use a hybrid approach that utilizes dynamic and static rendering for increased efficiency and faster load times. Because of these features, Next.js is an excellent choice for programmers looking to create modern, powerful web applications.

The next topic that we will cover is authentication. So, let's take a look at how certain security measures can enhance our defenses.

What authentication is available in Next.js applications?

The security of online apps is a high priority as they become more essential to our daily lives. A key component of protecting these applications is authentication, which is the method of confirming a user's identity. Providing authentication in a Next.js application can be done using a variety of techniques, including the following:

- Auth.js
- **JSON Web Tokens (JWTs)**
- Auth0
- OAuth2
- Login and password authentication

By utilizing these technologies, engineers can defend their applications against online threats such as hackers' attempts to steal user data. This high degree of verification guarantees users a safe and reliable environment while also safeguarding their private data. A Next.js application must use proper authentication procedures given the growing significance of online privacy.

Speed is a high-priority requirement when building our app infrastructure, but how does SWR make it better? We will find out now in the next section.

How does SWR allow fast data retrieval?

It is not surprising that quick and effective data fetching has elevated to the top of developers' priorities as the world becomes increasingly data-driven. And that's where **stale-while-revalidate**, or **SWR**, comes into play. SWR is a remote data fetching React Hooks library that prioritizes speed, caching, and revalidation. Fetching data is made simple with SWR, since it does away with annoying loading boxes and makes sure the data is continuously current. Additionally, it has a user-friendly API that makes it simple for programmers of any experience level to utilize.

Now, we will take another look at GraphQL to see why it has become the best choice for modern application architecture.

How can GraphQL integration optimize our data fetching?

The need to optimize productivity and simplify operations grows as technology develops. In response, GraphQL integration has become more common. GraphQL significantly boosts the speed and accuracy of data retrieval by enabling optimized data fetching. With GraphQL, queries can be customized to meet particular needs rather than having to get several datasets and sort through them to find the necessary information. The outcome of this is that data can be retrieved more quickly and accurately, which can aid companies in staying current. Because of these advantages, many businesses have adopted GraphQL integration, given its capacity to improve data fetching procedures.

Deployment is where our application goes live online for the public to use and we get to show off our creation to the world. So, let's now learn about this crucial step in the next section.

How do we deploy our Next.js applications online?

Deploying apps on cloud platforms is the conclusion of all of our hard work, and this process can be both challenging and rewarding. The best feature (which makes Next.js a favorite among developers) is that it allows SSR. Our Next.js application will now be accessible at all times and from any location when we deploy it on a cloud infrastructure. Numerous cloud providers are readily accessible on the market, each with distinctive characteristics.

One of the most popular online cloud host providers is **Vercel**, the creators of Next.js, meaning that their platform is the perfect place for deploying our Next.js apps. Other popular serverless host providers include Netlify, AWS, Azure, Render, Firebase, and Supabase. There are countless others out there to choose from. The important thing is to find a platform that is cost-effective and offers many good features and services. The majority of the ones mentioned here offer free services.

Finally, we will end this section by checking out ways to scale and maintain our application once it has been deployed to manage its growth.

What strategies can we use for scaling and maintaining our application architecture as it grows?

It's critical to have a plan developed for expanding as well as sustaining our architecture as the popularity and usage of our application grows. Without proper planning, our application might not be able to cope with the surge in traffic, which could turn off prospective customers. Forecasting and taking into account potential future growth, along with the tools and technology that might assist us in getting there, are necessary for a scalable design. The continuous effectiveness of an app is also greatly dependent on the upkeep of our architecture as it develops. Adding user feedback to enhance the user experience, testing our software for faults and problems, and routinely reviewing and revising the code base are all part of this. Our apps can thrive for a very long time if we put the correct plans in place.

Having an in-depth knowledge of authentication, SWR data fetching strategies, GraphQL integration, and deployment strategies will greatly benefit us as we start to develop the architecture of our Next.js application. With these plans in place, we can start thinking about scaling and managing our application as it grows, which is a vital component of any effective application architecture. The strength of Next.js, combined with these strategies, will result in an excellent user experience and contribute to the efficiency of the development process.

Working on our coffee restaurant project

With the theory out of the way, let's start building our website. The first thing we need to do is set up our project, so let's do that now.

Our technical stack is as follows:

- **Next.js**: React framework
- **styled-components**: CSS styling
- **apollographql**: Data API
- **authjs**: Authentication
- **React Testing Library** and **Jest**: Testing
- **GitHub**: Version control
- **Vercel**: Serverless online web host

We are going to create a restaurant application for this project. There will be five main pages, and two of them will require you to be authenticated to access them. The authentication will be taken care of with Google or GitHub, so you can use either account to sign in.

This is what the final project will look like for our app:

Home   Nutrition   Menu   Profile

Figure 12.4: Next.js final project home page

The project and code base can be found online at `https://github.com/PacktPublishing/React-Interview-Guide/tree/main/Chapter12/coffee-restaurant`

and there is a link on GitHub to a working website, so you can see all of the pages.

Building the business logic

Now, with the theory completed, we are ready to do some practical work as we build our application. It's going to be a fairly simple application; the main aim here is to understand how we connect all of these technologies. The application will be a restaurant website that has some restricted pages that require an authenticated user to access them. These authenticated pages will only show the data from our GraphQL API if the user is logged in; otherwise, they will be presented with a sign-in page.

With that introduction out of the way, let's begin building the business logic.

Create a folder on your computer, such as on the desktop, and then run the following Next.js command to create a Next.js project:

```
npx create-next-app my-app-restaurant
```

You can use the following settings:

- Would you like to use TypeScript with this project? … No/Yes

- Would you like to use ESLint with this project? … No/Yes

- Would you like to use Tailwind CSS with this project? … No/Yes

- Would you like to use `src/` directory with this project? … No/Yes

- Use App Router (recommended)? … No/Yes

- Would you like to customize the default import alias? … No/Yes

Now, we have to install all of the dependencies and packages for our project. So cd into the my-app-restaurant directory and run the following commands to install the packages.

Run the following script to install the regular dependencies:

```
npm i @apollo/client @apollo/server @as-integrations/next @testing-
library/user-event graphql graphql-tag next-auth styled-components@
latest
```

Run the following script to install the development dependencies:

```
npm i --save-dev @testing-library/jest-dom @testing-library/react jest
jest-environment-jsdom
```

> **Note**
>
> If you encounter any errors when trying to install these packages you could try adding the --force command or using sudo if you are on a Mac like this: sudo npm i --save-dev @testing-library/jest-dom @testing-library/react jest jest-environment-jsdom --force

Now, add the following test run script to the `scripts` section in the `package.json` file in the root folder:

```
"test": "jest --watch",
```

Now, run this command inside the root of the `my-app-restaurant` folder. This will create all of the files and folders we will need for this project:

```
mkdir data
touch data/menu.js data/profile.js
touch .env.local jest.config.mjs
cd src/app
mkdir account account/menu account/profile
touch account/menu/page.js  account/profile/page.js
mkdir api api/auth api/auth/"[...nextauth]"
touch api/auth/"[...nextauth]"/route.js
mkdir components graphql lib nutrition queries rewards utils
touch components/GlobalStyles.js components/MainMenu.js components/
Provider.js
touch graphql/route.js
touch lib/registry.js
touch nutrition/page.js nutrition/page.test.js
touch queries/clientQueries.js
touch utils/withApollo.js utils/cors.js
touch not-found.js page.test.js
```

Before we start to work on the main app files, let's sort out the configuration files first.

Configuration files setup

Put this code in the `api/auth/[...nextauth]/route.js` file. We will use this code for setting up our authentication layer, in which GitHub and Google will be used for signing in to the protected routes:

```
import NextAuth from 'next-auth';
import GithubProvider from 'next-auth/providers/github';
import GoogleProvider from 'next-auth/providers/google';

export const handler = NextAuth({
  providers: [
    GithubProvider({
        clientId: process.env.GITHUB_ID,
        clientSecret: process.env.GITHUB_SECRET,
```

```
    }),
    GoogleProvider({
      clientId: process.env.GOOGLE_ID,
      clientSecret: process.env.GOOGLE_SECRET,
    }),
  ],
});


export { handler as GET, handler as POST };
```

Next, put this code in the `lib/registry.js` file. This code is used for configuring `styled-components` to work with Next.js:

```
use client';

import React, { useState } from 'react';
import { useServerInsertedHTML } from 'next/navigation';
import { ServerStyleSheet, StyleSheetManager } from 'styled-components';

export default function StyledComponentsRegistry({ children }) {
  // Only create stylesheet once with lazy initial state
  // x-ref: https://reactjs.org/docs/hooks-reference.html#lazy-initial-state
  const [styledComponentsStyleSheet] = useState(() => new ServerStyleSheet());

  useServerInsertedHTML(() => {
    const styles = styledComponentsStyleSheet.getStyleElement();
    styledComponentsStyleSheet.instance.clearTag();
    return <>{styles}</>;
  });

  if (typeof window !== 'undefined') return <>{children}</>;

  return (
    <StyleSheetManager sheet={styledComponentsStyleSheet.instance}>
      {children}
    </StyleSheetManager>
  );
}
```

Now, add the following code to the `jest.config.mjs` file in the `root` directory. This file can be used for setting up the Jest test runner:

```
import nextJest from 'next/jest.js';

const createJestConfig = nextJest({
  // Provide the path to your Next.js app to load next.config.js and
.env files in your test environment

  dir: './',
});

// Add any custom config to be passed to Jest

/** @type {import('jest').Config} */

const config = {
  // Add more setup options before each test is run

  // setupFilesAfterEnv: ['<rootDir>/jest.setup.js'],

  testEnvironment: 'jest-environment-jsdom',
};

// createJestConfig is exported this way to ensure that next/jest can
load the Next.js config which is async

export default createJestConfig(config);
```

Now, update the `next.config.js` file in the `root` folder with this code, which will enable `styled-components` to work as well as the app directory setup:

```
/** @type {import('next').NextConfig} */
const nextConfig = {
  compiler: {
    styledComponents: true,
  },
};

module.exports = nextConfig;
```

We just have one more step to complete, which is the GitHub and Google authentication setup section. We must create IDs and secrets for our `.env.local` file. The authentication setup can be found at `https://authjs.dev/getting-started/oauth-tutorial`. The tutorial shows you how to do the authentication setup with GitHub. However, the setup is fairly similar for other authentication providers, and you can find the one for Google at `https://developers.google.com/identity/protocols/oauth2`.

Just remember that when we run our app locally, the callback URL will look something like this if we use GitHub as an example: `http://localhost:3000/api/auth/callback/github`.

When we deploy it online, it might look something like this: `https://your-app-url.vercel.app/api/auth/callback/github`.

This is important because our authenticated routes won't work unless we use the right URL. Finally, we just need to add the IDs and secrets to our `.env.local` file. This file also needs a secret to be created for our NEXTAUTH_SECRET key-value pair, which is required for NextAuth.js:

```
NEXTAUTH_SECRET="yournextsecret"
GITHUB_ID="yourgithubid"
GITHUB_SECRET="yourgithubsecret"
GOOGLE_ID="yourgoogleid"
GOOGLE_SECRET="yourgooglesecret"
```

You can create your own secret key, and it can be anything you want; I would suggest making it secure by generating a random string of characters as you would if you were creating a strong password. There are many free tools that can do this for you, or you could just randomly make one yourself, such as this example: `Y@q7LH@6YoBa$Dkz`. It uses both uppercase and lowercase alphanumeric characters and it also has special characters. We all know how to create secure passwords; just use the same thinking when creating your secret key.

Building the app

Let's go for it! There are quite a lot of files because the build phase has many files. But after this section, we will be close to completion! We have a data layer that will act as our database. Basically, there is an array of objects that we will fetch using GraphQL and then display on our frontend.

Use the following code inside the data folder we created. This code will be for the data we show on the **Menu** page, so put it in the `data/menu.js` file:

```
export const menu = [
  {
    id: '1',
    foodType: 'Drinks',
    name: 'Latte',
    description: 'Steamed milk',
  },
  {
    id: '2',
```

```
      foodType: 'Drinks',
      name: 'Cappuccino',
      description: 'Espresso',
    },
  ];
```

Now, the following code is for `data/profile.js`:

```
export const profile = [
    {
      id: '1',
      bio: `Born and raised in London, my name is Jordan Brewer and I
am a passionate coffee aficionado with a heart as warm as a freshly
brewed cup of java.`,
    },
  ];
```

Moving on, the next batch of code is for the authenticated pages for the menu and profile.

The following code is for `account/menu/page.js`.

This code is quite long so let's break it down into smaller code blocks. This first code block has our imports and color theme setup:

```
'use client';
import { useSession, signIn, signOut }  from 'next-auth/react';
import { useQuery } from '@apollo/client';
import { GET_MENU } from '@/app/queries/clientQueries';
import withApollo from '../../utils/withApollo';
import { styled, ThemeProvider } from 'styled-components';
import GlobalStyle from '../../components/GlobalStyles';
import MainMenu from '../../components/MainMenu';

const theme = {
  colors: {
    primary: 'rgb(15 23 42)',
  },
};
```

The next code block has our CSS and `styled-components`:

```
const MainContainer = styled.div`
  margin: 2rem auto;
  max-width: 120rem;
  padding: 2rem;
  width: 100%;
```

```
`;

const PageTitle = styled.h1`
  color: #ffffff;
`;

const LoginStatus = styled.p`
  color: #ffffff;
`;

const SignInOutButton = styled.button`
  color: #ffffff;
  padding: 0.5rem;
  cursor: pointer;
  margin: 2rem 0 2rem 0;
`;

const ContentContainer = styled.div`
  display: flex;
  flex-flow: column wrap;
`;

const Content = styled.p`
  color: #ffffff;
  font-size: 1.4rem;
`;

const ItemContainer = styled.div`
  display: flex;
  flex-flow: row nowrap;
  margin: 2rem 0 2rem 0;
  border: 0.1rem solid black;
`;

const ItemDescription = styled.div`
  margin-left: 1rem;
`;
```

And lastly, we have the rendered data for our application:

```
const Menu = () => {
  const { loading, error, data } = useQuery(GET_MENU);
  const { data: session, status } = useSession();
```

```
const userEmail = session?.user?.email;

if (loading) return <Content>Loading...</Content>;
if (error) return <Content>Something
  went wrong</Content>;

if (status === 'loading') {
  return <Content>Hang on there...</Content>;
}

if (status === 'authenticated') {
  return (
    <>
      <ThemeProvider theme={theme}>
        <GlobalStyle />
        <MainMenu />
        <MainContainer>
          <PageTitle>Menu</PageTitle>
          <LoginStatus>Signed in as {userEmail}</LoginStatus>
          <SignInOutButton onClick={() => signOut()}>
            Sign out
          </SignInOutButton>
          {!loading && !error && (
            <ContentContainer>
              {data.menu.map((items) => (
                <ContentContainer key={items.id}>
                  <ItemContainer>
                    <ItemDescription>
                      <Content>{items.name}</Content>
                      <Content>{items.foodType}</Content>
                      <Content>{items.description}
                      </Content>
                    </ItemDescription>
                  </ItemContainer>
                </ContentContainer>
              ))}
            </ContentContainer>
          )}
        </MainContainer>
      </ThemeProvider>
    </>
  );
}
```

```
  return (
    <>
      <ThemeProvider theme={theme}>
        <GlobalStyle />
        <MainMenu />
        <MainContainer>
          <PageTitle>Menu</PageTitle>
          <SignInOutButton onClick={() => signIn('')}>
            Sign in</SignInOutButton>
          <LoginStatus>Not signed in. Sign in to view
            the menu.</LoginStatus>
        </MainContainer>
      </ThemeProvider>
    </>
  );
};

export default withApollo(Menu);
```

Now, the following code is for `account/profile/page.js`.

Like last time, let's break it down into smaller code blocks.

First, we have the imports for our page:

```
'use client';
import { useSession, signIn, signOut }  from 'next-auth/react';
import { useQuery } from '@apollo/client';
import { GET_PROFILE } from '@/app/queries/clientQueries';
import withApollo from '../../utils/withApollo';
import { styled, ThemeProvider } from 'styled-components';
import GlobalStyle from '../../components/GlobalStyles';
import MainMenu from '../../components/MainMenu';
```

Now, we have the color theme and `styled-components` code:

```
const theme = {
  colors: {
    primary: 'rgb(15 23 42)',
  },
};

const MainContainer = styled.div`
  margin: 2rem auto;
  max-width: 120rem;
```

```
  padding: 2rem;
  width: 100%;
`;

const PageTitle = styled.h1`
  color: #ffffff;
`;

const LoginStatus = styled.p`
  color: #ffffff;
`;

const SignInOutButton = styled.button`
  color: #ffffff;
  padding: 0.5rem;
  cursor: pointer;
  margin: 2rem 0 2rem 0;
`;

const ContentContainer = styled.div`
  display: flex;
  flex-flow: row wrap;
`;

const Content = styled.p`
  color: #ffffff;
  font-size: 1.4rem;
  margin-top: 2rem;
`;
```

Lastly, we have the rendered content for the page:

```
const ClientProtectPage = () => {
  const { loading, error, data } = useQuery(GET_PROFILE);
  const { data: session, status } = useSession();
  const userEmail = session?.user?.email;

  if (loading) return <Content>Loading...</Content>;
  if (error) return <Content>Something went wrong
    </Content>;

  if (status === 'loading') {
    return <Content>Hang on there...</Content>;
```

```
    }

    if (status === 'authenticated') {
      return (
        <>
          <ThemeProvider theme={theme}>
            <GlobalStyle />
            <MainMenu />
            <MainContainer>
              <PageTitle>Profile</PageTitle>
              <LoginStatus>Signed in as {userEmail}
              </LoginStatus>
              <SignInOutButton onClick={() => signOut()}>
                Sign out
              </SignInOutButton>
              {!loading && !error && (
                <ContentContainer>
                  {data.profile.map((account) => (
                    <ContentContainer key={account.id}>
                      <Content>{account.bio}</Content>
                    </ContentContainer>
                  ))}
                </ContentContainer>
              )}
            </MainContainer>
          </ThemeProvider>
        </>
      );
    }

    return (
      <>
        <ThemeProvider theme={theme}>
          <GlobalStyle />
          <MainMenu />
          <MainContainer>
            <PageTitle>Profile</PageTitle>
            <SignInOutButton onClick={() => signIn('')}>
            Sign in</SignInOutButton>
            <LoginStatus>
              Not signed in. Sign in to view your profile.
            </LoginStatus>
          </MainContainer>
```

```
        </ThemeProvider>
      </>
    );
};
```

```
export default withApollo(ClientProtectPage);
```

Now, let's work on some component files. The first code is for components/MainMenu.js:

```
import Link from 'next/link';
import { styled } from 'styled-components';

const MainNavigation = styled.nav`
  position: relative;
  z-index: 1;
  display: flex;
  flex-flow: wrap;
  justify-content: space-around;
  font-size: 2rem;
  padding: 1rem;
  background: rgb(250 250 250);
`;

export default function MainMenu() {
  return (
    <MainNavigation>
      <Link href="/">Home</Link>
      <Link href="/nutrition">Nutrition</Link>
      <Link href="/account/menu">Menu</Link>
      <Link href="/account/profile">Profile</Link>
    </MainNavigation>
  );
}
```

Next, the following code is for the components/Provider.js file, which is required for authentication and session state:

```
'use client';
import { SessionProvider } from 'next-auth/react';

const Provider = ({ children }) => {
  return <SessionProvider>{children}</SessionProvider>;
};

export default Provider;
```

Our next file has our GraphQL schema, resolvers, and our Apollo server. The following code goes in `graphql/route.js`:

```js
mport { ApolloServer } from '@apollo/server';
import { startServerAndCreateNextHandler } from '@as-integrations/
next';
import { gql } from 'graphql-tag';
import { menu } from '../../../data/menu';
import { profile } from '../../../data/profile';
import allowCors from '../utils/cors';

// Define the GraphQL schema and resolvers
const typeDefs = gql`
  type Menu {
    id: String
    foodType: String
    name: String
    description: String
  }

  type Profile {
    id: String
    bio: String
  }

  type Query {
    menu: [Menu]
    profile: [Profile]
  }
`;

const resolvers = {
  Query: {
    menu: () => menu,
    profile: () => profile,
  },
};

// Create the Apollo Server
const server = new ApolloServer({
  typeDefs,
  resolvers,
});
```

```
const handler = startServerAndCreateNextHandler(server, {
  context: async (req, res) => ({ req, res }),
});

export async function GET(request) {
  return handler(request);
}

export async function POST(request) {
  return handler(request);
}

export default allowCors(handler);
```

Now, use the following code to build nutrition/page.js:

```
'use client';
import { styled, ThemeProvider } from 'styled-components';
import GlobalStyle from '../components/GlobalStyles';
import MainMenu from '../components/MainMenu';

const theme = {
  colors: {
    primary: 'rgb(15 23 42)',
  },
};

const MainContainer = styled.div`
  margin: 2rem auto;
  max-width: 120rem;
  padding: 2rem;
  width: 100%;
`;

const PageTitle = styled.h1`
  color: #ffffff;
`;

const PageIntro = styled.p`
  color: #ffffff;
  margin-top: 2rem;
  font-size: 1.4rem;
`;
```

```
export default function Nutrition() {
  return (
    <>
      <ThemeProvider theme={theme}>
        <GlobalStyle />
        <MainMenu />
        <MainContainer>
          <PageTitle>Nutrition</PageTitle>
          <PageIntro>Nutrition is good for health
          and diet!</PageIntro>
        </MainContainer>
      </ThemeProvider>
    </>
  );
}
```

GraphQL queries are next, so the following code is for the `queries/clientQueries.js` file:

```
import { gql } from '@apollo/client';

const GET_MENU = gql`
  query {
    menu {
      id
      name
      foodType
      description
    }
  }
`;


const GET_PROFILE = gql`
  query {
    profile {
      id
      bio
    }
  }
`;
export { GET_MENU, GET_PROFILE };
```

Now, the important `utils/cors.js` file is needed so that we don't get CORS errors when our app is deployed online. This will allow us to access our GraphQL API on the authenticated routes:

```
const allowCors = (fn) => async (req, res) => {
  res.setHeader('Access-Control-Allow-Credentials', true);
  res.setHeader('Access-Control-Allow-Origin', '*');

  res.setHeader('Access-Control-Allow-Origin', req.headers.origin);
  res.setHeader(
    'Access-Control-Allow-Methods',
    'GET,OPTIONS,PATCH,DELETE,POST,PUT'
  );
  res.setHeader(
    'Access-Control-Allow-Headers',
    'X-CSRF-Token, X-Requested-With, Accept, Accept-Version,
      Content-Length, Content-MD5, Content-Type, Date, X-Api-Version'
  );
  if (req.method === 'OPTIONS') {
    res.status(200).end();
    return;
  }
  await fn(req, res);
};

export default allowCors;
```

Let's keep going. We have some more code here and it's for another GraphQL setup page; this time, it has the endpoints for GraphQL, which is how we will access our queries later. This file is in `utils/withApollo.js`:

```
import { ApolloClient, InMemoryCache, ApolloProvider } from '@apollo/
client';
import { useMemo } from 'react';
import { SessionProvider } from 'next-auth/react';

export function initializeApollo(initialState = null) {
  const _apolloClient = new ApolloClient({
    // Local GraphQL endpoint
    // uri: 'http://localhost:3000/graphql',
    // Your online GraphQL endpoint
    uri: 'https://coffee-restaurant.vercel.app/graphql',
    cache: new InMemoryCache().restore(initialState || {}),
  });
```

```
    return _apolloClient;
}

export function useApollo(initialState) {
  const store = useMemo(() => initializeApollo(initialState),
    [initialState]);
  return store;
}

export default function withApollo(PageComponent) {
  const WithApollo = ({ apolloClient, apolloState, session,
    ...pageProps }) => {
    const client = useApollo(apolloState);
    return (
      <SessionProvider session={session}>
        <ApolloProvider client={client}>
          <PageComponent {...pageProps} />
        </ApolloProvider>
      </SessionProvider>
    );
  };

  // On the server
  if (typeof window === 'undefined') {
    WithApollo.getInitialProps = async (ctx) => {
      const apolloClient = initializeApollo();

      let pageProps = {};
      if (PageComponent.getInitialProps) {
        pageProps = await PageComponent.getInitialProps(ctx);
      }

      if (ctx.res && ctx.res.finished) {
        // When redirecting, the response is finished.
        // No point in continuing to render
        return pageProps;
      }

      const apolloState = apolloClient.cache.extract();
      return {
        ...pageProps,
        apolloState,
      };
```

```
    };
  }

  return WithApollo;
}
```

Almost done! We are now on the `layout.js` page file:

```
import './globals.css';
import { Dosis } from 'next/font/google';
import StyledComponentsRegistry from './lib/registry';

const dosis = Dosis({ subsets: ['latin'] });

export const metadata = {
  title: 'Resturant App',
  description: 'Generated by create next app',
};

export default function RootLayout({ children }) {
  return (
    <html lang="en">
      <StyledComponentsRegistry>
        <body className={dosis.className}>{children}</body>
      </StyledComponentsRegistry>
    </html>
  );
}
```

The 404 error `not-found.js` page has the following code:

```
'use client';
import { styled, ThemeProvider } from 'styled-components';
import GlobalStyle from '../../src/app/components/GlobalStyles';
import MainMenu from './components/MainMenu';

const theme = {
  colors: {
    primary: 'rgb(15 23 42)',
  },
};

const MainContainer = styled.div`
```

```
    margin: 2rem auto;
    max-width: 120rem;
    padding: 2rem;
    width: 100%;
`;

const PageTitle = styled.h1`
  color: #ffffff;
`;

const PageIntro = styled.p`
  color: #ffffff;
  margin-top: 2rem;
  font-size: 1.4rem;
`;

export default function NotFound() {
  return (
    <>
      <ThemeProvider theme={theme}>
        <GlobalStyle />
        <MainMenu />
        <MainContainer>
          <PageTitle>Page Not Found</PageTitle>
          <PageIntro>Could not find requested
            page :(</PageIntro>
        </MainContainer>
      </ThemeProvider>
    </>
  );
}
```

And lastly, the page.js file is in the root folder, which is our home page.

The code is split in two for readability. First, we have the imports and CSS section:

```
'use client';
import { styled, ThemeProvider } from 'styled-components';
import GlobalStyle from '../../src/app/components/GlobalStyles';
import MainMenu from './components/MainMenu';

const theme = {
  colors: {
    primary: 'rgb(15 23 42)',
```

```
    },
  };

const MainContainer = styled.div`
  margin: 0 auto;
  width: 100%;
`;

const CoverHeadingBG = styled.div`
  margin: 2rem auto;
  display: flex;
  flex-flow: column;
  align-items: center;
  background-color: rgb(6 95 70);
  color: rgb(255 255 255);
  border-radius: 2rem;
  padding: 2rem;
`;

const CoverHeading = styled.h1`
  text-transform: uppercase;
`;

const CoverIntro = styled.p`
  font-size: 1.4rem;
  margin: 2rem 2rem;
`;

const Hero = styled.div`
  margin: 2rem auto;
  background-image: url('https://res.cloudinary.com/d74fh3kw/image/
    upload/v1692557430/coffee-restaurant/coffee-shop_zlkf7u.jpg');
  background-repeat: no-repeat;
  background-size: cover;
  background-position: center;
  background-color: rgb(4 120 87);
  height: 67.5rem;
  width: 100%;
`;

export default function Home() {
  return (
    <>
```

```
      <ThemeProvider theme={theme}>
        <GlobalStyle />
        <MainContainer>
          <MainMenu />
          <CoverHeadingBG>
            <CoverHeading>Summer time is here!</CoverHeading>
            <CoverIntro>
              Our summer menu has arrived. Freshen up your day with
                our creamy
              and delicious coffee range, iced teas and mouth watering
                snacks.
            </CoverIntro>
          </CoverHeadingBG>
          <Hero></Hero>
        </MainContainer>
      </ThemeProvider>
    </>
  );
}
```

And now for the function where we render our components in JSX with HTML:

```
export default function Home() {
  return (
    <>
      <ThemeProvider theme={theme}>
        <GlobalStyle />
        <MainContainer>
          <MainMenu />
          <CoverHeadingBG>
            <CoverHeading>Summer time is here!</CoverHeading>
            <CoverIntro>
              Our summer menu has arrived. Freshen up your day with
                our creamy
              and delicious coffee range, iced teas and mouth watering
                snacks.
            </CoverIntro>
          </CoverHeadingBG>
          <Hero></Hero>
        </MainContainer>
      </ThemeProvider>
    </>
  );
}
```

That's it! We are done with the bulk of the code base, and our app is almost complete! All that is left is a `GlobalStyles.js` file and the images for the frontend. We will do this in the upcoming section.

Building the presentation layer

Our project uses `styled-components`, which means the component and page files already have localized CSS. We do have one global CSS file though, which is a styled component with global style. Here is the code for `components/GlobalStyles.js`:

```
import { createGlobalStyle } from 'styled-components';
const GlobalStyle = createGlobalStyle`
  html,
  body {
    color: ${({ theme }) => theme.colors.primary};
    padding: 0;
    margin: 0;
    font-size: 1rem;
    background: rgb(6 78 59);
  }

  * {
    box-sizing: border-box;
  }
`;

export default GlobalStyle;
```

We have waited long enough; it's time to finally see our application running!

Make sure that you are in the `root` folder for `my-app-restaurant` and run the application with the `npm run dev` command.

Our application should be running on `http://localhost:3000` and our GraphQL API should be on `http://localhost:3000/graphql`.

The GraphQL API has built-in documentation for testing our queries. Here is an example query that should return the menu data:

```
query {
  menu {
    id
    name
    foodType
    description
  }
}
```

Before we put our app on GitHub and deploy it online, we will finish off with some unit tests for some of the files so that we get used to test-driven development.

Implementing testing

We have two test suites. First, we have the code for `nutrition/page.test.js`:

```
import { render, screen } from '@testing-library/react';
import '@testing-library/jest-dom/extend-expect';
import Nutrition from './page';

describe('Nutrition', () => {
  it('renders without crashing', () => {
    render(<Nutrition />);
  });

  it('displays the correct title and intro', () => {
    render(<Nutrition />);
    expect(
      screen.getByText('Nutrition is good for health and diet!')
    ).toBeInTheDocument();
  });
});
```

And lastly, the following code is for the `page.test.js` file in the `root` folder:

```
import { render, screen } from '@testing-library/react';
import '@testing-library/jest-dom/extend-expect';
import Home from './page';

describe('Home', () => {
  it('renders without crashing', () => {
    render(<Home />);
  });

  it('displays the correct heading and intro', () => {
    render(<Home />);
    expect(screen.getByText('Summer time is here!')).
      toBeInTheDocument();
    expect(
      screen.getByText(
        /Our summer menu has arrived. Freshen up your day with our
          creamy and delicious coffee range, iced teas and mouth
          watering snacks./
```

```
      )
    ).toBeInTheDocument();
  });
});
```

Run the npm test command, and all tests should be passing. You can press the *A* button to rerun all of the tests.

Our app is more or less complete. Let's now put it on GitHub so that we can version control it. It is also preparation for getting our app to work online when we deploy it to Vercel, our serverless host.

Creating a Git repository with README documentation

Go to GitHub and create a new repo for our project. If you are new to or still unfamiliar with GitHub, then you can follow the *Get started* guide here: https://docs.github.com/en/get-started. Then, simply follow the commands to push your project to GitHub. These are the commands I used. Replace them with your own repo:

```
git init
git add .
git commit -m "first commit"
git branch -M main
git remote add origin https://github.com/yourname/yourprojectname.git
git push -u origin main
```

Our project is now on GitHub! We only have one thing left to do – to deploy our app on Vercel – and then we are done!

Deploying the application for public access

Sign in to your Vercel account and then, on the dashboard, there should be a button to add a new project. Add a new project and import the Git repository you just created for the project.

Before you hit the **Deploy** button, you must enter your environment variables, which you will find in the .env.local file in the root folder of your project. This file was not uploaded to your GitHub repo because it has your GitHub and Google IDs and secret keys, which you don't want people to see! When you're done, hit **Deploy** and wait for the build to complete.

Our app should be live online now. However, the **Menu** and **Profile** pages will be broken. Don't worry! This is expected because, in our code in the utils/withApollo.js file, the URL is set to http://localhost:3000/graphql; our app is online now and is not running on our machine, so the address needs to change. Update it to the address of your app on Vercel, as in the following example: https://your-app-url.vercel.app/graphql. Push the latest changes to your GitHub repository, and Vercel will automatically update and deploy with the new URI.

The following commit message should be fine:

```
git status
git add .
git commit -m "vercel graphql endpoint for uri"
git push
```

And remember from earlier, when we run our app locally, the callback URL will look something like this, if we use GitHub as an example: `http://localhost:3000/api/auth/callback/github`.

When deployed online, it will have the following type of URL structure: `https://your-app-url.vercel.app/api/auth/callback/github`.

So update the authentication for your app on GitHub and Google to get the **Menu** and **Profile** pages working online.

It should be all done. Now, our application should be available online for the whole world to see. Well done!

Summary

We have made it to the end of this chapter and leveled up our programming skills considerably. Right at the beginning of this chapter, we learned about REST APIs and how they help us to fetch data on the internet, which we can then use in our applications. Afterward, we had an introduction to planning application architecture, where we talked about authentication followed by SWR, an HTTP cache invalidation strategy. The next topic was GraphQL, the popular alternative to using REST APIs, which requires fewer API requests as it's possible to fetch only the data we require. We then touched upon deployment because it's important to remember this setup from the get-go.

In the next sections, we dived into business logic and learned why our code needs to be well refined. This section was followed up by the presentation layer as we created a design that used styled-components. Testing was factored in, and we learned how to test the code that we wrote for our project. With our application completed, the final step was its deployment, and this is where we learned about creating a Git repository that has a README file with our documentation. In this step, we also put our application online so that it was publicly available for everyone to use.

With everything that we have absorbed, it's safe to say that we have taken a huge leap forward in terms of learning and have become much more talented programmers in the process. We are now better prepared to tackle interviews as job seekers.

Index

‹packt›

Packtpub.com

Subscribe to our online digital library for full access to over 7,000 books and videos, as well as industry leading tools to help you plan your personal development and advance your career. For more information, please visit our website.

Why subscribe?

- Spend less time learning and more time coding with practical eBooks and Videos from over 4,000 industry professionals
- Improve your learning with Skill Plans built especially for you
- Get a free eBook or video every month
- Fully searchable for easy access to vital information
- Copy and paste, print, and bookmark content

Did you know that Packt offers eBook versions of every book published, with PDF and ePub files available? You can upgrade to the eBook version at packtpub.com and as a print book customer, you are entitled to a discount on the eBook copy. Get in touch with us at customercare@packtpub.com for more details.

At www.packtpub.com, you can also read a collection of free technical articles, sign up for a range of free newsletters, and receive exclusive discounts and offers on Packt books and eBooks.

Other Books You May Enjoy

If you enjoyed this book, you may be interested in these other books by Packt:

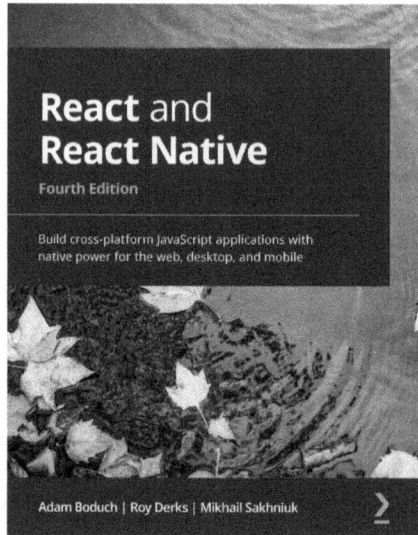

React and React Native

Adam Boduch | Mikhail Sakhniuk | Roy Derks

ISBN: 978-1-80323-128-0

- Explore React architecture, component properties, state, and context
- Work with React Hooks for handling functions and components
- Implement code splitting using lazy components and Suspense
- Build robust user interfaces for mobile and desktop apps using Material-UI
- Write shared components for Android and iOS apps using React Native
- Implement Apollo-driven components
- Write GraphQL schemas to power web and mobile apps.

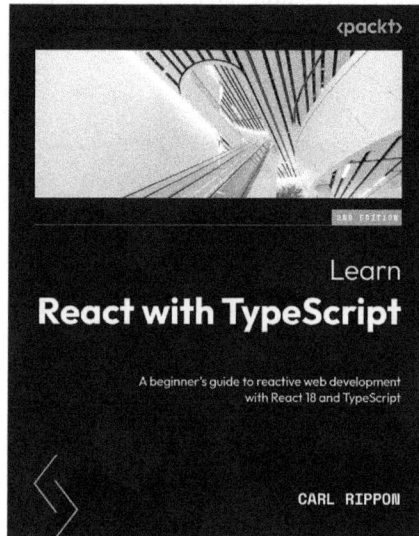

Learn React with TypeScript

Carl Rippon

ISBN: 978-1-80461-420-4

- Gain first-hand experience of TypeScript and its productivity features
- Understand how to transpile your TypeScript code into JavaScript for running in a browser
- Build a React frontend codebase with hooks
- Interact with REST and GraphQL web APIs
- Design and develop strongly typed reusable components
- Create automated component tests

Packt is searching for authors like you

If you're interested in becoming an author for Packt, please visit authors.packtpub.com and apply today. We have worked with thousands of developers and tech professionals, just like you, to help them share their insight with the global tech community. You can make a general application, apply for a specific hot topic that we are recruiting an author for, or submit your own idea.

Hi!

We are Sudheer Jonna and Andrew Baisden, the authors of *React Interview Guide*. We really hope you enjoyed reading this book and found it useful for increasing your chances in cracking a React interview along with increasing your productivity and efficiency.

It would really help us (and other potential readers!) if you could leave a review on Amazon sharing your thoughts on this book.

Go to the link below or scan the QR code to leave your review:

`https://packt.link/r/1803241519`

Your review will help us understand what's worked well in this book, and what could be improved upon for future editions, so it really is appreciated.

Best wishes,

Sudheer Jonna

Andrew Baisden

Download a free PDF copy of this book

Thanks for purchasing this book!

Do you like to read on the go but are unable to carry your print books everywhere?

Is your eBook purchase not compatible with the device of your choice?

Don't worry, now with every Packt book you get a DRM-free PDF version of that book at no cost.

Read anywhere, any place, on any device. Search, copy, and paste code from your favorite technical books directly into your application.

The perks don't stop there, you can get exclusive access to discounts, newsletters, and great free content in your inbox daily

Follow these simple steps to get the benefits:

1. Scan the QR code or visit the link below

https://packt.link/free-ebook/9781803241517

2. Submit your proof of purchase
3. That's it! We'll send your free PDF and other benefits to your email directly